IN HIS SERVICE

IN HIS SERVICE
THE MEMOIRS OF A MODERN-DAY MESSENGER OF GOD

ERIC C. WHEELER

The problem is that Jesus is more real to people as a past figure of history than as a present reality.

YorkshirePublishing
www.yorkshirepublishing.com
Write Now.

ISBN: 978-1-947247-75-8
In His Service
Copyright © 2009 by Eric C. Wheeler

Scripture quotations marked "NKJV" are taken from the *Holy Bible, New King James Version*, Copyright © 1982 by Thomas Nelson, Inc. Used by permission. All rights reserved.

For permission requests, write to the publisher at the address below.

Yorkshire Publishing
3207 South Norwood Avenue
Tulsa, Oklahoma 74135
www.YorkshirePublishing.com
918.394.2665

"I realize that many who read this will find it too fantastic to believe, but as God is my witness, every bit of it is true and accurate."

—Eric C. Wheeler

TABLE OF CONTENTS

PREFACE

A number of people have asked me to write a book about my experiences as a servant of God. I have been hesitant to do this in the past, not wanting to put any focus on myself, but rather let all eyes be upon the Lord, and upon Him only. However, I have now come to realize that since my whole life is a credible witness to the greatness, mercy, and grace of God, as well as the fact that all of my spiritual experiences in Him are a real testimony, and because "faith comes by hearing" (Romans 10:17), I have agreed to relay some of my personal experiences in this book in order to help others. It is my hope and prayer that whoever reads this will be edified and strengthened in his or her faith in Him. For He alone is worthy of our praise, adoration, and worship. I realize that many who read this will find it too fantastic to believe, but as God is my witness, every bit of it is true and accurate.

"WHICH ONE OF THESE TWO MEN DO YOU CHOOSE TO BE?"

When I was eighteen years old, I was lying on my bed alone one evening in a little house my parents owned near the college I was attending, when the Lord gave me a vision. As I was resting, there suddenly appeared in front of me two men suspended in the air. One was younger looking and the other much older. Floating in front of me and on my left was the younger man who appeared to be in his midthirties. He was well dressed, incredibly polished, good looking, and quite debonair in his demeanor. I could tell that he was very successful (at least as far as the world's standards go) and was quite wealthy; he had a new sports car, a number of gorgeous girlfriends, Armani tailor-made suits, an Ivy League college degree and education, and the envy of the entire world. Outwardly, he represented all the celebrity and brilliance of the American dream. However, inside, as a person, I could tell he was hollow and shallow. It was obvious to me that he had no knowledge of God or any sense of meaning to life—other than "appearance" to others—and that he was empty of all truth and any divine purpose. While appearing to "have it all," I could tell that he actually had nothing.

In contrast to him was an old man suspended in front of me to my right. This elderly man was the direct opposite of everything that this younger man represented. He was much older (seemingly in his seventies); was visibly weaker; wore dirty, tattered clothes; and smelled of body odor. His hair and long beard were unkempt and unshaven, and he obviously was not someone who was respected or admired. The world had little regard for him, and I could tell that he had no money, that he was somewhat transient, and that he was probably classified by the world as "a little kooky and homeless." However, despite his awkward and undesirable appearance and demeanor, he had an incredibly sharp gleam in his eye. He obviously *knew* something—something that nobody else did! I could tell by the very subtle, yet distinct, smirk in the corner of his mouth. It was almost a small grin, you could say. As I stared at the sharp gleam in his eye, I began to realize that this man knew God! He knew the Eternal One—the only true God! The One and Only God of the Universe! He truly *knew* Him—intimately. I was amazed by him. It didn't matter to him how he looked or what he smelled like; he simply didn't care what other people thought of him. Yet, it was very obvious to me that this guy understood something very deeply—something that the rest of us in the world could not even comprehend. It soon became obvious as I studied him that he was a friend of the Almighty. And although the world had little regard for him, God jealously and protectively watched over him.

As I gazed and longed to speak to this old man, admiring the incredible depth and knowledge of God that he surely possessed, I

"Which One of These Two Men Do You Choose to Be?"

immediately heard a loud Voice ask me, "Which one of these two men do you choose to be?" Dumbfounded and surprised at first by the divine question being posed to me, I quickly responded without hesitation. "The old man, of course!" I suddenly blurted out, not being dissuaded at all by the inherent physical costs involved in choosing this spiritual package. "And so shall you have it!" the Voice exclaimed, and then the heavenly vision ended.

It wasn't long after this that I was led to tell my parents that I needed to quit the college in Ohio that I was attending on a full-tuition paid scholarship at the time (my mom worked for the college), and move to California to study theology at my church's small private Christian college. Although my father had been initially against the idea of me going to this Christian college when I had first mentioned the idea to him years earlier in high school, the Lord nonetheless began opening doors for me, and by the time I approached him this second time, he cheerfully received me, announcing enthusiastically, "No problem, Eric. I will help you pay for it!" He added, "Somehow, I already *knew* you were going to be going there. In fact, I already told my mother— your grandmother—a few weeks ago that you would probably be going there soon." This was a real shock to me, because I had never mentioned my interest in going there again since being a freshman in high school—five years earlier! Little did I realize it at the time, but it was part of my destiny.

It was required of all freshmen attending Ambassador College to be employed by the college either serving in its kitchen—as part of the dish-washing crew, or working in the custodial department scrubbing floors and toilets, or working on the grounds crew providing landscaping services to the college and church headquarters. The college required all new first-year freshmen, regardless if a student had had previous college credit or not, to serve in one of these departments during their freshmen year as a way to help pay their college expenses. Thankfully, I was assigned to work in the kitchen as a pots and pans scrubber. To my surprise though, halfway through my freshman year, I was suddenly asked to assist our church denomination's pastor general and college president's personal chef—despite the fact that I didn't have any cooking experience or culinary knowledge or skills whatsoever. I couldn't figure it out or believe it at the time—*what a stroke of luck,* I remember thinking to myself. In a matter of just five months, I went from being a lowly dishwasher to being the assistant chef to our church's and college's most important personnel figure— the pastor general himself—the very man that I was erroneously raised to believe was in direct leadership working under Jesus Christ Himself. The remarkable thing about this was that now, as a young man, I was going to be given a firsthand look and view of what actually goes on "behind the scenes" of religious institutions and ecclesiastical hierarchies (i.e., church organizations)— something that I had long dedicated my life and tithe money to supporting, not to mention my own personal faith and trust.

Every Tuesday, the chief administrators and faculty members of the college and the upper echelons of the church hierarchy would gather together for a "special luncheon meeting" in Memorial Hall. While I was a student, it was generally understood that Memorial Hall was for the most part "off limits" to the student body as well as to the general membership of the church. It was a beautiful mansion that had been donated and gifted to the church and college many years before by former (and now presumed deceased) church members. The church's original founder and previous pastor general had used it as his own personal home and residence. I realized as a student, especially as a freshman, that it was a very special treat and honor for me to be able to work and serve regularly inside this mansion during these luncheon meetings. It was understood that all servers and students helping out during these meetings inside Memorial Hall were to remain "behind the scenes"—that is, they were not to be seen, were expected to remain silent unless spoken to, and were to be as "courteous and meek and smiling" as could be expected. The luncheons usually consisted of filet mignon, roasted lamb, and/or some expensive fish or game hen, and were always garnished with the finest trimmings available. The real surprising part to me was not the food itself, but rather the shocking fact that all of these gourmet dishes were literally served on gold plates! To my horror and shock, all of the eating utensils, serving dishes, cups, wine glasses, and trays were all made of exquisite gold and handcrafted silver, and each piece had to be hand washed with the utmost care. Each dish and eating utensil probably cost more than all of my college education and then some.

I remember feeling so sick to my stomach as I stood there hand washing those gold and silver dishes, thinking of all of the poor widows that I knew back home who had sent in their "last dimes" in tithe money so that these sons of bitches could eat off gold plates. I was so angry about this as a young student! I kept hearing the words of Jesus written in the Bible echo through the back of my mind as I stood there washing those kingly dishes:

Woe to you, scribes and Pharisees, hypocrites! For you devour widow's houses, and for a pretense make long prayers [and hold meetings]. For you bind heavy [financial and social] burdens, hard to bear, and lay those on men's shoulders; but you yourselves will not move them with one of your own fingers. But all your works you do to be seen by men. You make your phylacteries broad and enlarge the borders of your garments. You love the place of honor at feasts, the best seats in the churches, greetings in the marketplaces, and to be called by men, "Rabbi, Rabbi." Woe to you, scribes and Pharisees, hypocrites! For you shut up the kingdom of heaven against men; for you neither go in yourselves, nor do you allow those who are entering to go in. You travel land and sea to win one proselyte, and when he is converted, you make him twice as much the child of hell as yourselves. Blind guides, you who strain out a gnat and swallow a camel! Woe to you, scribes and Pharisees, hypocrites! For you wash the outside of the cup and dish, but inside you are full of extortion and self-indulgence. Blind Pharisees! First cleanse the inside of the cup and dish, that the outside may become clean also. For you are like whitewashed tombs which indeed appear beautiful outwardly, but inside are full of dead men's bones and all uncleanness. Even so you also outwardly appear righteous to men, but inside you are full of hypocrisy and iniquity. Woe to you, scribes and Pharisees, hypocrites! Because you build the tombs of the prophets and adorn the monuments of the righteous, and say, "If we had lived in the days of our fathers, we would not have been partakers with them in the blood of the prophets." Therefore you are witnesses against yourselves that you are the sons of those who murdered the prophets. Fill up, then, the measure of your father's guilt. Therefore, indeed, I will send you prophets, wise men, and scribes. Some of them you will kill and crucify, and some of them you will scourge in your churches and persecute from city to city, that on you may come all the righteous blood shed on the earth, from the blood of righteous Abel to the blood of Zechariah. Assuredly, I say to you, all these things will come upon this generation.

Matthew 23:1–36, *paraphrased*

Little did I realize then that these powerful words of Jesus spoken over two thousand years ago would still have spiritual significance and prophetic meaning today. I did not fully understand nor comprehend then that Jesus' words are "living" and that all of His words are just as alive and relevant today as when He first spoke them. I would spend the next twenty-two years of my life learning and experiencing just how real and alive the "resurrected Jesus" truly is. This book is a true and accurate account of those experiences and the dear costs associated with living them.

BEGINNING TO "HEAR" FROM HIM

It was seemingly every young man's dream who was a student at Ambassador College upon graduation to be hired on as a "minister"—that is, a person who is employed by the church to serve in a "pastoral role" in the local church congregations. Although a number of my fellow classmates were hired by the church, to my dismay and disappointment, I was never called in for an interview, despite having a clean college record and above average grades. At the time, I couldn't figure it out. In a sense, I felt like "the only girl without a prom date" so to speak. In actuality, there were many other fellow classmates who were not interviewed or hired as well, but I couldn't help my feelings of utter disappointment upon graduation. I *knew* that I was supposed to be there. I knew that God had opened doors for me to attend that college. *Why then wasn't I being hired by the church?* I sincerely wondered. After earnestly praying about my situation one day, I suddenly had this strange feeling and sense that somehow I wasn't allowed by God to be religiously "owned" or employed by anyone; no man could have anything over me or have the power to control anything that I said or did. I somehow began to sense deep down in my soul that in the future I was not permitted to be controlled or manipulated by anybody, but that I was answerable only to God—and to Him *only*. I suddenly was made aware of the fact in my spirit that anybody that worked for "man" was owned by man and answerable to him—and therefore they were not able to freely speak the whole truth of God without fear of losing their paycheck. A number of years later, the Lord would clearly state this to me, by saying, "Eric, whoever a man looks to to put food on his table, *owns* him—whether that be God, or whether that be man!" Although I didn't fully understand the timing or meaning of certain things during this time, I remember getting the strong sense back then that everybody that had just been hired by the church was going to be losing their jobs soon anyway or leaving the church altogether eventually, so it didn't really matter; therefore, I didn't need to fret about it or be disappointed in my being passed over for employment upon graduating. Sadly, within five to six short years, this would prove to be true.

Immediately upon graduation, I was blessed by the Lord with a beautiful wife. Teresa and I had met at college, fell in love, and were married in June of 1990. Not able to find work in California and not really wanting to lay down permanent roots there anyway, Teresa and I decided to move to Denver, Colorado, where she is from, in November of 1990. Our plan was to find suitable, stable work and eventually start building a family. After trying to start a family about three and a half years into our marriage with no success, we began to get deeply concerned regarding fertility. Nothing seemed to work. Eventually, we decided to seek professional help, so we went to a fertility specialist. After conducting diagnostic tests on both of us, the doctor concluded that both of us have "fertility problems." Apparently, Teresa had severe endometriosis and I had a very low sperm count. I asked the doctor how bad it was, and he retorted, "It ain't going to happen! In fact, you may want to consider adopting." Needless to say, Teresa and I were severely crushed at this disheartening news.

It was during this five-year period that our church denomination was going through some major churchwide doctrinal changes. Some of our long-held doctrines and beliefs were being called into question, and were now being re-examined and re-interpreted by our church denomination's leadership. Almost monthly, it seemed the local congregations were being notified of yet another doctrinal change that was being made and administered by the ecclesiastical authorities at church headquarters. As these doctrinal debates heated up within the church and among its leadership, many of the congregations began to split as a result, and many members and church pastors began to leave our fellowship. Unfortunately, a great number of families and marriages were torn apart as a consequence, and many sincere Christians became disillusioned. I remember writing the following entry in my personal spiritual diary during this critical time:

12/26/95—Many people both in the church and out of the church are hurting and are lost. I want to help in some way. I'm not sure where I am going or if I have a great purpose or not. Even though God has given me a lot and has blessed me in so many ways, I truly feel lost and as if I am supposed to be preparing for something, and yet, I don't know what. I can see God's hand in a lot of things in my life, and yet, where I am going, I cannot tell. I wish so badly that I had someone to talk to that would believe me and give me some godly advice.

I feel so alone. My wife only "half-believes" me. She thinks that I "take too much on myself." Am I? I don't know. I only know that I really wish God would use me somehow. I would give up everything that I have, just to know that I knew God and His will, and that He was pleased with me as His servant. I can't think of any greater honor or fulfilling purpose.

God has been very good to me, and extremely merciful. My job is going very well. I am making lots of money and the people there like me and respect me. But every day, I can't help but think that I am just wasting precious time. I don't feel like I am making a difference in this world for God. I don't know what to do?! I am constantly asking God to use me in some miraculous way, but right now I don't see it. I believe that God has something in mind for me, but I have no idea what. I don't want to live my life and then die having not made a difference to the world. I want to know God, to see God, to be part of what God is doing on this earth. I don't want to be like most everyone who has ever lived—just live and breath, and then die, not ever knowing why they lived, or by what power they lived, or even knew the One who created them.

There have been a couple of times that I'm sure that I heard God's voice. Sometimes He has talked to me in dreams, sometimes in visions, and sometimes by a voice internally. Some of the things that I can remember are: (1) That my wife was to give birth to a baby girl and that I was to name her Elizabeth. (2) That if I indeed worked hard and studied diligently, then God would surely use me. (3) That now were the "fat years" of physical prosperity, and that the "lean years" were coming. (4) That one day in the near future, I was going to speak with the "mouth of God" by His Holy Spirit and say some marvelous things (not of myself), and that the whole congregation and the pastor were going to be dumbfounded. (5) That when I had begun speaking under this divine inspiration, that I would eventually come to speak to great multitudes of people and that some would believe, and many would not. (6) That I would know that "my time had come" to begin the "Lord's Work" when I would suffer some kind of injury to my left arm. This would serve as a "sign" to *me*.

I don't know why I am writing this. I just need to get it off my chest. I don't have anybody to talk to. My wife thinks I am a hypocrite and a "self-proclaimed prophet wanna-be." Perhaps she's not far from the truth. I don't know why I am writing these things. Perhaps, I too, feel that I am a fake. Only God knows for sure. I pray, dear God, for guidance and humility, and that You would have mercy on me continually.

A lot of what I had written above in my diary referred to some of the "revelations" that I had privately been given by God earlier that spring in 1995. After the church began changing some of its core teachings, I, too, like many of my spiritual brothers and sisters, began questioning things as a result of this "doctrinal shaking." As a consequence, I began praying to the Lord constantly to reveal Himself and His will to me. I sincerely wanted to *know* the truth. To my surprise, after a few months of seeking His face day and night in prayer, coupled with listening to the Bible on audiocassette daily in my car on the way to work, I began having visions and was given astounding revelations from Him. The Lord began showing me things about the future—my own personal future, as well as the future of my local church community, our denomination as a whole, Christianity in general, and the future of the world. I was astounded and speechless at what I saw. I wasn't able to immediately recall or fully understand some of these revelations at the time—let alone share them with anybody.

Although I could "see" them all in my mind's eye, the minute that I tried to communicate them to anybody in any form, either verbally or in written form, they would immediately be "snatched" from my mind and lips. It became very clear to me that I was not "allowed" to share these revelations with anybody at the time because most of them were for yet "a time appointed." Although it personally was a very awesome and enlightening time for me, it was also a very frustrating and lonely time as well. Needless to say, these spiritual revelations were going to personally cost me a lot to secretly carry them in my heart.

As I mentioned above, during this time my wife and I were considered completely "barren" by a fertility specialist—that is, we were unable to have children or even to conceive. After enduring months of anguish over the prospect of not being able to have children, one night out of emotional exhaustion and utter despair, I cried out to God in desperation about it. I said to Him, "Lord, You promised in the Bible that if a man delighted himself in You that his wife would be a fruitful vine and that his children would sit around his table like olive plants. You also said that children are a gift from You! Why then, God, have You made us barren? Why have You chosen to do this to us? I trusted You, Lord. I have served You all the days of my life. I have sought to please You. Why then, oh why, have You done this to us?" My bed and pillow were covered with my tears as I pleaded with God for answers. Totally unexpectedly, I suddenly heard a booming, loud Voice speak to me out of the darkness of my room: "Eric, don't worry!" The heavenly Voice said, "Your wife shall give birth to a baby girl. And you shall call her name Elizabeth." Needless to say, I was astonished at hearing these words, as well as the fact that He was speaking to me and that He specifically called me by my name!

As I sat up from my prayer in joyous amazement upon hearing His magnificent Voice, with tears running down my face, I immediately and inadvertently began protesting in my thoughts what I heard. *Elizabeth?* I questioned, *But I don't like the name Elizabeth. Can't I make her middle name Elizabeth, and call her something else instead?* Before I even realized what my evil and ungrateful mind had been thinking, the Voice answered, "That's fine." At first I was afraid, but then I had to laugh at myself when I realized that God had literally just read my childish thoughts. Consequently, my wife and I conceived two weeks later. We now have three children—Kate, Rachel, and Evan. Our eldest is a twelve-year-old daughter aptly named Kate *Elizabeth* Wheeler. Incidentally, the name Elizabeth means "oath of God" or "God promised."

EARLY COMMUNICATIONS FROM THE LORD

In order for my reader to better understand where I have been and where I am going in this book, it is probably prudent that I give a little backdrop to some of the promises and prophecies that the Lord has given me over my life. The earliest recollection and revelation from God that I can recall is a dream that I had when I was probably around six or seven years old. Before I relay this dream, I must give you a little backdrop first. I was born with an internal cleft palate, which left me with severe ear problems that I have experienced all of my life. As a result of this cleft palate and the subsequent ear problems, I have had many sets of tubes placed in my ears over the years. In the early seventies, it was believed by the medical profession that water could not get into my ears with these tubes in them or I could possibly go deaf. I was never allowed to go swimming or take showers without some sort of ear protection, and putting my head under water was strictly forbidden. With this in mind, one night I had this frightening prophetic dream when I was about six years old: I dreamed that I was sitting on the roadside across from my house with my finger-painting set in my lap just enjoying the bright beautiful sunny day, when all of a sudden a flashy red sports car came barreling down the road toward me at a high rate of speed. A man and his girlfriend sped right past me, barely missing me, and went careening off the side of the road over a steep canyon. As their car hit the bottom, it exploded, and instantly set off a series of explosions all around me. Immediately, the blue sky turned dark as fire and smoke began to permeate the atmosphere. All of the rows of houses across the street caught fire, and sirens were going off everywhere. I ran back to my house just in time to meet my family members who were coming out of the house and gathering on the front porch. Nobody knew what to do or how to get out of the city, which by now was completely engulfed in terrifying flames. Standing on the porch, I looked down to the side of our house and noticed a small hidden river that flowed out of the city. I knew that it was the only means of deliverance for us. However, because of my ear problems and the fact that I could possibly lose my hearing if water were to get into my ears, I realized that it was going to require a great amount of faith and personal sacrifice on my part in order to deliver our lives. I instructed my parents and sisters to jump into the river, as I myself stood on the porch contemplating my crisis of belief. I then woke up.

Even though I was only six or seven years old at the time, I recognized that this dream was prophetic and that it was from God. I knew that it had supernatural meaning and significance. Even at a tender young age, a prophet is able to tell the difference between a dream (or communication) that comes from God, and a dream that originates from eating a spicy burrito the night before. Although the prophet Samuel was very young, the

Lord nonetheless began speaking to him at a very early age. The same was true for Joseph, Jeremiah, and Josiah. God says that He reveals Himself to His prophets through dreams and visions (Numbers 12:6). Although I was very young, I understood this dream to mean that there is great calamity coming in the future and that it will take great faith and, in some cases, would require costly personal sacrifices for some, in order for people to be delivered. This worldwide calamity will happen all at once, but only the "hidden little ones" in God will know how to escape it. These "hidden little ones" will be required to personally give up much in order to help deliver others. It will also require great faith in order to do so. Up until I was eighteen years old, when I was given the vision of the two men in my bedroom, this was the only communication that I knowingly received from the Lord. But I quietly kept this dream hidden away in my heart all of these many years knowing that it was from the Lord—and that it would have prophetic meaning sometime yet in the future.

While I was attending Ambassador College, a number of strange occurrences happened that I didn't fully understand at the time. Although I had always had the sense that there was a special God-ordained "calling" on my life since first receiving that dream from the Lord at the young age of six or seven and having that belief confirmed by the subsequent vision at age eighteen, I nonetheless didn't understand where my life was going or heading. Every time I wanted to pursue a career or begin planning a vocation, I somehow knew in my spirit that I had to "work for the Lord" and that my "career path" was already predestined by Him. I *knew* this in my heart, yet I didn't understand what this looked like or how it worked in application. I kept wondering, *How was I to be paid—especially since I wasn't able to work for anyone ecclesiastically?* The Lord was beginning to show me during this time that no man was allowed to "own" me. No man could have any bearing on what I was to preach or permitted to say. *If I wasn't allowed to work for any church or religious organization,* I thought to myself, *then how am I supposed to work for Him?* These were the thoughts and questions that kept running through my mind shortly before graduation. "Why are You having me study both the Bible and history, God, and yet, how am I supposed to earn a living with that— seeing that I am not allowed to be employed by any ecclesiastical entity?" I asked Him. He never gave me an answer to any of my questions. I was beginning to realize that He expected me to just walk forward in faith trusting Him. Not really knowing Him or how He works, I couldn't understand it then and it became a real test for me. One afternoon though while I was lying on my bed at college, after having earnestly prayed about it, I heard a loud Voice speak to me as I closed my eyes to take a nap. The Voice sounded like someone was standing there next to me, yet I didn't see anybody, and it was incredibly loud and booming. The Voice literally knocked me off my bed and onto the floor. The booming Voice declared, "Study and work hard, and I will surely use you!"

A few months later at the end of November of that year, very early in the morning, I was awakened to the voice of an angel standing next to my bed. In my spirit I was aware of his presence standing next to me, although I didn't see anything with my human eyes—the room was still dark. Apparently, my three sleeping roommates didn't hear his announcement because they didn't awaken to the firm sound of his voice. The angelic voice said to me, "Your sister, April, has just given birth to a baby boy!"

I remember opening my eyes and then smiling as I clearly heard him speak these words to me. I went back to sleep.

A few hours later, a roommate woke me up to tell me that I had a phone call. When I answered the phone, it was my oldest sister, April, calling from the hospital, to tell me the good news: "Guess what?" she excitedly began.

"You gave birth to a baby boy last night," I interrupted.

"Ah, Mom already told you, huh?" she asked disappointedly.

"No," I said.

"Then how did you know?" she asked.

"I don't know; I just somehow already knew it," I sheepishly admitted.

Thankfully, she didn't press me any further about it, because I don't think she would have believed me at the time anyway. Incidentally, I wasn't to learn the significance or importance of my nephew's birth until many years later.

"HUMBLE" BEGINNINGS

As I mentioned earlier, upon graduation, I got married, and my wife and I moved to Colorado where she is from. After a short stint of five months of working for my father-in-law, I got laid off. Unfortunately, as a result of the Persian Gulf War, his aviation art business wasn't doing too well, and he could no longer afford to pay me. I began to search the want ads in the newspaper for work. I remember commenting once, upon graduating from college, when a man had offered me a telemarketing job, "I would rather scrub toilets or flip hamburgers than be a telemarketer!"—and little did I realize then that I was prophetically sealing my own fate. It seems that whatever position you think is "beneath you" is exactly what the Lord is going to give you in order to humble you and to teach you a few things. Looking back on it now (I am forty years old now), humbling is exactly what I needed during this time in my life. Like most college graduates, I too, felt like I had "put in my required time" at school, and therefore, the working world now owed me a pretty good living, a high-paying job, and a nice big house! "Look out, world, here I come!" was the proud battle cry of the day, and I felt that I was definitely entitled to my share of the spoils! But wisely, the Lord had other plans for me, and humbling was the first item on His wise agenda!

Fearing that my wife (who, incidentally, is very gifted and talented in the working environment) would get angry if she came home and found me "just watching television" instead of out interviewing for jobs, I quickly grabbed the want ads one afternoon and just called "any old place" to interview with in order to get out of the house before she came home from work. We lived in a cheap one-bedroom apartment at the time. It wasn't that I didn't want to work; I was just holding out for that "perfect high-paying job" which, as a recent college graduate, I felt that I was "entitled" to—you know the one—the one working for Merrill Lynch as a young successful stock broker! I had already interviewed with them twice, and so I was just basically sitting around waiting for them to call me and to tell me when to start. I knew in my gut that they were going to offer me a position with them. Although I had only interviewed with them for an entry-level customer service position, I just knew in my proud heart that it would possibly develop into something more—especially once they got to see how "talented and gifted" I was! After all, I knew that I was "talented and gifted" and that God was with me, so it was just a matter of waiting. But thankfully, God doesn't think like we do, and His ways are not our ways. He takes His servants by the "low and humble roads" and not by the "high and lofty ones." I was about to learn a great and much-needed valuable lesson.

As I called the first place that I found in the want ads that seemed to me to be eager to hire "just about anybody," I requested an immediate interview just so that I could get out of the house before my wife came home. The man on the other end of the telephone was impressed with my "boldness" in asking for an immediate interview and gladly asked me to come in. Little did

I know at the time that this "boldness" is exactly what he and the company he represented was looking for—telemarketers who weren't afraid to *boldly* ask for business. When I arrived at their small "boiler-room" type building, I remember arrogantly thinking to myself, *Who would work in a dump like this?* Dressed in my suit and leather coat, I pompously and proudly asked for the man who had invited me down for an interview. After a few minutes of touring me around and some brief discussion (neither of which I paid close attention to), he asked me if I wanted to speak to his boss. Looking at my watch and realizing that I had only been away from home for about forty-five minutes, I agreed to meet his boss, Tony, in order to waste more time and to appear to my wife to be earnestly "out interviewing and looking for work."

When I entered Tony's office, he was sitting behind a big cherry wood desk eyeing me very closely. I plopped down in one of his executive-type leather chairs and disdainfully looked around the room. "So what does it take to rise to the top in a place like this?" I arrogantly sneered.

"Here, the cream rises to the top!" He snapped back, taking the same arrogant tone that I had used to address him. "Why do you ask; are *you* the cream, young man?" he brazenly and defiantly asked, as he stood up, taking a challenging posture and position over me.

Feeling rather insulted and eager to put him in his place, I immediately jumped to my feet and pridefully declared, "When do I start?!"

He shrewdly replied, "Tomorrow morning. Be here by eight if you think you have what it takes to make it here!"

"I'll be here!" I flatly stated, thinking to myself, *I'll show you!* By the time I made it outside, I realized the gravity of what my arrogance and pride had done. I didn't want to work there! I didn't even know what the job was! I didn't know what I was to be paid, what the job entailed, or even what was expected of me. I didn't know anything! I had completely ignored everything that the interviewer had said to me about what they did, what they sold, or what the job was. I didn't want to work there—but I was stuck because my pride wouldn't let me cave into that "arrogant SOB" sitting behind the cherry wood desk that had insulted and challenged me. That "arrogant" man's name was Tony Dopp.

Over the next few days, I found myself literally sitting in the boiler room (the utility room) of a "boiler-room-type" telemarketing call center. I had reached a new low in my life (or so I thought). Here I was a college graduate with a respectable theology degree, sitting at an old desk in an ugly little cubicle, in the most undesirable available office, next to a furnace, doing the actual job that I swore upon graduation that I would never do—telemarketing. Surrounding me were all kinds of high school dropouts, drunkards, drug addicts, and weekend partiers whose seemingly only goals and purposes in life were to blow their paychecks on booze, drugs, and lap dances. I was embarrassed to tell anybody what I did for a living, but at the same time, too proud to quit. I didn't want to let Tony think that he, or the job, had beaten me and that I wasn't the "cream" that I had purported to be. It is funny to look back now and realize that my own pride had put me in a "prison" so to speak. It wasn't the first time that my pride had gotten me locked away in a corner, and as I was going to find out in a few more years, it certainly wasn't going to be my last.

God has a strange way of making you do what He wants. It was obvious that I was where He intended for me to be. Let me explain. I had figured that I would land a few deals just to show Tony that I could do the job, and then I would split just as soon as I heard from Merrill Lynch offering me a position. But God had other plans for me. On my second day there, He gave me a big order so that I would stay. It literally fell into my lap. I didn't even know what I was doing. I cold called a lady in Tennessee off a marketing list to try and sell her blank videotapes (that is what our company did), but she asked me if we offered video-tape duplication services instead. After checking with my floor supervisor, I assured her that we did, and she gave me an order for sixty-seven hundred videos. In those days, this was considered a really big order—especially since it was her first order with our company and I was a brand new salesperson. Since we got paid on a commission basis after the order was completed and the job shipped, I had to wait around for my commission check. I was planning to quit as soon as I got paid, which I was figuring would only take about two weeks. However, there was a delay in produc-tion on her end, and by the time the job was actually completed and shipped, and I finally received my commission check, a whole month and a half had passed! So by the time that I finally got paid, I had already landed a number of other good clients who each had quite a few orders pending—so I had to continue to wait around for those good commission checks. As you probably can guess, it was during this time that Merrill Lynch finally called me and offered me an entry-level position with their company. But by now, I was making pretty good money where I was and having fun, and I didn't want to just walk away from my easy and lucrative residual commission checks. Needless to say, God was obviously blessing me at VU Videos and wanted me to remain there, so I turned Merrill Lynch down.

As the weeks and months went by, I grew to absolutely love Tony as my boss and friend. In many ways, he was like a father to me. He taught me so much about business and sales that I will be forever grateful. Little did I realize then, but God had personally placed Tony in my life to teach me many things—especially humility. Although, Tony wasn't a Christian believer then, he always had a tender and kind spirit, coupled with great business savvy. The "arrogance" that I was initially feeling from him was actually really my own youthful arrogance being reflected back at me, and Tony knew how to "push my pride buttons" to motivate and challenge me. And that is what he did—in order to bring out the best in me. He was very good at reading people and giving them what they personally needed. I remember thinking to myself back then that if I were to ever go into business with somebody in the future I would want it to be him. He was such a great business manager, gifted both in leadership and in administrative skills, and had a wealth of experience. I had such a deep and profound respect for him that I had never had for anyone else in business. He was, and still is, the best manager that I have ever known.

After about four years of working for Tony though, sadly Tony's mother grew gravely ill, and so he had to quit his job with VU Videos and move to California to be with her during her final years on this earth. I continued on as a telemarketing sales person for another three years with great success. The Lord granted me a federal government contract, which in turn gave me a very lucrative sales commission every month. Things were going very well financially for Teresa and me. But spiritually, as I had mentioned before, it was during this time that our church began changing its long-held doctrines, and things began to spiritually change for me personally. It was about this time in the spring of 1995 that God would begin to regularly speak and communicate with me and my life would never be the same again.

REVELATIONS FROM THE LORD

I was twenty-six years old when I began having visions from the Lord. Other than that one time when I was eighteen, I had never had a vision before and had never heard of anyone having visions from the Lord (other than in the Bible), and so I didn't know what they were. Because my faith had been severely shaken as a result of the changes that my church was making denominationally, I had been crying out to God for many days and nights, seeking to know Him apart from man's institutions. I didn't want to rely on man or his interpretations anymore. I wanted to know God for myself! I didn't realize it then, but I really didn't know Him. I knew *about* Him, but I didn't *know* Him *personally*. I wanted a direct relationship with Him—and not through a man's organization anymore. Little did I realize, but I was soon about to meet Him and begin to know Him as He really is. One morning in March of 1995, around 7:30 a.m., I was waiting for Teresa to finish getting ready for work so that we could drive downtown together. (We both worked downtown about a half a mile apart.) As I was sitting on the couch waiting for her, I fell into a vision. I didn't realize it until it was over, but it is sort of like falling into a daydream, yet you can clearly see and hear everything as if it is really happening. This is what I saw: I was sitting in a chair at church, when all of a sudden, the pastor, Tim Snyder, came rushing in with his sermon notes all in disarray sticking out of his Bible and briefcase. He came over to me and said, "Hey, Eric, I don't have my sermon quite prepared yet, so can you please go up there (to the podium) for me and say a few words in order to stall, so that I can get my message ready?" Thinking it strange that he would choose me, I reluctantly said, "Okay," because he was my pastor and personal friend.

As I went up there on the stage and stood behind the podium, I wondered to myself what I should say to the people as I looked out over them. I finally thought to myself, *I know—I will tell them what I did this week.* As I proceeded to open my mouth to speak my own inane words, I immediately heard an authoritative Voice speak from directly behind me in my ear. The commanding Voice said this: "No, but speak these words that I say unto you!" As I heard Him speak, I was astonished at the words He was saying, and thought to myself, *I can't say these things! The people will kill me. These words are way too bold and authoritative!* Nevertheless, I said everything that the Voice commanded me, not even really understanding the words myself. When I finished repeating everything that was spoken in my ear, the people stared at me in utter disbelief and astonishment. All eyes were focused on me, and the room was so quiet that you could hear a pin drop. As I quietly and sheepishly slumped back to my seat, wondering what in the world I had just said, lowering my head as I sat down, the pastor came over to me and angrily said, "I want to see you out in the hall during break!"

The vision immediately flashed forward in time, and I was standing in the hall with the pastor who was bent over me, yelling at me, and demanding to know "why I was speaking like that!" I could see myself cowardly wincing and sheepishly drawing back not knowing why I had been saying the things that I had been saying. Then after a few moments, in this submissive and frightened position, with the pastor towering over me, the heavenly Voice suddenly reappeared behind me, and immediately spoke through my mouth again. The Voice had me forcefully say to Mr. Snyder, "As it is written: 'With stammering lips and another tongue will He speak to this—His people!'" At that moment, Mr. Snyder recognized the Voice that was speaking to him, and his eyes flew open, and he became afraid. He stepped back from persecuting me and humbly withdrew himself from towering over me. At that instant, the vision ended, and I was left sitting there on my couch wondering what in the world I had just seen.

After shaking my head for a few minutes in disbelief, trying to "snap out of it" and wondering if I had been daydreaming, I marveled at what I had just witnessed. *With stammering lips and another tongue will He speak to His people? Who the heck talks like that?* I thought to myself. *Stammering lips? What the heck does that mean?* I kept asking myself over and over again. As I sat there on the couch, my mind racing and still wondering if I had dreamed it, I suddenly remembered that in the vision I had said the phrase, "It is written." The only time that I had ever heard that phrase used was when someone was quoting the Bible like when Jesus was talking to Satan or to the Jewish people, He would say, "It is written..." I ran to grab my Bible concordance to look up the words "stammering lips" to see if this phrase was used in the Bible. As I looked, to my surprise, there it was written in Isaiah: "For with stammering lips and another tongue He will speak to this people" (Isaiah 28:11). Needless to say, I was astonished, and greatly perplexed, as well as a little bit scared. *What did this vision mean? Was it something that my own subconscious mind had concocted? Is it possible for a human mind to quote Scriptures that it has never even read before?* These are some of the thoughts that raced through my mind as I went to work that day. But as I was about to find out, this was only the beginning! For the next solid week, I saw nonstop visions about a great many things. I heard and witnessed unspeakable things—things that are too incredible to mention (2 Corinthians 12:3–4). I was shown interpretations and illustrations of Scriptures that I had never known or understood before. I was given revelations that only a spiritual mind could identify with. Certainly, I didn't have one of those spiritual minds! In fact, my own human carnal mind was struggling to resist and reject everything that I was being shown—but to no avail. God was beginning to reveal Himself, His will, and His incredible plans to me that was leaving me astonished, without breath, in tears, unable to speak, and at times, on my face like a dead man (Daniel 10:8–11, 15–17). These visions and revelations lasted an entire week.

That whole week I could neither cuss nor think in the natural (physical) realm. Every time that I would try to form my lips to say something unclean or profane (God forgive me), my mouth would literally contort, and I would be unable to speak at all. As I would go to work, I would see barren trees in front of my office building instantly bud, leaf, bear fruit, and then wither away, becoming totally barren again all in a single instant, right before my very eyes.

Everything before me became spiritual, and I could see. It was as if my eyes had been spiritually opened, and I could see things that were not visible to the natural world. In my mind, I would see whole scenes of people, congregations, and nations, being dramatized and illustrated before me, as the Holy Spirit would narrate from the Scriptures, so that I could understand their true spiritual meanings and prophetic significance. What went on that week with me can only be described in the words that Luke wrote when he described how Jesus had "unlocked the disciples' minds so that they could now understand the Scriptures" (Luke 24:45)—even though His disciples, being Jews, had heard and studied the Scriptures all of their lives just as I had. It wasn't until Jesus *unlocked their minds* did they really begin to understand and comprehend the Scriptures' hidden meanings. Just like what happened to the disciples in the Bible, my whole spiritual world and scriptural understanding was being turned upside down. I was beginning to realize the true meaning of what God says in His Word—that it is *impossible* to understand the things of God without the Spirit of God revealing it to a person (1 Corinthians 2:10–14).

During that week, I thought that I was going crazy, losing my mind, and possibly being tormented by demons (God forgive me). I was so new to the Spirit and how He works that it certainly can be said about me as it was said about young Samuel, that "he did not yet know the Lord, nor was the word of the Lord yet made manifest to him" (1 Samuel 3:7). At first, I too, was ignorant of the Lord's ways and did not yet fully recognize His voice or His Spirit. Believe me, it is a process. Although a little child almost immediately recognizes the authority of his parents' voices from birth, it takes a while for him to come to understand the wisdom behind what his parents are saying and to realize what his parents' underlying motivations are for saying it. I am not saying here that I fully understand God or His ways. That is impossible—His ways and mind are beyond searching out. I am just saying that it can sometimes take a while (and a lifetime) to understand just a few things that God reveals—let alone, during this one particular week in which He was seemingly revealing a lot to me. I was overwhelmed! I felt like I was losing my mind during this time. And I wasn't the only one who thought I was going crazy. My darling wife, Teresa, thought so as well—and to some degree, she still thinks that I am. And unfortunately, this would prove to be a real trial and personal struggle for me for many years to come.

Shortly before the week of visions began is when God told me that we were going to be having a baby girl whose middle name we were to call Elizabeth. After He told me that, my wife, Teresa, became pregnant approximately two weeks later. She had gone in for her routine pap smear when the nurse insisted that she take a pregnancy test there in the office because she suspected that my wife might be pregnant. Indeed, she was. Over the next three months, however, Teresa became severely ill. She could not hold anything down—she would vomit excessively. In fact, I had to take her to the hospital three times to be treated for dehydration. I believe that it was in the third or fourth month of her pregnancy that we went to the doctor's office to do an emergency ultrasound. You can imagine the pain and shock that we felt when the doctor told us that the baby's heartbeat had stopped—and that it was dead. In grief, my wife had a DNC a few minutes later—which is a medical procedure in which they go in and clean out her uterus and dispose of the nonviable fetus. It was a sad time for us. It was the first conception that we had ever had, and now it was gone.

To our surprise and joy though, my wife conceived again a short time later. We were so excited! This time the early ultrasound showed two fertilized eggs in her womb. But sadly, after about two more weeks, those embryos died as well. I remember being in the doctor's office with my wife when we received the sad news. Again, we were heartbroken and grief stricken. Teresa and I had driven separately to the doctor's office that day because I was originally planning to return to work after the ultrasound. However, instead of immediately returning to work, I went back to my car and just sat there in the doctor's office parking lot and wept. "Why, God? Why have You done this to us? Why have You given us hope and then stripped it away?" I asked in tears. I was deeply broken and saddened. My insides ached for my wife and for the children that would never be.

Suddenly, even though my car windows and doors were tightly shut, what appeared to be a faint wind quickly moved through my car, and delicately spoke to me. It sounded like a breathy whisper; yet I could clearly hear it speaking to me. This heavenly Presence gently said, "Eric, remember, I said, 'Do not worry. Your wife *will* give birth to a baby girl.'" I knew then that the Lord had just spoken to me and that everything was going to be fine. And for the first time in my life, I suddenly understood the Scriptures that describe the Holy Spirit as being our Comforter, and sometimes coming to us as a wind or sounding like a faint whisper (John 3:8; Acts 2:2–4; 1 Kings 19:12). I now *knew by firsthand experience* what Jesus meant when He said that the Holy Spirit would comfort us by bringing all things to our remembrance that He had spoken to us (John 14:16, 26). "For He will not testify of Himself; but what-soever He hears and receives of Me," Jesus said, "that He will declare unto you" (John 16:13–15). This faint windlike whisper was the Holy Spirit reminding me of the promise that God had made Teresa and me regarding being given a daughter by Him. Now all I needed to do was believe and persevere, and learn to trust and relax, and let Jesus deliver on what He had promised. I was greatly encouraged after I heard the Holy Spirit remind me of God's promise to me, and I drove to work that day truly comforted and excited that God was indeed with me. And to our delight, approximately three weeks later, my wife became preg-nant again! This time, the pregnancy took, and nine months later we received our precious long-sought-after baby. It was our Kate Elizabeth—the beautiful daughter that God had promised us.

As Kate steadily grew, and as time went by, my wife and I were beginning to wonder if Kate could have any brothers or sisters, or if she was to be an only child. Silly me, not wanting to appear ungrateful to God or greedy, I was hesitant to outright ask Him about it. Even though, He had already proven to me (in terms of the naming of Kate Elizabeth) that He can read our thoughts, I tried to hide my true concerns and feelings about it from Him. Being spiritually immature and foolish, my wife and I both kind of fell into superstitious thinking regarding having more chil-dren. We foolishly reasoned that if we outright tried to have more children, we might receive a handicapped or deformed child "as punishment" for not being satisfied with having just Kate. On the other hand, if we "accidentally" had one, then maybe it wouldn't clearly be "our fault," and God would forgive us and bless us with another one since it was an "accident." How stupid and foolish we are! But God knows that in comparison to Him, we have the minds and spiritual maturity of two-year-olds. After a few months of not knowing what to do, and trying to "perform my part as a man" under such indecisive and anxiety-filled circumstances, I quit trying to get my wife pregnant altogether and just resigned myself to the fact that maybe "it just wasn't meant to be." Neither Teresa nor I shared our predicament and concerns over this with anybody.

One day, though, after church as I was getting ready to leave, the Spirit of the Lord said to me, "See that man over there walking in the courtyard. Go to him!" I didn't really know the man too well, but I obediently walked up behind him and tapped him on the shoulder.

He was alone, and he callously turned to look at me as if to say, "What do you want and why are you bothering me?!"

I said, "Hi, sir. Do you have something for me?"

He quickly said, "No."

I insisted, "Yes, you do. What is it?"

He snapped back, "No, I don't!" and he turned to leave.

I grabbed his sleeve and said, "Yes, you do!" as I pulled him back to me.

Seemingly annoyed, he half turned around and suddenly looked up as if he was having a conversation with somebody over my head. After nodding, he looked at me with a smile on his face and said, "The Lord God says that you can have as many children as you want and that you are going to have a boy!" After saying this, the man quickly walked away. He was a black man that I didn't know very well at the time but who would later become a very close friend and spiritual mentor.

EARLY ASSIGNMENTS

As you have probably realized by now after having read the previous chapters, it was during this time from 1995 to 1999 that the Lord was beginning to regularly communicate with me. Shortly after the week of visions in the spring of 1995, God began continually speaking to me, although it seemed to be mostly a word spoken directly in my ear from behind me. As I am relaying this now, the following Scripture comes to mind: "Your ears shall hear a word behind you, saying, 'This is the way, walk in it,' whenever you turn to the right hand or whenever you turn to the left" (Isaiah 30:21). This Voice behind me kept telling me what to do, and I was learning to trust it. Before I go any further, I need to give a little background information first. I had been raised a Christian. I belonged to a church denomination that taught the validity and authenticity of the Bible. We believed and taught that the Bible is the absolute truth and word of God and that Jesus Christ is the Son of God. We taught our members to be God-fearing people who sincerely and earnestly practiced what we preached, and we were people who dedicated our lives and earnings to what we felt was right and what was expected of us. Although we preached and believed that Jesus Christ is living, and that the Holy Spirit is real, like most churches, we didn't claim to see Him or hear from Him. So now that God was personally talking to me, I found myself in a real quandary. I didn't really tell anybody what was going on. For the most part, during this time, I chose to just remain quiet and withdrawn.

On one particular day in 1997 however (I think it was about then), God instructed me to go and tell Andy Benavides that his son Eddie was going to be healed. Eddie was about fifteen or sixteen at the time and had been born severely handicapped. (I had had a vision two years earlier showing me what the Lord is planning to do, and how He is going to heal Eddie and others in due time, after a period of prophesying, in order to spiritually wake people up.) One particular night after Bible study, I was getting into my car to leave when the word of the Lord suddenly came to me. God said to me (in my ear), "Tell Andy Benavides, 'Thus says the Lord God: I will heal your son, Eddie, not because *you* don't believe, but because *others* don't believe. For the Lord your God *knows* that you believe.'"

I looked up from putting my key into my car door, and Andy was there in front of me getting into his car in the driveway. I called to him, and as he approached, I said the words that the Lord had commanded me to speak to him. Upon hearing these words, Andy grabbed me and tightly hugged me, with tears running from his eyes, he exclaimed, "I knew it! I knew it! I knew that God had heard me, and that he is going to heal Eddie!" Stunned, I got into my car in a state of disbelief, wondering what in the world was going on.

God had already previously told me that those who believed would weep when they heard His words spoken to them. During the week when I was given the visions two years earlier, one particular vision given to me was that I was standing on a small platform down in an "underground basement of a church" so to speak, speaking to a small group of people. All of the people who were there I recognized as being from my local church congregation. Most of the people in the small audience were bored, sleeping, looking at their watches, and yawning. I could tell that they just weren't "getting it." In the vision I was standing on a very small platform speaking to them, by way of a steady stream of water which was coming down out of heaven and flowing down through my head and out my mouth unto the people, but they just weren't receiving it. Only a very small handful of people (two or three at most) sitting in the front row of the audience were receiving what I was saying. This small handful of people had their eyes looking up toward heaven with their hands outspread rejoicing and praising God for the satisfying water that they were drinking in that flowed out of my mouth. To them the words that I was speaking were cool and refreshing, and greatly thirst-quenching, and tears of joy were streaming down their faces as they tasted the "holy water" that was coming out of my mouth. As I was witnessing this in the vision, the Lord said to me, "Behold, the believers will weep at the hearing of My words." Now, here I was telling Andy what God had just commanded me to speak to him, and he started crying. Obviously, Andy Benavides believed. As soon as he heard the words of the Lord coming out of my mouth, he unashamedly wept tears of joy in praise to God. I was amazed by his show of faith, because at the time (I now realize), I really didn't have much faith.

A couple of days later as I walked into church, the Lord said to me, "Behold, Al Thornton! Go to him and tell him these words: 'Thus says the Lord God: 'I will heal your son, Paul; not because *you*

don't believe, but because *others* don't believe; therefore I will do this!'"
I went over to him (he was standing in the hallway) and pulled him
away privately from the others and said those exact words to him. He
immediately threw his arms around me and excitedly jumped up and
down and shouted, "I knew it! I knew that God is going to heal Paul!
Thank you! Thank you! Thank you so much!" Again, I was stunned
at both Andy's and Al's mighty faith.

To my own shame (because of my lack of belief) I walked
away from Al Thornton greatly discouraged and mad at myself.
How could I do such a thing? I thought to myself. *How could I give
such kind sincere men as Al Thornton and Andy Benavides such false
hope about their sons? How could I be so heartless and cruel?* I hated
myself. I couldn't figure out why I was doing such "wickedness."
How could I do such evil to these kind men? I wondered. As I sat in
church that day with my head down, contemplating what had
transpired, and my part in it, I loathed myself. I thought of poor
Al Thornton and his severely handicapped wheelchaired son,
Paul, and how I had given Al such false hope of his son's complete miraculous healing. I detested myself and promised myself
that I would never do such an evil thing again. When the church
service concluded, a black man who had been sitting to the left of
me, whom I didn't know, suddenly came up to me.

He was apparently a stranger who had just relocated to Denver
from California, and this was his first time attending our local
church congregation. He said to me, in somewhat of a Southern
drawl, "Wow! That was a great sermon now, wasn't it?"

Because I was so preoccupied and concerned with my distressing situation, I didn't even really hear the sermon that day. So I
sheepishly muttered, "Yeah, I guess so."

"Can I tell you something?" he politely asked.

"Sure." I responded.

"Do you know when that pastor was up there speaking, and when he stopped in the middle of his sermon and asked us all to join him in prayer?"

"Yeah." I nodded.

"Well, as soon as I put my head down in prayer, I heard a loud Voice speak to me that said, 'Lift your head up and look upon that boy over there.' (He was pointing at Eddie Benavides). 'I will do this!' And immediately I saw that disfigured boy become completely whole in front of me from head to toe! And then the Voice said to me again, 'Look up, see that man over there sitting in a wheelchair.' (He was pointing at Paul Thornton). 'I will do this!' I saw that handicapped young man literally just get right up out of his wheelchair and begin walking!"

My knees buckled underneath me, and I thought that I was going to pass out when I heard these words! I began shaking, and tears filled my eyes, as I realized that *I* hadn't done these things at all. God, in His mercy, was sending another to let me know that I hadn't imagined these things, nor was I orchestrating them, and that He was surely going to bring to pass all that He had told me. (I have tears rolling down my face even now as I recall this. It has been so long. I have struggled so much. I have endured much heartache to faithfully proclaim what He has privately whispered in my ear so long ago.) I quickly bolted out the door, skipping, and jumping, and dancing all the way, rejoicing at what my God had done for me and praising Him for what He is shortly going to do.

A few months later after this, I went to a Feast of Tabernacles planning meeting. This was an annual churchwide event that at the time our church denomination felt was commanded in the Bible to be observed. After the meeting, as we were leaving, I found myself in a casual conversation with another member of the church. His name was Jerry Olson. I didn't know Jerry very well, but nonetheless, we were standing in the parking lot talking about modern technology, when all of a sudden "that Voice" began talking to me again, this time directly over Jerry's head. The Lord said to me, "Tell him!" I knew what that meant. Up to this point, I had not told anybody what had been happening to me. I kept it to myself. But I was learning to trust Him. Gradually and steadily, I was learning to obey what God was telling me to do. After all, I was beginning to realize and *know* that it was Him talking to me. God was slowly and methodically increasing my belief (faith) in Him. I was beginning to recognize His voice and trust Him. And as a result, the frequency and size of my assignments were shortly going to increase as well. As Jesus said, "If you only have but the faith [belief] the size of a mustard seed" in Him it will steadily grow and increase until you can say unto a mountain, "Go and cast yourself into the sea," and it will obey you—if you have learned not to doubt in your heart (Matthew 17:20; 21:21). I was slowly learning how to trust Him by obeying what He was giving me to do.

At that moment when God told me to "tell Jerry," I immediately grabbed him and hugged him and joyfully told him that he had found favor with the Lord. As Jerry looked at me with a bewildered look on his face, I hugged him so fondly and tightly that he later told me that it was like receiving a hug from "a father that had finally found his long lost son." This is funny because Jerry at the time was probably twice (if not three times) my senior. As we slowly walked to my car, I proceeded to tell him that the Lord had a word for him and that I was sent to give it to him. Because it was after dark and cold out, we got into my car where I asked him if we could take a moment to pray first. I did this because I didn't yet know what specifically I was to tell him from the Lord. After we prayed together, the Lord immediately opened my mouth and I told him what the Lord wanted me to. We spoke and fellowshipped together for over two solid hours! I can't even tell you what we talked about except to say that the Lord was upon me and filling my mouth for the entire time. Jerry believed and rejoiced at what God told him. Shortly after that, the Lord began using Jerry to miraculously heal people of many different illnesses and diseases. I will write more about Jerry later.

A "CRISIS WEDGE" IN THE CHURCH

It was about this time that the Lord's prophecy concerning me being used as a "wedge" by Him in my local church congregation began to come to pass. I vaguely alluded to this in my diary entry dated 12/26/95 that I quoted from earlier:

> There have been a couple of times that I'm sure that I heard God's voice ... Some of the things that I can remember are: That one day in the near future, I was going to speak with the "mouth of God" by His Holy Spirit, and say some marvelous things (not of myself), and that the whole congregation and the pastor were going to be dumbfounded; that when I had begun speaking under this divine inspiration, that I would eventually come to speak to great multitudes of people and that some would believe, and many would not.

Although I didn't mention it specifically in my diary entry here, I was also told at that time that I would unwittingly become "a wedge" to my local church congregation—being used by God to begin dividing people by causing them to have a crisis of belief. At the time that this was said to me by the Holy Spirit, I had no idea what it meant. Little by little though, things began heating up in church. Out of the blue, my pastor, Tim Snyder, asked me to serve as the youth pastor. He wanted me to begin teaching and instructing the teens and young adults, by holding Bible studies for them, as well as counseling them in the things of the Lord. I reluctantly accepted the job, wondering why he was asking *me* to do it. Soon afterwards, he ordained me a "deacon," and began inviting me to the "deacons and elders meetings." These deacons and elders meetings were official church meetings for the local church leadership that discussed the goals, visions, and overall management of the church and its affairs. The whole time that I was in these meetings, I felt uneasy because unbeknownst to anyone else there, the Lord was all the while revealing things to me in my ear and in my heart that seemed to contradict and oppose the very plans that the church leadership was intending to enact. It was hard sitting there obediently and submissively listening to men make religious plans that God was going to thwart in order to fulfill His sovereign purposes. I was definitely caught between two worlds. I did not want to be divisive nor disruptive; neither did I want to be disloyal to Mr. Snyder and the elders, whom I considered my friends; but I couldn't stop the Spirit from speaking to me, nor did I necessarily want to. But I was being put into a situation that I couldn't stop or control, and it was severely testing my loyalties and my conscience. I tried, best as I could, to just remain silent and supportive.

Every time that I had a Bible study for the teens and young adults, God would not allow me to prepare ahead of time. Somehow I knew in my spirit that I was not allowed to prepare a message, study a subject, or think about what I was going to say or teach them.

Instead, whenever the meeting would begin, God would suddenly appear in my mouth and begin expounding on a whole range of pertinent biblical subjects. All of the teens and young adults would eagerly listen, ask questions, and become personally inspired and filled with hope. The numbers kept increasing. The teens would bring their friends from school, neighbors, relatives, and eventually, even their parents. Their younger preteen siblings were beginning to come too. I never told anyone to bring anybody, but pretty soon, other parents and adults were asking if they too could come to my Bible studies. Before long, and because of growing demand, I was holding two to three Bible studies a week for anyone and everyone who was interested; one on the west side of town and one on the east side of town and one at my house for the teens. It was all happening so fast! Although I was excited and amazed at what was happening and the seemingly insatiable spiritual hunger of the people, I was quickly becoming exhausted and still wasn't quite sure why I was the one teaching them. Within a few weeks, I received a phone call from Connie Armstrong. She was in charge of the upcoming "church campout" that was going to be taking place up in the mountains in a month. She asked me if I would be willing to give the sermon at the church service during the church-wide campout. She indicated that Mr. Snyder had already given his approval for me to do so. Realizing that this "assignment" was from God and not from man, I gladly accepted the honor. A few weeks later as the campout weekend drew near, I grabbed my Bible and a pen and paper, with the intent to begin preparing my sermon message. As soon as I had these supplies in hand, I knelt down and asked God what He wanted me to speak about. Immediately, He spoke to me and told me to get up and to not think about it anymore, but to take only my Bible on the day of the service, and that He would give me at that moment what He wanted me to say to the people *then*. Needless to say, I was both shaken and scared. This was a real test for me. The sermon is typically ninety minutes long. How was I supposed to go up there in front of a crowd of people with no sermon notes, no prepared message, and no idea what I was supposed to talk about, for an hour and a half, just trusting that this Voice that had been privately talking to me was going to show up? Speaking to a bunch of teenagers (and a few adults) "off-the-cuff" in an informal-type setting is one thing, but speaking to the entire church body in an official service-type setting, as the main speaker giving the sermon "off-the-cuff" is quite another! And according to the Lord, I was only allowed to bring my Bible with me and nothing else. Needless to say, I was scared to death—all the more so as the campout weekend fast approached.

About an hour before church services, I remember pacing back and forth in the woods, begging God to please show up and either tell me what it was that He wanted me to say or to get me out of the assignment altogether. Neither request was granted. I sat in my seat during church with a sickening feeling of extreme anxiety in my stomach as the song leader led the congregation in singing hymns and sharing the church announcements. Afterwards, he announced that I would be giving the sermon and then proceeded to introduce me as the main speaker. I took a deep breath, grabbed my Bible, and obediently walked up to the podium with the beautiful mountain wilderness behind me as my backdrop. Clutching the makeshift podium, and still not sure what I was to speak about, I asked the congregation if we could take a moment to pray together first. As soon as the prayer ended, the Lord suddenly filled my mouth with His words! I can't tell you what I said that day, but all I know is that I was literally "a voice crying in the wilderness," and when I was done speaking about ninety minutes later, the people were stunned and sat there speechless with their mouths hanging wide open. A woman suddenly and uncharacteristically stood up and immediately began praising God out loud with her hands extended in the air. She began singing praises to God and leading everyone in a prayer of repentance and thanksgiving. This had never been done before in our congregation. We were a very quiet and conservative church and our women usually remained extraordinarily quiet. The people began both openly repenting and praising God, while some of the elders began to curiously stare at me, scratching their heads and wondering why (and how) I was speaking that way. Mr. Snyder was not there, but somehow I knew that he was soon going to be hearing about it. It seemed that the vision that I had had three years earlier regarding Mr. Snyder unwittingly granting me a platform from which to speak to the congregation was now coming to pass.

Later that night, a few people who had been at the church service came over to me at the campfire and began asking me questions. Strangely though, each time that I tried to answer their spiritual questions, my mouth locked up so tight that I couldn't utter a word. After a few strange looks of bewilderment from them, and some rather uncomfortable moments, my friend, whom I had confided in earlier, suddenly saw what was happening, and immediately spoke up for me. He said to them, "Please don't be offended by Eric's silence. He doesn't intend it to be so. But sometimes God will not allow him to speak about things that God Himself has hidden for a time yet appointed." I was truly grateful for this man to have said this, because it was extremely awkward for me to not be able to speak to some people who sincerely wanted to know certain things. I would suddenly become mute in front of them, not able to even speak, and I am sure that they thought that I was being discourteous and rude toward them, seemingly ignoring them. One man in particular wanted to know if he should still pay his tithes or not. I knew the answer because the Lord had previously answered that question for me. However, the Lord would not let me answer him then. For it was not yet time for me to become a division and a wedge within my local church congregation.

A few months later, Mr. Snyder called me and told me that he wanted me to begin preparing a sermon to give to the congregation. He and I had become close friends and had talked often on the phone. Although, I rarely shared anything with him that God was telling me and showing me, Mr. Snyder could see that I was daily growing more and more in faith, and so he wanted me to give a message on faith to the congregation. I eagerly accepted his invitation and asked the Lord regarding it. This time God had me write the whole message out—and it literally just flowed out of me unto the paper. God began to show me things that I had never personally understood before from the Scriptures regarding truly believing (faith). He showed me what it truly means to believe, and that each of us needs to ask ourselves whether we truly *believed* or not. He explained to me that *true belief requires action*. He reminded me that in the Bible He declared that "faith without works [actions] is dead" (James 2:17–26). In other words, faith without actions does not exist—there is no faith or belief therefore. The Lord had me warn the congregation in my sermon that if they did not begin to believe and then demonstrate that faith through works, then they would find themselves doing the same thing that their spiritual ancestors under Moses did—they, too, would waste away in the desert place and their carcasses would fall in the wilderness just like the first generation of Israelites did that came out of Egypt. He also had me quote to them what was written in the prophets: "Behold, I will work a work in your days, says the Lord that is so marvelous that you will not believe it; even if a man were sent to tell you these things" (Isaiah 29:14; Habakkuk 1:5; Acts 13:41). The sermon was well received, though the people were astonished at my words—including Mr. Snyder. It was quickly becoming apparent to me that what God had foretold (in my earlier vision) was indeed being fulfilled.

As the Bible studies continued and increased, God was giving me more and more boldness in preaching and teaching His Word. After one particular Bible study, God said something to me regarding a very sincere and God-fearing woman who had been assisting me by opening up her house for the Bible studies. He said to me, in regard to her: "Behold, Mary Magdalene!" Perplexed, I then proceeded to tell her what the Lord had just said to me about her. The lady was greatly honored and deeply touched. At the time, I didn't know anything about her past. I didn't even know why the Lord had said that to me. But she proceeded to tell me about herself after I told her what God had said. Her name is Gail Schwindt. She apparently has had a very checkered past—with many broken relationships, numerous husbands, abusive boyfriends, and sexual sins, etc. Because of this troubled and sinful past, today she is a very humble and giving person. I can honestly say she is one of the most loving and kind and sincere women that I have ever met. She is dear to the Lord and loves Him with all of her heart. As Jesus once said, "Whosoever is forgiven of much, the same loves much" (Luke 7:47). In truth, this lady has served the saints and the people of God with much love and humility. She has also personally shown me much honor. Later, when many people were beginning to reject me and scorn me, she would often come to my aid, and comfort me, both supporting me and reminding me of the promises and faithfulness of our Lord. As Jesus said, "Whosoever receives a prophet in the name of a prophet, shall receive a prophet's reward. And whosoever receives a righteous man because he is a righteous man shall receive a righteous man's reward" (Matthew 10:41). Because of her kindness and graciousness toward the Lord's servants, the Lord had me tell her that although she has always been poor in terms of this world's goods, "she would never lack for a chicken on her table!" I didn't even know why the Lord specifically had me say "a chicken" to her, but that is what He said. After I said this to her according to His command, she humbly wept and joyfully explained to me that a few weeks earlier she had gone to the grocery store and, using her last bit of money, had bought a chicken for her family to eat and then bought a second one for another family that she barely knew that didn't have anything to eat. She felt at the time that the Lord wanted her to, so she did it, spending her last dimes to do so in order to honor and obey the Lord, and love and serve His people. Therefore, God had me declare to her that *she* would never lack for a chicken on *her* table—even during the soon-coming economic famine.

On another occasion, the Lord had me point at Jerry Olson and declare openly that he was a type of Stephen. Stephen was "one of the seven" whom the Lord had chosen to help with the daily distribution of the church's goods to the poor and needy within the church (Acts 6:1–6). The Bible says that he went on to preach and to do "great wonders and miracles among the people" describing him as being "full of faith and power" (Acts 6:8). He withstood the Sanhedrin—that is, the priestly ruling class of the Jews—witnessing to them, and ultimately gave his life in service to Jesus Christ being one of the Lord's first martyrs in the New Testament. At the time that the Lord first said this to me regarding Jerry being a type of Stephen, Jerry hadn't done any miracles, nor laid his hands on anyone in order to heal them, and he certainly wasn't in charge of the local church's treasury or funds distribution. Soon afterwards, however, Jerry was given a position with another church body, and to his surprise was immediately put in charge of the church's finances and church charity distributions. As was mentioned earlier, he also has since been given the gift of healings and miracles by the Holy Spirit and has been faithfully utilizing these gifts as the Spirit leads him. At the time of this writing, he is steadily growing in his faith in the Lord, and it will certainly be exciting to see what mighty things the Lord will have him yet do in His service in the future—martyrdom notwithstanding.

A TYPE OF JOHN
THE BAPTIST?

I need to relay one more biblical character type and modern-day counterpart here. I realize that some readers might find these biblical character types and modern-day counterparts distracting, unorthodox, offensive, and maybe even heretical. Believe me, that is how I viewed it too initially. However, keep in mind that the Holy Spirit was the One giving them to me, and when I questioned the veracity of it within my own mind, the Spirit quickly answered by saying, "Behold, it is written that they shall call their names after the surnames of Israel" (Isaiah 44:5). Obviously, I didn't know this Scripture beforehand. The Spirit quoted it to me when I was wondering about these things. Please bear in mind that the Lord often changes people's names or calls them by a different name which has spiritual significance and prophetic meaning: Jesus changed Simon's name to "Peter or Cephas" which means "a stone" (Mark 3:16; John 1:42). The Lord called John the Baptist "Elijah" thus pointing out the spiritual work he was doing (Matthew 11:12–14; 17:12–13). Moses changed Hoshea's name to "Joshua" meaning "savior and/or deliverer" (Numbers 13:16). In this way, Joshua became a prophetic type representing Jesus. The name Joshua was used to prophetically illustrate the fact that the Law (personified by Moses) could not deliver the children of Israel from their sins into the promised land; but rather God needed to appoint a "savior" who would deliver His people into the true "promised land"—the kingdom of God. The point is that God calls things (and people) before they are known to serve as prophetic types in order to fulfill His purposes and to impart spiritual understanding (Romans 4:17).

This brings me to an elderly black man named Tucker. Actually, his name is Welton Tucker. He is seventy-two years old, and by the world's standards, he is poor, uneducated, uncouth, undesirable, and insubordinate. According to his own mouth, he literally was "a castaway baby whose own teenage mother put him in a shoebox as an infant under her bed and left him there to die." His grandmother heard him crying, came and found him under the bed, and fed him biscuits and coffee because he couldn't digest milk. He never really knew his father, seldom interacted with his mother, was the eldest of twenty-four kids, and grew up in the backward hills of Tennessee when the Jim Crow laws of racial segregation were at their peak. The Lord called him at age twenty-three, revealed Himself to him at age twenty-eight, and then later told him that he was going to be "sat down for thirty years hidden away in white churches sitting amongst the Jews" waiting until the day when the Lord was going to reveal him (Luke 1:80). This is that same man that sat next to me one day while visiting our church, and who told me that the Lord had just told him that "that young boy over there [Eddie Benavides] and that man over there sitting in the wheelchair [Paul Thornton] are going to be healed one day by God." This is also the same man that the Spirit later sent me to who told me that the Lord said that Teresa and I could have as many children as we wanted and that we were going to have a boy.

One day while I was practically falling asleep during a deacons and elders meeting (I was getting really tired of how spiritually dead it was in church and in the planning meetings. I do not say this to be mean-spirited or disrespectful. It's just that once you have tasted the living and thirst-quenching waters of God [the Holy Spirit], you don't want the bitter, dead waters of man anymore.), Mr. Snyder stood up and announced that a new couple had relocated to Denver from California and that they were going to be serving with us. (Apparently, he had been ordained a deacon in a sister congregation in California.) At that moment, Welton and Sandra Tucker stood up and introduced themselves. I remember at the time I was doodling on my notepad, out of sheer boredom, and that I was literally knocked out of my chair when Tucker first opened his mouth to speak. All he did was introduce himself, but I heard what seemed like a bolt of lightning and thunder come out of his mouth! It was like a great big sonic boom, and it literally jolted me awake and out of my chair. *Who is this man?* I wondered. I sat there totally perplexed and fixated on him. I knew that he definitely was "somebody in the Spirit" because I recognized the Spirit of God coming out of his mouth, but I had no idea who he was.

A few weeks later, my wife informed me that she had invited a "new couple from church" to our house for dinner. I was surprised when she told me that it was an older black couple. Being originally from the northeastern part of the United States (Ohio) and raised by parents who were from the Deep South, I had never really fellowshipped that much with black people. As a family, we weren't prejudiced or anything; I had just not had that much opportunity to interact with people of a different race. Also, the fact that they were so much older than us (both Teresa and I were in our late twenties at the time), I thought that it might be a bit awkward and uncomfortable. (Needless to say, I was very immature and inexperienced—both mentally and spiritually speaking.) To my surprise and relief though, we all got along very well, and we laughed and laughed together talking about what it was like growing up with the different misconceptions and racial stereotypes of each other. Later, I would come to realize the deep-seated anxieties and racial scars that Tucker was struggling with as a result of growing up with years of racial segregation and prejudices. (Tucker would later confide in me that he and Sandra were both really surprised that a white couple would invite them over for dinner—let alone get along so well together.) Because we had so much fun that night being together, we all decided a few weeks later to go out to dinner to a restaurant.

I had never shared with the Tuckers, or my wife for that matter, the fact that something had spiritually "quickened within me" at that very first moment when Tucker introduced himself months earlier at the deacons and elders meeting. I use the term "quickened within me" to describe the spiritual jolting or a heightened spiritual awareness that occurs when you hear or notice something in the Spirit. To describe this spiritual "sixth sense" further, it is like being able to pick up a high, piercing frequency that most human ears can't pick up. I suppose this is what some might call "being in tune with the Spirit." Anyway, we went out to dinner, and Tucker began to share some dreams that he had been having.

He began to describe in great detail some incredible, futuristic things that God had been showing him in dreams. As Teresa and I listened, I began to realize that he was actually describing the very same things that I had seen previously in visions from God that I hadn't shared with anybody. I was awestruck. As we quickly began comparing spiritual notes, we both began to get excited and started rejoicing—realizing that God had no doubt been working among us. For it is written in the Bible that in the last days God would pour out His Spirit upon His people and that "young men would see visions and old men would dream dreams" (Acts 2:17). The Bible also further states that God will once again pour out His Spirit upon His servants, both male and female, and that they would prophesy during these last days (Acts 2:18). These are the things that we are now beginning to see happen! God is doing what He said—and Tucker and I were both rejoicing as we were just then beginning to realize it.

Before I go any further, I need to relay something here that is quite remarkable. In March of 1995 when I was experiencing that solid week of non-stop visions and revelations from the Lord, one of the things that I was shown during a vision was that I was going to be "sent to the Jews." (I will explain what that spiritually means later.) I had never mentioned that specific revelation and vision to anyone. Curiously, however, about a year or so later, I was hosting a small Bible study at my house and a man that I barely knew, named Mike, called me and asked if he could come. I thought that it seemed a bit strange at the time for him to want to come, but nevertheless, I told him that he was always welcome. After the Bible study ended and everyone else left, he oddly hung around for a few minutes and then asked if he could pray with me. Thinking this an unusual request, I cautiously agreed. As we knelt down together holding hands, he began to pray quietly to himself. All of a sudden, Mike sat up from prayer and stared at me with his face all contorted with a puzzled look, and he declared, "You! You are sent to the Jews!" He paused for a moment and then added, "And not you only. But also a man named Tucker." I was flabbergasted because I had never shared with anyone what was said or revealed to me during those visions. How did he know that? Furthermore, the man that I would later come to know by the name of "Tucker" hadn't even arrived in Denver yet from California—that was still a year and a half off!

Now back to our dinner with the Tuckers. Soon after our pleasant evening together at the restaurant, where Tucker and I had both compared a few "spiritual notes" of what the Lord had been individually showing us, Tucker and I drifted apart. In fact, I don't think that we spoke again of any real consequence until almost a year later in the summer of 1998 when the Lord instructed me to "go to that black man standing over there" in regards to whether or not Teresa and I were going to be given any more children by Him. By that time, I had forgotten who he was, and I really didn't recognize him—and judging from his cold reception of me that day, I doubt that he really remembered too much about me as well. It was during this same time that I was asked to be the youth pastor and quickly became very busy teaching the teen Bible studies.

Skipping ahead for a moment to April of 1999, I want to relay a quick story here that might help shed some spiritual light on Tucker. I assure you that I didn't come up with this on my own— God gave it to me. I was sitting at my desk in my home one morning, wondering and praying to God about some of the visions and revelations that He had given me concerning the future. I was asking Him, "When will these things be, Lord—the things that You have been showing me?" Immediately, the Lord answered me and said, "Just as the Scripture says—when John the Baptist is taken away." He immediately showed me Welton Tucker's face and the actual verse in Mark 1:14 that He was referring to in my mind's eye. I remember thinking, *What?! What does that mean? And what do You mean by saying that Tucker is a type of John the Baptist?* He didn't answer me. (But later, the Holy Spirit explained it to me and also expounded on this theme showing me prophetically what is coming upon the whole earth and what these things prophetically mean—I will address some of these themes in later chapters.) Needless to say, this revelation of "Tucker being a type of John the Baptist" came as a real shock to me! I found out later though that I wasn't the only one that the Holy Spirit was revealing this truth to. Apparently, two years earlier, God confirmed it by the mouth of one of His other servants—literally by Tucker's own admission. Read on.

Unbeknownst to me at the time, about a year or so earlier at church, Mr. Snyder had gone up to Tucker and put his arm around him and hugged him and said, "I am so glad that you are here with us."

To which Tucker sharply replied, "No, you're not—because to all of you I am nothing but a nigger!"

Shocked and horrified, Mr. Snyder stepped back and said, "Now, Welton, why would you say something like that? We don't think of you as that."

"Yes, you will," Tucker replied. "To you, I am just a poor, uneducated black man. But I have been sent here to speak against you! For I am a mouth sent to cry against you and to tell you to repent! I am a nobody sent here to tell everybody about Somebody who can save anybody. And I am here to let you know that He is coming soon. But you will not hear me nor receive me—to you I am just a nigger—a poor, uneducated black man whom you will reject. Behold, God will indeed raise up another witness—one of your own, even from among yourselves. He will be white, blond-haired, and educated—yet, you will reject him too. But woe be unto you if you reject the third witness whom He will send!" (Presumably, this "third witness" that Tucker was speaking about here is the witness of the Holy Spirit which is coming soon to work miraculous signs and wonders among the people; some of which will be the miraculous healings of Eddie and Paul still yet in the future. I will explain more about this later.) As God's own words in the Bible testify—"Surely the Lord God does nothing, unless He reveals His secret to His servants the prophets." (Amos 3:7). And again, He says, "By the mouths of two or three witnesses shall every word be established." (Deuteronomy 19:15; 2 Corinthians 13:1). God always sends two or three prophets and/or witnesses to warn the people before He does anything. Incidentally, true to the prophecy that he gave, Tucker was indeed later rejected and run-off by the ministry of this church; and as I will describe in later chapters, I too (being white with blond hair) was soon afterwards cast out and disfellowshipped by them as well.

"UNTO THE LEAST OF THESE MY BRETHREN"

By 1998, the Lord was speaking to me pretty regularly and teaching me many things. In fact, over the next three years (from 1998 to 2000), God gave me some pretty amazing and astounding experiences in order to teach me some very valuable lessons about the truthfulness of His Word. One particular day, Teresa asked me to go downstairs into the basement crawlspace where we had hidden and buried a safe and retrieve some important business documents. As I opened the safe, I noticed that all of the documents were fine, but that the cash that we had stashed there only a few months earlier, still bundled in its bank-issued white envelopes, was all covered in green and brown mold. To my horror, I opened the cash envelopes and found that all of the money inside, representing our life savings, was moldy and rapidly falling apart. I rushed upstairs in a panic to the bathroom sink, and quickly tried to salvage the money, by washing off the mold and corrosion. As I did so, the money—which were all $100 dollar bills—began crumbling and disintegrating in my hands. The money was literally turning to dust right before my very eyes! As I cried out panicking, the Lord immediately said to me, "Did I not say, 'Do not lay up for yourselves treasures on earth where moth and rust corrupt, and where thieves break in and steal. But rather, lay up for yourselves treasures in heaven, where neither moth nor rust destroys and where thieves do not break in and steal'?" (Matthew 6:19–20). Needless to say, I was stunned by the Lord's remark. I was only able to salvage three-thousand dollars. Unfortunately, I do not know how much cash was there to start with.

I hid the remaining three-thousand dollars (three envelopes containing one-thousand dollars each) up on a high shelf in our pantry. It represented our entire life savings at the time. We had no other money. A few days later, the phone rang. It was Tucker. I hadn't talked to him in a very long time. He sheepishly confessed to me that he had just been praying about his finances moments before, and complaining to the Lord that he didn't have enough money to pay his electric bill that month. The Lord had told him to "Call Eric." He told me that at first he refused to do so. But then the Lord said to him a second time, "Call Eric!" Realizing that he had better obey God, he reluctantly called me.

Before I go any further, I need to first relay a few details here. A couple of years earlier, I had asked God about paying tithes to Him. Many churches teach that a believer's tithes should be given to their local church or sent in to their denomination's headquarters—as ours taught. But over the last few years I had been feeling kind of reluctant to do so because I kept thinking about how when I was in college all they were doing at church headquarters with our tithe money was eating off gold plates. It made me sick to think about it. I could see how tithing (giving a tenth of your income to God) was commanded in the Bible, yet I wondered how a person might be able to give their money directly to Him without having to send their money in to a man's organization. I didn't want my holy sacrifices and offerings going to pay for some Pharisee's or Sadducee's extravagant lifestyle or to help pay for his college's expensive dichondra (special landscaping grass).

When I asked the Lord about paying my tithes to Him, He said to me: "It is written that whosoever gives anything, or does anything, to the least of these My brethren, has given it, and done it unto Me, right? So then, whenever you give anything to the least of My brethren—that is the poor and needy among you—you are actually giving it to Me." The Lord continued, "And another thing, Eric. In the Old Testament, I required the bare minimum from My people—which was ten percent of their livelihood. In the New Testament, I require much more than that! I require *all* that you have and *all* that you are. In the New Testament, did I not commend the poor widow woman for throwing in her last two mites? Was it not said of her that she threw in 'all that she had' and 'her entire livelihood' as an offering into the treasury? Is it not written that you are to present your whole being as a living sacrifice and that you are to give up all that you have to come follow Me? In the Old Testament, I required the bare minimums. Isn't that what the Ten Commandments are? The bare minimums? Where is the love that I require within the Ten Commandments? Where is the kindness that is required? The forgiveness? And the patience that I require? Is it truly loving your neighbor just not to kill him or not to steal from him or not to sleep with his wife? Under the New Testament, I have many more commandments that you must obey and keep. You must love your enemies and do good to those who hate you, and pray for those who spitefully use you. You must give to those who would take from you and sue you, and must willingly lay yourself down in service to others, as I do. You must bless those who curse you, and forgive those who harm you. I tell you the truth, unless your righteousness exceeds that of the Pharisees and Sadducees, you will in no wise enter the kingdom of heaven. In order to be My follower, you must go far beyond what the Old Covenant requires!"

Ever since the Lord said these things to me—and that giving to others ("to the least of these My brethren") was actually literally giving it to Him—Teresa and I began from that day forth setting aside our tithe money in a special account just waiting for one of His "little ones" to call us. We figured that it was His money and that He would bring forward whomever ("the least of His brethren") He wanted us to give His money to. As soon as we began setting the tithe money aside, the Lord's "little ones" began coming out of the woodwork. We didn't tell anybody about the account, but every time that we set aside this "tithe" money, somebody would call us. And they would always request the exact amount of money that we had put into the account. If we put $150 into the account, someone would miraculously call us out of the blue and request exactly that same amount from us. If we had $600 in the account, someone would show up on our doorstep to claim exactly that amount. The comforting thing for me and Teresa was that we would never tell anybody the actual amount that was available. The person would have to tell us exactly what they needed first, and every time it would match exactly how much we had set aside for the Lord's purposes! And it was always someone new who would call us or show up on our doorstep—we never heard from the same person twice. It was a very exciting and confirming thing to witness, and it went on like this for many months.

It was during this time that I received Tucker's phone call. I wasn't surprised at all by his claim that God had sent him to me. Because this was what had been happening for the past year or two—some people we knew, others we did not. We didn't care—we knew that God was the One leading them to us to claim what was His. When Tucker first called though, I was a little perplexed because the "tithe account" had just been emptied by another claimant earlier that week. A bit confused, I asked Tucker how much he needed to pay the electric bill.

He answered, "Sixty-two dollars and fifty cents."

Realizing in my spirit that this was an assignment from the Lord, I immediately asked God in my mind what He wanted me to do. The Lord said, "Double every dollar amount that comes out of his mouth."

So I said, "No problem, Mr. Tucker. I will give you one-hundred and twenty-five dollars."

There was a slight stutter in his voice, as he said, "Yes, thank you. One-hundred and twenty-five dollars would be nice. Thank you!"

"Okay," I responded, "I will bring you two-hundred and fifty dollars. Where do you live?"

After a brief pause and momentary silence, Tucker replied, "Wow! Two-hundred and fifty dollars! That's incredible. Thank you so much."

"No problem, sir, I will bring you five-hundred dollars. Where should I meet you?" I asked.

Obviously stunned at what was transpiring between us, he

softly replied, "There is a Denny's restaurant near I-225 off of 6th Avenue. Can we meet there around twelve o'clock today?"

"Sure, I will see you then!" I happily agreed, taking special notice that he didn't repeat the five-hundred dollar amount. But when I hung up the phone, it was obvious to my spirit that the Lord wasn't done with this conversation yet. So I got down on my face and asked Him, saying, "Lord, what do You want me to do?"

He answered, "What does the Scripture say? 'If a man compels you to go with him one mile, go with him two' (Matthew 5:41). Therefore bring him one-thousand dollars."

I remember gulping when the Lord said this to me, realizing that now I was going to be dipping into one of those thousand-dollar envelopes that my wife and I had hidden away in our pantry. That was exactly one-third of our entire life savings that the Lord was now telling me to just freely give away. Yikes, what was my wife going to think? As I got up from conversing with the Lord, I reluctantly agreed, saying, "Okay, Lord. You're the boss!"

I told my wife, grabbed one of the envelopes, and quickly headed out the door to meet him.

When I met Tucker at Denny's a half hour or so later, I could tell that he was somewhat embarrassed and a little ashamed. I tried to make him feel at ease by treating him to lunch and engaging him in conversation. We shared a few lighthearted laughs, and pretty soon, I could tell that he felt at ease with me and more comfortable about the situation. After a few minutes of sharing, I slipped him the envelope with the thousand dollars in it, saying that it contained one-thousand dollars, and that it was his. He sat there quietly with his head down, motionless, and I watched as tears began to slowly fill his eyes and roll down his face. After a few moments of shaking his head and wiping his tears with a napkin, he said the following to me: "You know, God told me that I didn't believe Him. When I was praying to Him this morning about my financial situation, and how I couldn't pay my bills, He told me that He could do anything. He then told me to call you. I didn't want to. I was ashamed and embarrassed to ask for help—especially from a white man. But then God spoke to me again and commanded me to call you, saying 'There is neither Jew nor Gentile in Me; there is no male or female; there is no black or white, or bond or free in Me. All My people are one in Me. You do not believe that I can do all things. Therefore, I will show you. Call Eric now!' So I called you not knowing what to expect. Before I told you the dollar amount that I needed, God then said to me while I was on the phone with you, 'Watch! This man will double every amount that you say.' I couldn't believe it when you actually started doing it! Every time that I would say an amount, you would double it. I could hardly believe what I was hearing! After a while, I was afraid to speak anymore. Every time you would say a dollar amount, it would literally be double what you had just said moments before. And each time that you did it, God would say to me, 'See, I can do whatever I want, and nothing is impossible for Me.' When I hung up the phone astonished at what God could do, He then said to me, 'You still don't believe. Therefore, I will have this man bring you one-thousand dollars!' And now, here it is." He sat there clutching the envelope, slowly shaking his head in disbelief and utter amazement, being absolutely astounded, with tears still flowing down his face.

About two months later, I found myself working on negotiating a large business deal between our company (which we had named TW Graphics) and a company representing Royal Caribbean Cruise Lines. A few years earlier, with my former company's blessing and patronage, Teresa and I had started our own company, working out of our house, doing multimedia packaging and design. After only a couple of years, our company was doing quite well, and we were really growing. Now, almost out of nowhere, I found myself in the middle of negotiating a sizable order that promised to net Teresa and me exactly one-hundred-thousand dollars profit! We had never run across anything like this before. It just virtually landed in my lap one day soon after this had happened with Tucker. After I landed the deal, and after we paid out everybody and all of the pertinent vendors, we were left with exactly one-hundred-thousand dollars in our pockets! Realizing that this had to be a God-thing, I immediately went upstairs to pray and to thank Him for it. (By this time in my spiritual walk, I was beginning to realize that there are no coincidences and that only the blind "bump into things by chance." This is not only true for the physically blind, but for the spiritually blind as well.) I asked God why He had given me the money. He said to me, "Remember when you gave Welton Tucker that thousand dollars of your own money? Well, did I not say in My Word that whosoever gives up anything for My sake will be repaid a hundredfold in this life, and in the age to come, given eternal life (Matthew 19:29; Mark 10:29–30)? You gave Me, by way of the least of these My brethren, a thousand dollars, and I have repaid you one-hundred-thousand, just as I said that I would." Once again, I was amazed and left utterly stunned by the goodness and truthfulness of the Lord.

After consulting with the Lord, Teresa and I later used the

money to purchase some undeveloped land down in Perry Park, Colorado. Teresa had grandiose ideas of eventually wanting to build a big beautiful log house down there.

When I asked the Lord if purchasing the land was what He wanted us to do with the money, He replied, "What does the Scripture say?"

"I don't know," I answered.

Immediately, He showed me the following verse in my mind's eye: "Those who were possessors of lands or houses sold them, and brought the proceeds of the things that were sold, and came and laid them at the apostles' feet" (Acts 4:34–35). I took this to mean at the time that it was okay to go ahead and buy the land, not really knowing for what future purpose it was going to be used for.

After we purchased the land, we immediately set out to begin making plans to build on it. However, when Teresa contacted the district utility manager to inquire about utilities being accessible to the property, she was promptly informed that in its current state it was impossible! In fact, the person that she spoke to there asked if we had bought the piece of property from "so and so" (the previous owner's name). When my wife confirmed that we indeed had, the person on the other end of the phone from the utilities office then said, "Well, he knows that you can't get utilities to that piece of land; he's been trying to do that for the past two years. He knew that you can't build on it right now. That is why he obviously dumped the property off on you!" When we were initially negotiating to purchase the property, both the owner and his Realtor, as well as our personal Realtor all assured us that the land was readily accessible to utilities and immediately available to build upon. They clearly deceived us and defrauded us. I was livid! I told Teresa to contact a real estate attorney that very instant and that we were going to sue the previous owner, his real estate agent, and our real estate agent as well. She immediately got on the phone and promptly set up a consultation meeting for us with a real estate attorney for the following morning.

That night I was sitting outside in my hot tub, still fuming because of the situation and angry at how that previous owner had purposely defrauded us. As I was sitting there alone in the hot tub, the Lord suddenly spoke to me as I was looking out at the starlit night sky. He said, "Eric, am I your God or not?" There was a brief pause as I contemplated the Lord's question and wondered why He was asking me this. He continued, "Am I your Shield—that is, am I your defense? Am I your Sword—your offense? Am I your Healer—your physician? Am I your Advocate—your attorney? Am I your Rock—your security? Am I your Protector and your Provider? Eric, I am either all of these things to you, or I am none of these things. Now which is it?" Speechless, I couldn't answer Him. I couldn't figure out why the Lord was asking me these things. After a momentary pause, the Lord continued: "Eric, it is written that all of the earth is Mine and everything that is in it and that I own all of the land and all of the cattle upon a thousand hills. It is written that all of the silver and gold are Mine and that they are Mine to do with as I please, and as I see fit. It is also written that I give good gifts unto My children. I gave you this land, Eric. Yes, what this man [the previous owner] did, he meant it unto you for evil, but I meant it for good. Do nothing with this land but sit on it, and it will turn to gold in your hands." Totally shocked at what the Lord had just revealed to me, I nonetheless believed Him, and so I went back into my house and promptly canceled our appointment with the real estate attorney. (Incidentally, as I am writing this, I still own that piece of land in Perry Park, and I have done nothing with it, according to the word of the Lord.)

It was during this time in the summer of 2000 that "Rick" (not his real name) came to work for me. Here was a man whom I loved deeply. He was like the little brother that I never had. He worked for a competitor of mine at the time, but when he came to work for me, I insisted that he not take anything from his former employer. Although he wanted to, I did not allow Rick to bring any former clients, clientele lists, contacts, pricing information, or trade secrets to his new job with me. I didn't want to be guilty of stealing from another company in order to build my own. To do so would have been utterly foolish—not to mention sinful. It would have been like trying to build a loyal army out of a bunch of former AWOL soldiers and deserters! If the soldiers weren't loyal to their former superiors in the past what makes a person believe that they are now going to be loyal to their new one?! As Jesus said, "He who is faithful with little will be faithful with much also" (Luke 16:10). Looking back, I guess I should have realized then what was likely going to happen later on in my future with Rick. But Rick was very gifted, and he was very likable, and I truly loved him as my "little brother." Perhaps my love for him is what blinded me from truly seeing Rick's grave character flaws.

One day, not long after Rick first began working for me, I was walking down the stairs to my office when the Lord suddenly spoke to me. Teresa had just told me how wonderful Rick was doing and how he was writing a lot of business and landing all kinds of new deals. Excited at what she had just told me, I thought to myself regarding my "new hire," *Wow, he's really working out great. He's going to do very well for our company.* Whereupon immediately, the Lord declared to me, "He has no part in this inheritance!" I stopped on the stairs, completely flabbergasted at what I had just heard the Lord say. "What, Lord?" I asked. "What inheritance? What does that mean?" I diligently inquired. The Lord did not further respond nor comment. I went and sat at my desk completely puzzled at what the Lord had just stated to me. It would be years before the Lord would ever clarify or expound on what He said to me that day regarding my new employee.

KEEP YOUR HEAD DOWN!

As I have been describing in the preceding chapters, many things spiritually occurred and happened to me over the course of the initial first six years (from the spring of 1995 through the year 2000) when God first began revealing Himself to me. As I continue to describe what happened, I will try my best to relay these occurrences in such a way that they make sense to my reader. The problem in relaying these stories is that many of them unfolded over time, often overlapping with other lessons and stories so that the overall timeline and chronologies might seem a little hard to follow. But please bear with me, and I will try to the best of my ability to bring everything "full circle" so that it makes perfect sense at the end.

As things at church began heating up for me, I found myself the unwitting participant of a great move of God. The whole time that these things were unfolding, I was truly just trying to do what was right and submit to the church leaders and elders and yet remain faithful to the Lord—whom I was finding to be more "real" than I had ever known or believed before. It was a real struggle for me. Although, I had always believed in Him and believed in His overall sovereignty, I guess I had never really known how much of a *personal* God He truly is—searching the hearts and thoughts of His people, and masterfully correcting and leading each one of us on our own personal journey through this life. He is involved with each one of us on a personal level—as a great Father who deeply cares for the tender development and evolving character of each and every one of His dear children. That is not to say that He doesn't let each of us make our own mistakes though. He surely does! How else are we going to grow and learn how to overcome and begin to realize *by firsthand experience* that "Father truly knows best!"? And that we need to learn to always trust Him. As it is written: "As many as I love, I rebuke and chasten," says the Lord (Revelation 3:19). And again, He says, "My son [and daughter], do not despise the chastening of the Lord, nor be discouraged when you are rebuked by Him; for whom the Lord loves He chastens, and scourges every son whom He receives" (Hebrews 12:5–6).

Because God was beginning to communicate with me more and more during this time, I often found myself caught between two worlds—especially at church. The revelations that God was giving to me in my ear, as well as by way of visions, were increasingly bringing me into more and more conflict with what I had always believed, as well as what our church denomination had always taught and was teaching. I had always felt (and been taught) that "division" in the church was unacceptable and that to be at odds with the church leadership was sinful. Like many Christians, I too loved God but felt that I needed to be in "subjection" to the pastor and church hierarchy in order to be right with Him. I guess I had never realized before that in the Bible, it was "the majority" and the church leadership who were often the ones that were not right with God and the very ones who rejected Him and who were always resisting the leading of the Holy Spirit (Acts 7:51–54). In the Bible, it was the majority of Israel that rejected God from personally ruling over them and who wickedly wanted and desired a *human* king to lead them. It was the majority who set up a false idol and worshiped the golden calf, proclaiming that it was the "god" who had led them out of Egypt. It was the majority who rejected Christ and who called for Him to be put to death on the cross. And sadly, it was their misguided and self-righteous church leaders that persuaded them all to do so!

One thing I am learning in my walk with God is this: No matter who you are, or think you are, you better keep your head down at all times—both in prayer and in humility. You better always be teachable and reachable. If you think that you are "untouchable" and that you are "above" others and that you don't ever need to be corrected or admonished, you better watch out! The Bible clearly warns, "Let him who thinks he stands take heed lest he fall" (1 Corinthians 10:12). And again, it says, "Do not think of yourself more highly than you ought, but think soberly, as God has dealt to each one a measure of faith." (Romans 12:3). And again, "Better is a poor and wise child than an old and foolish king who will no longer be admonished" (Ecclesiastes 4:13). Unfortunately, many church pastors and leaders have fallen into this gross deception and have become stubborn and obstinate—not willing to be broken by God. They are no longer humble and teachable and reject all calls by God to become pliable and to once again become *His* follower, instead of promoting themselves as being someone to be followed. Some have erroneously come to think that they are the head instead of realizing that they are the body. Somewhere down the line, they quit following God and serving Him (and consequently, His people) and instead began expecting others to start serving them or to pay them homage.

It is a very subtle and evil deception that creeps in unawares, and no one is immune to it. Just when you think that you are "somebody special" and begin to lift up your head in pride, God will come and quickly let you know the truth of the matter. Case in point—it happened to me. One particular night when I was lying in bed with my wife, who was fast asleep beside me, I began thinking about all that had been happening to me over the past few months. I began thinking about all of the Bible studies that I was teaching at the time and all the supernatural experiences that I was having, and my heart began to be lifted up in pride. All of a sudden, as I was lying there thinking about myself, and the "spiritual success" I was having, I looked up and saw Jesus in a vision above me. He had His back to me and was bending over as if He were weeding in a garden or something. To my surprise, He was dressed very humbly. Although He was a glorious King—the King of kings in fact—He was dressed very modestly. He wore a dingy, old-looking cloak, apparently soiled from working in the garden. He had gardener's gloves on, and He was seemingly ignoring me as I proudly spoke.

I self-righteously asked Him, "Lord, how come in the Bible, when You addressed or sent a message to one of Your servants, You always greeted them with an affectionate name or phrase such as 'Daniel, a man greatly beloved' or 'Mary, one who is highly favored'? But to me, You never say such things. You only call me 'Eric' when You address me or talk to me. Aren't You pleased with what I am doing and what I have done for You, Lord?"

At that moment, the Lord stood up and turned around and glared at me with His soul-piercing eyes. "Why? What have *you* done for *Me* that I should be pleased with *you*, Eric?" He angrily asked. "Is it not written that those servants who have done only that which has been expected and commanded of them are *still* considered unprofitable servants? What then have You done for Me that I should be pleased with you? Tell Me, therefore, Eric, how have *you* profited *Me* that I should give *you* thanks?" When He finished speaking, He immediately turned back around and went back to doing what He was doing, presumably weeding in His garden.

I lay there stunned and frozen! His convicting words pinned me to my bed so that I couldn't move or talk. Feeling like such a heel and a complete idiot, I began to see myself as the foolish and arrogant man that I had become. Knowledge had begun to "puff" me up and cause me to become prideful just as the Scripture had forewarned: "Knowledge puffs up, but love edifies [builds up]" (1 Corinthians 8:1). As I lay there watching Him and contemplating what a self-righteous ass I had become, I began to become ashamed and embarrassed at my behavior and my foolish human pride. After a few minutes, I sheepishly said, "Lord, I'm sorry. I only want to please You."

Immediately, the Lord turned around again and quickly lowered His eyes at me, while pointing His finger, and sharply said, "*You, you* want to please *Me*?"

"Yes," I nodded.

"Then *follow* Me!" He screamed, His voice echoing and reverberating through my soul like sonar through water. At that instant, both He and the heavenly vision that I had been seeing disappeared.

I lay there on my bed, both afraid and very sobered by what had just happened. It was obvious that the Lord cannot be fooled or manipulated. He read the wicked thoughts and intents of my proud heart. He is not a respecter of persons; neither does He care what we humans think. He unapologetically told me the truth and yet left me with such a profound respect and admiration for Him that I longed to remain in His presence and to be close to Him. He efficiently (and mercifully) put me back in my proper place that night—and yet, He did it with an incredible amount of love and grace—He Himself being clothed in humility.

After a few minutes, as I lay there very still in the darkness thinking about the whole episode and all that had just transpired, I began to take a good hard look at myself. Spiritual knowledge and supernatural experiences had puffed me up in pride, and I had lost sight of God as being the true and only "focal point of every-thing." Sadly, I had begun putting focus upon myself instead. I had pridefully started thinking that I somehow deserved "recogni-tion," and that I was the Lord's helper and assistant. I am not the Lord's helper and assistant—I am His bondservant—His slave! He doesn't *need* me; I am not profiting Him one iota. I am only doing that which is expected of me. After all, isn't this what Jesus said when He was still on the earth? He said to His disciples, "Does the master thank his servant because he did the things that were com-manded of him? I think not. So likewise you, when you have done all the things which you are commanded to do, say, 'We are still unprofitable servants—we have only done that which was our duty to do'" (Luke 17:9–10). As I lay there contemplating these things, I began to see myself as I really was and how foolish and prideful I had become. Once I got past the initial shame and embarrassment, I started laughing. I laughed so hard at my utter foolishness and stupidity that I woke my wife up. She asked me what was going on.

I answered that I had been conversing with the Lord, to which she promptly turned over and went back to sleep.

Speaking of sleeping, this is what we in the church have been doing for many years now. Just like the disciples in the New Testament, while Jesus is busy doing His marvelous works all around us, we are fast asleep, unaware that our hour of temptation (testing) is drawing near (Mark 14:37–38). I realize now, looking back, that this is what was happening to me while I was a member in the Denver South congregation. As God began speaking louder to me, I was being forced to go where I—that is, my flesh, didn't want to go. I didn't want to be forced out of my comfort zone—where I had been spiritually fast asleep, comfortably sitting in my church pew. God was making me do things and say things that I didn't want to in order to not only personally shake me out of my comfort zone and wake me up, but in order to wake others up spiritually as well. (Remember, He told me years earlier that He was going to use me as "a wedge" in order to bring about division and cause people to go through a crisis of belief in order to begin spiritually waking them up.) None of us enjoys having to leave our complacent comfortable beds in order to get up and to go to work. This is precisely what He is going to do (and is doing) among the churches right now—waking up the "ten virgins" who are all fast asleep (Matthew 25:1–13).

It is interesting to note my wife's reaction above—how when I was busily "conversing with the Lord" that night, she just rolled over and went back to sleep. A few years later, the Lord would tell me that my wife, Teresa, is prophetically "a type of the church." While I am having regular communications with God (not necessarily by my choice—remember I was once spiritually asleep too!), she, like most of the church, is sleeping and is not aware of what is spiritually going on. Just like the disciples during Jesus' day (before they were given the Holy Spirit), they were all sleeping, even on the eve of Jesus' suffering and excruciating death. They were just too tired to keep their eyes open to understand the significance of what was going on. They were completely unaware of the momentous events and earth-shaking days in which they were living—their eyes being too heavy and too tired and not able to stay awake. But Jesus had to go on without them—all alone to Golgotha—the place of His suffering and death. His wife—that is, the church (in the form of the disciples)—couldn't go with Him at this time; He had to "go it" alone in order to prepare a place for them. Afterwards, they would be able to join Him where He is, for they *only* would be able to see Him, but the rest of the unbelieving world would not be able to see Him nor receive Him (John 14:18–29; 16:16–22).

In a sense, Jesus also didn't want to leave *His* "comfort zone" either (that is, His flesh). He asked the Father three times to "take His cup away" (Matthew 26:36–44). But His suffering and fleshly death was necessary in order to "wake many people up" both spiritually in this life, as well as speaking of the resurrection yet in the future. He said that it was necessary for Him "to go away," in order that we might live! The same was true in type for Joseph when he was betrayed by his brothers and sold into slavery. Joseph had to go away and prepare a place for his brethren—so that they might be able to be with him and live. (In fact, I remember a few months after I was disfellowshipped from the Denver South congregation I was complaining to God about how the pastor and the elders had put me in a "prison of isolation," and then God promptly interrupted my prayer, by declaring, "Eric, *I* put Joseph in prison!")

IN CONFLICT WITH
THE CHURCH ELDERS

As I said before, things were quickly beginning to accelerate at church. Over the course of the following year since I first began giving messages to them from the Lord, many people were now beginning to question what I was saying. At first, most people graciously received what I was telling them, with some of them even showing signs of truly believing me, but as time went on and doubt and fear began to creep in, they soon became offended. It all quickly began to culminate. Within one year of giving my sermon on "believing," which was at first graciously and warmly received, the church would collectively reject me and kick me out of their fellowship! I didn't realize it then, but Jesus had already predicted two thousand years ago how things would turn out. Speaking to His own hometown church in Nazareth, He told them that they would graciously receive His words at first—even wanting Him to do among them the same miracles that they had heard that He had performed elsewhere. But then, He said, they would quickly become offended and reject Him—casting Him out of both their church and their city (Luke 4:16–29). He told the people that they would do this because "a prophet is without honor among his own people" (Luke 4:24; Matthew 13:57). He also warned those servants who would come after Him: "If they have done this unto Me, they will do it unto you. For the servant is not greater than his Master, and the disciple is not above his Teacher" (John 15:20; Matthew 10:24). A few months before I was kicked out in June of 1999, the Lord had me perform an amazing miracle in front of one of the elders as a testimony and witness to the people. I assure you that I was an unwitting participant at the time, but I did what the Lord had commanded me to do. Let me explain.

Our local church congregation had one pastor (Tim Snyder) and four ordained "local elders." I was good friends with all of them. One of the local elders by the name of John had also gone to Ambassador College with me, so I knew him quite well. One day, John and I were playing basketball at a city recreation center. We were playing against two other young guys who were seemingly in their early twenties. One of the young men was very tall, about six feet four inches, and was very hot headed. In fact, I was extremely shocked at his arrogant demeanor, his angry attitude, and his filthy mouth. He kept cursing and taking God's name in vain and stomping around the basketball court as if he had something to prove. Not being intimidated by his aggressive play and demeanor, John and I were easily beating them, which only proved to heighten his frustration and sullen attitude. John's little four-year-old son was standing by watching us play. After a few intense games, John excused himself to take his young son to the bathroom and to get a drink of water. Wanting to lighten things up, and also to try and curb the vulgar profanity, I calmly walked over to this tall young man and politely asked him to "try and tone down on the language a little bit for the sake of the young child who was watching us."

He looked at me with contempt and said, "F—you!" I was totally taken aback and felt quite disrespected and slapped. This young man was at least ten years my junior! I couldn't believe his audacity and his arrogance.

A few minutes later, we resumed playing. As he and his teammate were trying to do a fast break down the court, this angry young man leapt up into the air to dunk the basketball and came down hard on his knee, completely blowing it out. As he landed, his knee wrenched, causing it to separate, and he hit the floor screaming in unimaginable pain. As he was writhing around on the floor, holding his knee, and suffering, I wickedly thought to myself, *Well, I guess he got what he deserved!* At that precise moment, I heard a loud booming Voice shoot straight down from the heavens like thunder and shout, "No! That is *not* the mind of Christ! Now go to him." Stunned, I looked around to see whether or not anyone else in the gymnasium had heard this booming commanding Voice. Apparently they didn't because no one else reacted. Knowing that it was the Lord speaking to me and that He was angry at my condemnation and lack of compassion, I reluctantly obeyed and slowly walked over to the injured young man, joining the crowd that by this time was beginning to encircle him.

As I walked over, I could see the tears of pain streaming down his face. He was lying on the floor, holding his shattered knee, trembling in pain, and screaming in agony. The Voice that had told me to go over to him then said to me, "Now, pray for him!" I didn't want to, but I obediently began praying quietly to myself while I stood among the crowd. Immediately, the Voice interrupted me, "That isn't doing anybody any good! Go to him, and pray out loud so that everybody can hear you."

Very hesitantly, I knelt down beside him and picked up his trembling head that was now wet with tears and sweat and held him in my arms and lap and sternly asked, "What is your name?" His lips trembling, and his eyes pleading for mercy, I think he answered that his name was Justin (I don't really remember what his name was now). Closing my eyes, mostly because of embarrassment, I looked up toward the heavens and prayed out loud, asking, "Lord, have mercy on this man. Please forgive him. He doesn't know what he is doing. Please forgive him for blaspheming and for taking Your name in vain. Please heal him, Lord, according to Your tender mercy and according to Your great kindness. In Jesus' name, I ask this." Instantly, the young man became calm in my arms and stopped shaking. I opened my eyes and turned to him and said, "Get up, Justin, the Lord has had mercy on you and has forgiven you. Get up!"

He looked up at me, still lying in my arms, his eyes wide open, and his mouth dropped in utter disbelief and then began to sit up. He stared down at his knee in amazement, which had miraculously come back together, and looked back at me, being completely stunned. His friends lifted him up and stood him on his feet, and he began testing the strength of his knee, by jumping around on it in delicate apprehension. When he realized that it was true and that it was going to hold, he began dancing and skipping around the gymnasium, he and his friends being completely overcome with amazement and joy! He looked like a man who had just been spared a death sentence and released from prison. He was so happy and yet completely humbled. I have never seen anyone so humbled and yet joyful in all of my life. It was truly amazing! God had spoken to him (and to all of us) in a very meaningful and profound way.

Nobody spoke to me, but everybody stared at me as I went over to get my clothes to leave. I was too embarrassed to hang around anymore; besides, I didn't know what to say. God had never used me to do anything like that before.

As I left, Justin humbly called over to me. "Sir?" he meekly asked. "Can I tell you something?"

"Sure" I replied.

Justin continued, "I have had two surgeries on this knee before, and it has never been this good. I can't believe how good it feels! I have never been able to move it like this before." (He moved it all around excitedly.) "Thank you, sir, for what you've done!"

I smiled and nodded, assuring him that it was the Lord's doing and not mine, and then quickly exited.

John and I rode together, so I waited for him in the parking lot. We both got into his car, neither one of us saying a word. We just sat there in his car for a long time, contemplating what had just happened. He finally said with a big exhale, "I don't know what I just witnessed in there, but that was absolutely amazing! I was praying for him as I was standing there in the crowd, but how did you know to go over there and lay your hands on him and that God would answer?"

"I don't know," I answered. "God just told me to."

"I sure wish that I was the one who had done that!" John replied.

A few days later, he told the whole church congregation what had happened.

It wasn't too long before jealousy and envy crept in. I had

already known that John was envious that Mr. Snyder had chosen me earlier to be the youth pastor. When Mr. Snyder had asked me to serve in this capacity a year before, John had not even moved into the area yet. But I knew in my heart when he came that he was jealous and wanted the position for himself. One day soon after this miraculous healing happened at the recreation center, John "volunteered" to come and "check out" one of my Bible studies in order to report back to Mr. Snyder on whether or not they were in line with church teachings. Mr. Snyder had never done this, nor had he requested John to do so, because he trusted me completely. But John indicated that he felt that it was necessary because he was an "ordained elder" and "needed to help protect the flock" as he put it. But I knew John's real motives, because the Holy Spirit had revealed them to me earlier. He was jealous and envious because people were beginning to talk about how great the Bible studies had been. Nevertheless, I welcomed John's visit, realizing that God's will must be done.

Another church elder, whose name is Tom, regularly attended many of my Bible studies and claimed that he had been learning a lot from them. After each one, he would warmly greet me and give his enthusiastic support and praise. After the particular Bible study that John attended, Tom once again came over to congratulate me on a "terrific Bible study." I turned to him and said what the Spirit had me say to him: "Do you really think so, Tom? I tell you the truth: very soon, you will be put into a vice—a crisis of belief—and you will have to ask yourself, 'What do I really believe?' What will you think then, Tom? And how will you choose?"

He looked at me strangely, with a very puzzled look, as if to say, "What are you talking about?" But the Spirit had me walk away before I could say any more or explain anything to him. The next day, Tim Snyder, the pastor, called me at home. He informed me without explanation that he was canceling my Bible studies for the adults until further notice, effective immediately! When I asked for an explanation, he said that he and the elders wanted to meet with me after church that coming weekend to discuss a few things. When I asked about the Bible studies for the teens, he surprisingly and strangely said that I could continue giving Bible studies for them, but not for the adults. Below is the entry from my spiritual diary from that time:

11/24/98—Yesterday was a miserable day. Mr. Snyder told me that he wanted me to stop giving Bible Studies. I have been giving them for a few weeks now, and the people have been astounded! Every person that has been coming has been returning, and making comments that they know it is God speaking to them through me. They have also said that they have gone away inspired and excited about what God is doing, and that they can't wait until the next one. I have been teaching every Tuesday night on the West side and every Friday night on the East side, in addition to an occasional Bible Study for the teens/pre-teens. And I know that God has been speaking through me. But now, Mr. Snyder has asked me to stop. It is so amazing to think that here is a church that calls itself after God's name, forbidding its members to study the Bible together. It reminds me of the Roman Catholic Church during the Middle Ages when it used to burn people at the stake for reading the Bible in their native languages.

I have been angry and hurt all day. It is amazing how we all pray that God would be a part of our services and fellowship, and lead us and teach us, and then when God does show up— we refuse to let Him in! It is just as Jesus said, "O Jerusalem

[Church], Jerusalem [Church], you that kill the prophets, and stone them which are sent unto you. How often I would have gathered your children together as a hen does gather her chicks under her wings, but you would not! Behold, your house is left unto you desolate!" (Matthew 23:37)

After Mr. Snyder called me, upon receiving John's evil report, he requested me to appear before him and the elders the following Sabbath after church. Not sure what I had done, I was very apprehensive. When we met together, they said, "We understand that you are claiming that God has been speaking to you and giving you messages. We also understand that you have been telling certain people that they are different biblical characters, such as Gail being Mary Magdalene, Jerry being Stephen, and Welton Tucker being John the Baptist. You have also stated that Eddie and Paul are going to be healed. Tell us, if these things are true, why wouldn't God tell *us* these things? After all, we are the ones that He has put in charge over this congregation. Surely, if God were going to do something among us, He would tell us first, don't you think?"

I did not answer.

As they continued, their tone of voice got a little stronger and more forceful. "Tell us, Eric, do you have a message for us?" they asked.

"No, sirs, I do not," I respectfully replied.

"But wait a minute; you claim that God is talking to you. If He gave you a message, surely He would want us to know it, seeing we are the elders of His church! What then is His message for us?" they demanded.

"I am not sent unto you. As you yourselves have said, you are *my* elders. What can you learn from *me*? I am not your elder, but rather you are mine; therefore, I am not sent unto you. Who am I that *I* should be sent unto *you* to give *you* a message?" I calmly answered.

As they looked at each other in puzzlement, they then said, "Then who *are* you sent to?"

I answered, "I am sent to the little ones. To those young ones among you who will listen. I am not sent unto you. For you are *my* elders and *my* teachers; as you yourselves have said, I am not *yours*."

One of them then stood up in anger and demanded, "Tell us! What message has God given you for us?! Surely, He has told you something for us!"

I calmly answered, "If you will receive a message from Him, then this is it: repent—for He is coming quickly! This is the only message that I have for you."

As they looked at each other bewildered, I heard one of them mutter to himself, "Repent? I don't need to repent. I did that a long time ago."

After a few moments of not knowing what to say, Mr. Snyder then said, "Eric, we are not sure that you are teaching in accordance with official church doctrine at some of your Bible studies. Some of your statements are concerning and disturbing. Therefore, we want you to suspend your adult Bible studies until further notice. You may go ahead and still have your teen Bible studies for the time being though, but not the adult ones."

After hearing this hypocritical and compromising directive, I asked them the following probing question: "If I am indeed the wolf that you claim me to be, then why would you throw your children to me?"

Mr. Snyder quickly spoke up and said, "Nobody thinks that you are a wolf, Eric. We just need time to sort this all out."

The meeting was then dismissed. Mr. Snyder informed me that they would get back to me with a decision in a week. As I left the meeting, I kept wondering, *A decision about what? Was I on trial here? What was I being accused of?* At the time, I was a bit naïve and slow to realize what was happening and what was spiritually unfolding.

The following week, I was instructed to meet with them again at one of the elder's homes. This time Teresa came with me. The Lord told me beforehand that one by one the five of them (the four elders and the pastor) were each going to state their individual reasons why they didn't believe me. The Lord instructed me not to say anything but to graciously hear each one's reasons for not believing. Oh, how I wish that I would have obeyed the Lord's command then!

Sure enough, each man one by one, beginning to my left, stated their personal reasons why they did not believe me and felt that I was a false prophet. Upon hearing Tom's reasons first, I looked at him and said, "How does that vice feel now, Tom?" Obviously, I disobeyed the Lord's command because that wasn't gracious, and furthermore, I was supposed to have remained quiet. As each elder in turn gave his reasons, it eventually became Mr. Snyder's turn. The Lord then said to me in my ear, "Tim Snyder is also going to state his reasons for not believing you, then he is going to ask you for your defense. You are to stand up and say, 'I have no defense. But as it is written, "The Lord is my defense."' And then you are to graciously hug each one of them, and then quickly leave."

Sure enough, Mr. Snyder did exactly that! He explained how that the words that I had at one time quoted earlier from the book of Isaiah were "ancient history," that they had already been prophetically fulfilled, and that they no longer had any bearing or prophetic significance on us today. He also stated that he had asked Welton Tucker if he were indeed John the Baptist, and that Mr. Tucker had denied it, saying, "I'm Welton Tucker. I'm not John the Baptist!" And then Mr. Snyder added, "I fear that demons are talking to you, Eric, and that you are being deceived." After saying this, Mr. Snyder concluded by saying, "Now it is your turn to speak, Eric. What is your defense?"

I had fully intended to answer and do exactly as the Lord had commanded me—that is, to say what He commanded me to say and then to graciously hug each one of them and leave. But foolish me, out of respect for my wife who was sitting next to me, I first asked her if *she* wanted to say anything, before I proceeded to do what the Lord had commanded me to. This was a grave mistake! Although, my intentions were good, I clearly disobeyed the Lord's precise commands. He did not tell me to first consult with my wife. (Remember the story in the Bible about the prophet who did not explicitly follow the Lord's clear commands to him, but instead, he hung around and visited with the people, and consequently, the Lord had him killed by a lion (1 Kings 13:7–26)? I should have known better than to have deviated at all from His clear instructions to me.)

Hearing all of the false accusations that were being made against me, Teresa, being a loyal wife, tried to defend me. Unfortunately, this opened a disastrous "can of worms" that I truly regret. I soon became incensed and enraged at their responses to her, and I lost control, emotionally, and flew off the handle! The Spirit of the Lord quickly stopped directing me at that moment, and I began accusing them all of self-righteousness and having an attitude of spiritual superiority. (When in truth, *I* was really the one who was being self-righteous and arrogant—having moved outside the will of God. God forgive me.) Later when things calmed down, they asked if they could lay their hands on me to pray for me. The Spirit of the Lord told me that it was okay to pray with them, but that "no one was to lay their hands on my head." My refusal to allow them to lay their hands on my head did not go over well. My out-of-control ungodly behavior that had been displayed only moments before, coupled now with my refusal to allow them to lay their hands on me, only helped confirm and solidify their growing suspicions that I was truly demon-possessed and in error.

The following week they called me in again to meet with them. This time, I was very meek and contrite. I had realized that I had given them "great occasion to blaspheme God and what He was doing." I was so sorrowful for what I had done. When I got home later that day from my previous meeting with them, I got down on my face before the Lord and greatly apologized for disobeying Him. He said to me, "What is done is done! Now get up and go on." I realized that I had just made things a lot harder for myself and especially for others. I had put a great stumbling block before their faith, and now I was going to see and hear the great harm to their belief that I had caused. Sure enough, when I met with them again, one week later, they each said to me, "Eric, I had my initial doubts about all of this and whether or not you are indeed a false prophet, but after witnessing firsthand your outbursts last week, and the fact that you refused for us to lay our hands on your head, now I am sure that you are indeed false and that you have demonic problems." I sincerely apologized to each one of them for my sinful behavior and pathetic display the week earlier, and I tried to explain to them that I had clearly disobeyed what God had commanded me, but it was too late. The spiritual damage had been done. Their minds and hearts had been made up. I could tell that I was now looking at a long, hard road ahead—and I really only had myself to blame.

The following week, as I was sitting in church, John (the local elder) gave the sermon. His message was on how Jesus had prophesied that in the last days many false prophets would rise up and deceive the people through false signs and by performing miracles and such. He told the congregation, that even so, there are now false prophets among us, who say great bold things, quote Scriptures, and heal people, but don't be deceived by them. They are of the devil, and they heal people by the power of demons. They are very cunning, and they even appear righteous, but don't be deceived by them.

As I sat there sadly listening to my own indictment, a teenage girl turned to me and whispered, "How can you let them say such things about you?" I assured her that no one can say or do anything against me except our Father in heaven allows it and that these things must be done. I also stated to her what the Spirit then prompted me to say: "Aleana, listen to me. The first generation under Moses gave their lives in order that their children might be free to enter the promised land and proclaim liberty and the goodness of God throughout the land. Likewise, the apostles too gave their lives in order that the succeeding generations after them might be able to proclaim the gospel freely and openly to all the nations. We too, those of my generation, must be expended also, so that you and others like you can be free from the religious bondage and institutions that now hold us all back, so that you might be able to one day freely proclaim this gospel to the whole world, so that the end may come."

I probably should clarify here that the reason that the Holy Spirit would not let the elders place their hands on my head earlier, in prayer, was two-fold. First, what is in me is not demonic. It is holy. It is of God and not of Satan. It is the Holy Spirit, not a demonic spirit. Therefore, allowing the elders to "cast it out" was not acceptable, not to mention, it could have had deadly consequences for them (both spiritually, as well as physically). No man can go into the holy of holies and try to "confront" the Spirit of God and live. Remember, our bodies are the temples of the Living God, and the Presence of God dwells there. Therefore, it would be like unlawfully storming into the Temple during the Old Testament days, and trying to enter into the holy of holies where the actual Presence of God dwells, and trying to cast Him out! In the Bible, men have died for a lot less (see 2 Samuel 6:6–7; Leviticus 10:1–2). The second reason is this: For me to have allowed them to do so would constitute *me* denying that God was actually the One who was doing these things in me. I can't deny God! To deny what I *know* to be God (of the Holy Spirit) is tantamount to me committing the unpardonable sin (Matthew 12:31–32; Mark 3:22–29). If I *know* something to be of God, yet I deny it and say that it might be of an unclean spirit or demonic, then I have just committed the unpardonable sin according to Jesus' own words. And by letting them place their unbelieving hands over my head, which represents them having "spiritual authority" over me, I am denying the very headship of Christ who is the One who is speaking in and through me. That is why it says that a man who is *prophesying* (as I was doing) should not have his head "covered"—else he is dishonoring his head who is Christ (1 Corinthians 11:3–4). Christ, who is my head (my immediate boss and direct superior), was speaking through me to them, and to try and cover that—to squelch that or to interfere with that—is a direct affront and insult to Christ Himself! As I mentioned before, no man is allowed to "own" me or allowed to control what Christ speaks through me. As a prophet and servant of God, I work for Him, and answer to Him only, and to nobody else (Romans 14:4, 8; Galatians 1:10; 1 Corinthians 2:15). The Scripture clearly states that "the spirit of prophecy [prophesying] is the testimony of Jesus"—not the testimony of man (Revelation 19:10). He is the One speaking, not me.

At the next meeting and "examination" which I am now going to describe (I believe there were five or six of these meetings in all), Mr. Snyder presented an "agreement" to me that he and the church elders had prepared, and were now insisting that I sign. I never actually got to see or read a copy of this agreement, but he read it out loud to me as I sat in front of him and the rest of the "examination board of elders" (curiously composed of the same five men). When I entered the room to appear before them, all five of them were sitting side by side in a single file row across the front of the room, and I was directed to sit in front of them in a single solitary chair facing them. As I sat before these now very visibly angry men, I remember thinking to myself how it felt like I had been strangely transferred back in time to the Middle Ages and was now about to experience what the poor "heretic" must have felt when he was being "examined" (interrogated) by the Spanish inquisitors. My "examination" began with Mr. Snyder addressing me sternly: "Eric, do you agree to abide by these rules that we—your church leaders and elders have laid out for you?"

I humbly asked, "What rules?" (I had not seen or heard of their proposed agreement prior to this examination.) He began reading out loud from the prepared document. I don't remember what he read exactly, but it was something to the effect of: "I, Eric Wheeler, hereby agree to submit myself to the church's governing authority and hierarchy and agree to abide by its rules, teachings, and beliefs; I also hereby promise to quit preaching, teaching and/or espousing heresies and false doctrines and any other teachings which have not been pre-approved and/or sanctioned by the church and its leadership. I also agree to refrain from giving other members and/or prospective members of this church any further prophetic words, interpretations of Scripture, and/or spiritual advice."

Upon hearing this, I was astonished at their demands. I then quietly asked, "And what if I am not able to abide by all of this?"

Mr. Snyder then angrily stood up and said, with his finger pointed directly at me, "Then you will be removed from this church!"

Realizing the gravity of this situation and wondering how in the world I had come to such a precarious predicament, I slumped back in my chair, searching my heart and mind for an answer, trying to find a response. I didn't want to be disfellowshipped. Afterall, these people were my brothers and sisters! I had grown up with them, and I loved them. I had gone to this church and been a part of their denomination since I was five years old. I had even graduated from their college. What evil had I done to deserve this? Why was this happening to me? All I had done was try to be a better Christian, and to try to follow Jesus more closely.

Sitting back down, Mr. Snyder sneered, "Well, Eric, what are you going to do?"

I asked, "Now, what precisely are you wanting me to do, again?"

Obviously frustrated and exasperated, he forcefully said the following: "We expect you to quietly sit in church and say nothing. You are not to give any messages to anyone, quote Scriptures, claim that God speaks to you, or purport in any way that you serve God!"

"You want me to stop being a Christian then?" I asked, realizing the true gravity of his demands. *I can't do that!* I thought to myself, realizing that now it had come down to choosing between them or God. As I came to the decision in my mind at that moment that I was going to follow God regardless of the personal cost to me—in this case my relationship with my beloved church congregation—that great Voice that had been previously speaking in my ear suddenly reappeared behind me, making His Presence known to me.

Mr. Snyder repeated his questioning again, by saying, "Well, Eric, what are you going to do? Are you going to abide by all of these rules that the elders have set forth, submit to our authority, and do as we have commanded, or are you going to continue to be obstinate and unrepentant and need to be removed from this church?"

The Lord suddenly said to me, "Tell him that you must obey Acts 5:29!" I didn't know what Acts 5:29 said, but nonetheless, I obeyed this time, relieved that God had now come to my rescue.

"Gentlemen," I said, "because you leave me no other choice, insisting that I must either choose between you or God, therefore, I must obey Acts 5:29!"

They all looked at me puzzled, and then at each other, asking each other up and down the line among themselves, "Acts 5:29? What does Acts 5:29 say?" Finally, after a few seconds, because none of them apparently had a Bible readily available, they turned to me and sternly asked, "What does Acts 5:29 say?"

The Lord immediately answered all of us, and had me say to them: "We ought to obey God rather than men!"

Upon hearing this, Mr. Snyder leaped to his feet, pointed at me, and angrily screamed, "Get him out of here! Didn't I tell you he has a demon?!" At that moment, two elders came over and escorted me out of the building. I remember walking to my car, praising God that He had come to my rescue and that I had apparently passed a test! I had shown that I was willing to obey Him and suffer for His name's sake, even in the face of what appeared to me to be "great threatenings" and personal loss. Obviously, as I look back now, these were only "baby steps" compared to what many other people have willingly suffered for His name's sake, but at the time, being accepted by others and being part of an organized church was something that I highly treasured and valued. Believe me, a kindergartener's test is every bit as intimidating and fearful to a kindergartener, as a sixth grader's test is to a sixth grader. God is not a respecter of persons; He doesn't show partiality. Each of us, no matter at what level of faith (belief) we are, a spiritual "pop quiz" and test is still that—a *test* of our faith! It is both difficult and intimidating. But we *must* overcome. As Christians, this is what we are *called* to do—to believe, persevere, and overcome.

DISFELLOWSHIPPED TO
THE LAND OF MIDIAN

I was officially "suspended" from church for three weeks. I was told that after that some of the elders would "visit" me to check up on my spiritual condition to see if I had repented or not and then they would decide at that point what to do with me further. I have included those entries from my diary below in order to give you, my reader, a little more insight into what I was feeling and experiencing during this time.

> 6/18/99—The last word that I feel like I have gotten from God was Psalm 40 and Isaiah 28. The Lord wants me to wait patiently on Him; for *He* is doing these things. I am truly learning a lot right now. Mainly, that I need to realize that the Lord alone is righteous, and that we *all* are carnal. I need to make sure that when I speak, I am speaking *His* words, and not my own; and that all of my words are spoken with both truth and grace (love), as His are.
>
> In regards to what is going on: I have met with the elders and Tim twice. They basically are giving me one week to repent and submit to their counsel—"to quit teaching and speaking" or I am going to be disfellowshipped. Tim called me yesterday, and asked me to meet with him and the elders

again tomorrow after church. Last week, they stripped me of all responsibilities in the church, including teen ministry. I can't say that through this whole ordeal I have been blameless. Last week at the meeting with them, I blew up and lost control. The Lord had told me to say that I did not have a defense, but rather, "As it is written, the Lord is my defense." But sadly, I didn't obey. Like Moses, I too let my own emotions and anger overcome me, and I disobeyed my Master's voice. I am so sorry, God. I have only given them great occasion to blaspheme that which You are doing, and have caused them to persecute me even more. God, forgive me. And please, hurry to my aid.

7/31/99—It has been exactly 6 weeks since I have been to church. I got suspended on June 19. My original suspension was supposed to be for only three weeks. But after meeting with me on July 12th, Mr. Snyder and Mr. Jordan suspended me until further notice. It's not all bad though. God told me in a dream about 6 or 7 months ago, before any of these meetings had happened that Mr. Snyder would "strip me of everything and push me off to some corner of the church in total isolation and spiritually bind me." And as is real apparent right now—God doesn't miss!

12/12/99—My wife and I were both disfellowshipped Nov.1. I still don't understand why she was kicked-out. She didn't do anything! Mr. Snyder called us up and told us that "it would be better if we went our separate ways." He stated that he felt that I was "listening to and being deceived by demons." We really haven't had any contact with hardly anybody the past month. I must say that Teresa and I have been really lonely and somewhat confused. Nevertheless, God has continued to show us favor and mercy. We have been so blessed lately—

seemingly more physically, than spiritually. Although, I realize that the blessings and lessons of God are taught simultaneously. During this time, I am reminded of how Elijah first prophesied to Ahab, and then was told by God to go out and hide in the wilderness by the Brook Cherith (meaning "cut off") and there God supernaturally preserved him by feeding him by the ravens.

One more interesting note that I should include is that I heard from Bob Bosh this morning that Eddie Benavides is scheduled to have facial surgery tomorrow morning. I prayed to God about this, because this is one of the things that God told me to prophesy—that He was going to heal Eddie and Paul Thornton supernaturally. I pray that God will do according to His will.

Oh Lord, my soul is weary and without direction. My heart has believed in You, yet I am lost. I have placed my trust in You, so why is my soul wandering aimlessly? My God, my Father, come take my hand and guide me. For You are the God of my salvation. You are my wonderful Counselor. Hear me, and don't delay to rescue me. The people make fun of me, saying, "He listens to and speaks for foreign gods; his fellowship is with demons." Why, oh why, oh God, do You let them speak this way? You are the only God that I serve! Oh Lord God, come quickly. Show them that I worship only Your great name. You are the God that I trust in alone. My own brothers have thrown me into a deep dark pit, and there is no escape. The walls are slick with mire so that I cannot take hold. Oh Lord, I do not wish to take hold, or find footing, if it is Your will to keep me here. But only, Lord God, let not my enemies lock me away. Let it be you, Lord. For it is You alone, Lord, that I fear. Please hurry to help me. My soul longs for You, and I cry out to You.

As is mentioned in my diary entries, I was originally suspended from the Worldwide Church of God in June of 1999. Five months later, Teresa and I were both permanently disfellowshipped. We both had attended their denomination since childhood. Thankfully though, the Lord had already informed me earlier that year in January by way of a dream that it was going to happen. I am going to relay here what transpired. It is not my intent to make anyone look bad or to assign blame. We have all had our sins and shortcomings in these matters. The Lord is working with all of us. It is a hard and arduous journey out of Egypt, and yet it is an even harder journey and struggle to get "Egypt" out of us! Unfortunately, we all still think in earthly and fleshly terms, with carnal minds, utilizing fleshly and worldly methods. We rely on that which we know humanly, which the world has taught us, and we unfortunately try to battle spiritual things with earthly devices and human methods. At the cost of digressing here, I want to illustrate this point further by relaying something that the Lord revealed to me when I was going through all of this. After being cast out into this "isolation wilderness" and placed within this spiritual prison that I have been in for quite sometime now (almost ten years), I began crying out to God in despair. One night, after suffering for a couple of years in spiritual isolation and loneliness, I asked God if what everybody is saying about me is true. Did my own vanity and self-righteous pride really cause all of this abandonment and isolation that I have been suffering? Was all of this my fault? Was I indeed being punished for my sins and for my vanity? That night God plainly spoke to me and revealed to me a profound truth and secret. I want to discuss that here:

He began by saying, "Eric, you are not prideful and vain as some men count pride and vanity. But, you, like all men, have the pride of life in you. It is common to all who are born of the flesh. That is, you all are self-reliant. You look to yourselves and to your own minds to determine what you should do and what you should not do. Therefore, you have all become gods unto yourselves. You obey your own judgments—those from your own minds—and not what I have said to do. This is the result of eating from the tree of the knowledge of good and evil. As a consequence, you all have become gods, judging for yourselves what is right and what is wrong, and what you should do and what you should not do, instead of looking to Me to lead you and to guide you—and to be your God." After a brief pause, He continued: "Eric, why did I make Moses leave Egypt and have him flee to Midian for forty years?"

"I don't know, Lord," I replied.

"It was to humble him. But why did I need to humble him, Eric, if it is also written that Moses was the meekest man who had ever lived (Numbers 12:3)?" God asked.

"I don't know, Lord. That is a good question. Why did you make him flee to Midian to dwell for forty years in order to humble him then?" I asked.

"Because he too, like all men, had the pride of life in him. It is true that Moses was very humble as a person and was the meekest of all men, and yet he too was self-reliant. He relied on the strength of his own right arm to deliver him and to deliver My people. He relied on his *own* wits and on his *own* judgments of what he felt was right and wrong to do, instead of relying on Me to deliver him and My people. As it is written in the book of Acts chapter 7, verse 25, Moses knew what his destiny was and how it would be by his hand that I would choose to deliver the children of Israel from their bondage. And yet he tried to take matters into his own hands by delivering his brethren by the strength of his own right arm when he slew the Egyptian that was abusing one of his fellow countrymen. He was using his own ways, his own methods, and his own wisdom—and not Mine! Notice what it says about him in Acts chapter 7 and verse 22: 'And Moses was learned in all the wisdom of the Egyptians, and was mighty in words and in deeds.' Egypt pictures the world, Eric. In other words, Moses was learned in all the *wisdom of the world*—and was mighty in *its* words and in *its* ways. But the world's ways are not My ways! The world's words are not My words! Moses was trained in all the ways of the world; so that he was both mighty in its words and in its deeds. This is not of Me. Therefore, I took Moses out of Egypt to humble him—to tear him down, to deconstruct what the world had made him into so that I could use him for My purposes. By the time that I got done with him, it is written of him that at the burning bush he couldn't even talk but had become a stutterer and that he lacked the self-confidence and self-assurance to go back to Egypt to deliver My people. Now he was ready to work for Me and to be used of Me to deliver My people, and not any earlier!"

I was beginning to see what the Lord had done—not only for Moses, but for me as well. I, too, in a sense, had been banished to Midian—to be humbled and to learn to rely on God—and upon Him alone. Praise be to the Lord for His marvelous wisdom! Praise be to His name forevermore! For His ways are not our ways; and His thoughts are not our thoughts. For even as the heavens are higher than the earth; so are His ways higher than ours, and His thoughts greater than our thoughts (Isaiah 55:8–9).

I probably should relay here that Eddie's complete and miraculous healing has not happened yet; neither has Paul's. Those things are yet for a time appointed. Right now is the time for prophesying. Just as God originally said to me earlier, "As it is written: 'Prophesying is for the believers; but [miraculous] signs are for the unbelievers' (1 Corinthians 14:22)." Jesus also said, "An evil and adulterous generation seeks after a sign" (Matthew 12:39). We are not called to look for signs, but rather, to believe; to believe all that God has spoken—which is what prophesying is—God speaking! The ancient Israelites saw many miraculous signs, but did it help them one iota when it came to entering into the promises of God (i.e., the promised land)? The Bible clearly says that it did not. In fact, it declares that they still didn't believe, although they saw many miraculous signs. And because of this perpetual unbelief "their carcasses fell and wasted away in the desert wilderness" (Hebrews 3:7–19). Yes, God does heal. Yes, He does many miraculous and wondrous things that cause many to believe. But as Jesus once said to me, "Do not rely on needing to see signs in order to believe what I have spoken to you!" At some point, you just have to believe God for who He is, and stop needing miraculous signs in order to believe. Keep this is mind, if you feel that you need to "see something" in order to believe—then the truth is—you *really* don't believe! As Jesus said to Thomas: "Thomas, because you have seen Me, you have believed. But blessed are those who have not seen and yet have believed." (John 20:29). I will address more on this subject later.

As was indicated in my diary entry, my poor wife, Teresa, was getting "innocently" caught up in all of this. She, too, was disfellowshipped by the church, although she never really said or did anything, other than write the letter below. The truth of the matter is all of it was by design anyway. Although, at this present time, even as I am writing this, she is at her "wit's end" wanting to leave me because of our current distressing financial situation and her lack of faith now that God is truly directing these things. Like with all of us, it is a constant struggle to believe, and yes, we wrestle to have faith and maintain it. But be that as it may, during the time when I was on official "suspension" from the church (during the summer and fall of 1999), Teresa was earnestly trying to find her way in all of this. She drafted the following letter, and presented it to Mr. Snyder and Mr. Jordan when they came to visit us before they permanently "disfellowshipped" both of us a few months later:

Dear Mr. Snyder:

Eric had a series of visions/revelations in the spring of 1995 (including an audible word about the birth of Kate). Since then, he has had a number of revelations about those visions, with the visions being brought into remembrance and then interpreted.

These "experiences" have almost always come during prayer, and Scripture is always given for confirmation. (By its very definition, the word "revelation"—"to make known something hidden or secret"—infers that the truth is not common knowledge, and that the Holy Spirit is revealing truth new to our understanding.)

What God Has Revealed to Eric:

Worldview:

Christ's second coming is at hand, and will be like unto the first only greater. (Matthew 24:34; Malachi 3; Luke 4:17; Isaiah 61:2)

Just as Christ did the first time, He will visit His own house first (John 1:11–12). Judgment will begin at the house of God (1 Peter 4:17). God is currently preparing His people to meet their Lord (Luke 1:17).

Once He has "cleaned up" His own house, He will use His people to go out to the world, and we will see a great revival as in the book of Acts, and then the end will come (Acts 1:8; Matthew 24:14).

Our Congregation:

God will use our local congregation for a mighty work *if and when* we start truly looking to God, trusting and believing in *Him, not men*. God has shown Eric, that you, Tim, would initially be in opposition, just as you are now, but that virtually overnight you would understand these things, and He would use you mightily (along with our brothers and sisters) for what He is going to do here in Denver.

Based on what Eric has shared with me for the last four years, what we're experiencing right now is exactly what God said would happen. He is training us all for what He will have us do in the near future. The point is that God will ultimately have us *all* on our knees looking to Him. (God does not come to take sides, but to take over!)

Eric, Personally:

God has told Eric to comfort, exhort and edify His people; focus them on their Lord and encourage them to put their trust in Him; and to seek Him with a continual sense of urgency.

Secondly (and this is being taken as divisive, or turning people from the organization), to believe that God empowers us individually and collectively, but only in as much as we seek and believe Him. God will work through us when we lay our lives down for Him, and seek Him directly instead of through men. We are called to a direct relationship with God. But like our forefathers, we still want a man to look to, *a king or ruler* to speak to us in place of God.

With a devotion to Jesus Christ as central to our being, God will provide everything else. We do not need to strive to *do* for God, because He will do through us, as we live in obedience to Him. God Himself will equip His people. *What house can we build for God? It is God who builds a house for us.*

God has shown Eric that this devotion to Jesus Christ is lacking in His Church today.

Now, what you're asking of us is to recant and repent of believing all of the aforementioned. And you must understand that as crazy as it all sounds, and that after beseeching God not just these three weeks, but for *four* years, that we believe with all our hearts and beings that this *is* of God.

And if it *is* of God, as we believe, then we *must* act in accordance with this faith.

As much as we respect and honor you as our elders, you are asking us to recant of the very existence of God working in our lives, which for us would be blasphemy.

We understand and appreciate that you also are acting in accordance to your faith.

—Teresa Wheeler

Apparently, the letter was not received well, because Teresa soon found herself being lumped in with me. Unbeknownst to me at the time, she had been praying to God to reveal to her whether or not what Tim Snyder and the elders had been saying was accurate regarding that we needed to submit to them instead of to what God had been showing us. She got her answer at the next meeting. Mr. Snyder turned to her during the meeting at our house and said, "You don't understand, Teresa, his teachings [pointing at me] are not in line with two thousand years of accepted Christianity!"

I said, "Of course they're not! They are not in line with the words and traditions of men, but with the Word of God!"

He got angry at my comment, but Teresa apparently got her answer. She knew enough about history to know that the last two thousand years of "accepted Christianity" is hardly a good spiritual measuring stick and that it certainly has not been representative of true biblical Christianity! More murders, robberies, and lies have been wickedly committed in the name of Christ by those who have falsely portrayed themselves to the world as being "His people and His church" than have been committed by the millions of heathens who don't even know His name!

"How can Mr. Snyder use 'two thousand years of *accepted* Christianity' as the definition and standard of *true biblical* Christianity?" she would later rhetorically ask me. That one comment alone by Mr. Snyder was proof positive to her that "*they* aren't right," she would later confess to me. As a consequence of this meeting (and letter), we were both "permanently disfellowshipped" a couple of months later.

TELL MOM MY LEFT ARM HURTS, BUT NOT TO WORRY

As I mentioned before in one of my diary entries, I already knew ahead of time that I was going to be "stripped of all responsibilities and positions in the church and banished to some small corner" by Tim and the elders—for God had already revealed this to me in a dream a few months earlier. However, I didn't realize that it was going to be as long and as hard as it has been. Being out in the "desert wilderness place" is a very lonely and trying time. It takes a toll on your soul and mind that sometimes is hard to relay in words. After a little while of being cut off from regular fellowship and spiritual interaction with others, loneliness begins to settle in. With loneliness comes emotional isolation, despair, mental anguish, and eventually, doubt. You begin to wonder if God has abandoned you; and if you had done and said the right things. Satan begins to play on these human emotions and feelings, tormenting your mind, and whispering into your brain thoughts of doubt and scenarios of fear. You begin to lose hope, and in some cases, become frustrated, bitter, and depressed—forgetting the wonderful and amazing things that God had previously done for you. Every servant of God, including Jesus, has spent time in the desert wilderness alone. It is the ordained "place of testing," and the place of suffering for the flesh. You enter into it clothed in the flesh and ideally come out of it naked in the Spirit. In the desert place, you are humbled and broken down by God, and your flesh is made to suffer in order that the Spirit that is in you might come forth in heavenly power (Luke 4:1–14). In the desert, you learn to rely on God *only* to sustain you, provide for you, and deliver you. It is an incredibly grueling time, yet a very necessary one. Out in the desert wilderness, God supernaturally sustains you with "bread and meat" (Psalm 78:24–28; 1 Kings 17:5–6). The "bread" picturing Jesus, the Word of God—the true Bread of Life—and the "meat" picturing the deep spiritual truths of God which only the Spirit can reveal, intended only for those who are "weaned from the milk" and for those who are maturing in Christ (Isaiah 28:9–10; Hebrews 5:12–14). Unfortunately, some never make it out of the desert place. They spiritually die there. Because their faith is weak, they give up and quit believing that God is able to deliver them and to bring about all that He has promised. They simply lose faith and, as a consequence, spiritually die in the desert— never seeing the promises of God fulfilled in their life. Let's face it—the flesh does not want to die. But it must in order that the Spirit might live! As Jesus said, "The flesh profits nothing; it is the Spirit that gives life. The words that I speak to you are Spirit, and they are life." (John 6:63).

The Bible says that the prophet Elijah "was a man with a nature like ours," and so, he too had to go and live in the desert in order to become spiritually strong in the Lord (James 5:17; 1 Kings 17:3–7). Likewise Jesus, being in the flesh, also had to spend

His appointed time in the desert wilderness alone where He was made to suffer, and where Satan continually badgered His mind and conscience, thus making Him spiritually stronger; the Bible assuring us that although He was a Son, Jesus too "had to learn obedience by those things which He suffered"—setting us an example that we should also follow in His footsteps (Hebrews 5:8; 1 Peter 2:21). Every servant of God must be humbled and "purified" by the grueling "desert wilderness experience." It is a necessary time of humbling and pruning—being "cut off" from fellowship and external influences. It is a lonely time of purification, character refinement, faith-building, and spiritual testing. When God first began working with Elijah, He commanded him to go and live in the desert next to the Brook Cherith where he was supernaturally fed bread and meat by ravens. The Hebrew name *Cherith* literally means "place of pruning" or "cut-off." After a certain amount of time dwelling in this desert, God then sent him to a Gentile city located outside of Israel called Zarephath (which means "place of refinement"), where Elijah's faith and character were further tested and refined by God. While in Zarephath, Elijah grew spiritually stronger and gained much-needed spiritual knowledge and understanding through his experiences dealing with a widow lady there that God had specifically sent him to. While she helped provide for his physical needs, he helped her spiritually by encouraging her and reviving and strengthening her waning faith in God, and by boldly demonstrating the Lord's redemptive and mighty power by literally raising her son from the dead. During his appointed "wilderness time" in both the desert and in Zarephath, Elijah learned how to trust God and faithfully rely on Him for all of his needs. He also learned how to lovingly minister to and lead God's "wounded" and "spiritually weak" people in the form of this poor widow lady. Through these trying experiences, God taught His servant Elijah how to humbly and courageously serve Him and His people, while at the same time, spiritually prepared and strengthened him for "Mt. Carmel" where the biggest spiritual battles and victories of his life and ministry would take place. After completing his "wilderness time" and spiritual training, Elijah was then ready to be used by God in an amazing and miraculous way at Mt. Carmel where he boldly called down fire from heaven in front of all of the Lord's people Israel (1 Kings 18:20–40). Clearly, everything that God did in Elijah's life, and still does in our lives today, is for a divine good purpose. All of His plans and ways have incredible spiritual meaning. It is just a matter of enduring, and believing, and of searching His marvelous ways out in faith. As I mentioned earlier in one of my first diary entries dated 12/26/95, God gave me a personal prophecy regarding a mysterious "injury" that I would suffer before beginning my public ministry:

> That I would know that "my time had come" to begin the "Lord's Work" when I would suffer some kind of injury to my left arm. This would serve as a "sign" to *me*.

I remember long ago when this prophecy was first given to me. This is how it unfolded: I was given a vision where I was "injured" somehow (I was shot, stabbed, hit, etc.) on my left arm. It severely hurt, and at first, humanly, I thought that I was going to die. I also was confused for a little while in the vision, in that although the injury actually occurred to my left arm, for a little while I erroneously thought that it had occurred to my right arm. After a while, I would come to realize that, yes, it had indeed happened to my left arm and that, in actuality, it was only a surface wound—that is, it was only a superficial "flesh wound." In the vision, I eventually was sitting in the hospital carefree, while the nurse bandaged me up—and by this time I had come to fully realize that it was definitely only a flesh wound or scratch (no big deal). During the vision as I was sitting in the hospital, my mom called my wife (who was there with me in the hospital) very worried and upset. I told my wife to tell my mom "not to worry, because this flesh wound was of God."

I realize that this whole vision and revelation might seem strange to my reader; however, God speaks to each of us in a language that we can understand or eventually figure out. Let me explain: First of all, in the Bible, a man's right arm is the arm that represents a person's strength—that is, what he relies on. The left arm is therefore subservient to the right arm and is considered not as important. Although I was definitely going to be injured, I would be confused for a time as to how bad the injury was actually going to be. For a time, I would not know whether or not it was going to be "life-threatening," and my initial confusion over whether or not it was my left arm or my right signified the fact that as I was going through this injury, I didn't know whether or not it was going to be serious (symbolized by my right arm) or insignificant (symbolized by my left arm). In time, I would come to realize that it was really nothing but a "flesh wound" and that what I had at first considered to be "life threatening" was indeed really not, but rather insignificant in comparison. This vision was a big metaphor describing my "desert wilderness time" that I was about to enter into. This is the "injury" that would happen to my flesh. At first, I thought that being disfellowshipped and "banished to the desert" was going to "kill" me. And so it did—it killed the fleshly part of me. But let's face it—this is exactly what the desert wilderness experience is meant to do—kill the flesh so that the Spirit might live and come forth in power! This vision and revelation was a prophetic metaphor speaking about my appointed "Midian time" that was coming. Remember Moses and how he at first tried to deliver the children of Israel by the "strength of his own right arm" when he slew the Egyptian? God wasn't his right arm (or strength) then during the time when he was in Egypt. He relied on his own human strength and methods. But after spending forty years in Midian, which hurt and humbled his flesh, he came forth with God now being his strength (his right arm), and not his own human strength and methods. After his very trying wilderness experience in Midian, Moses was now ready to be used by God to deliver His people. As the prophecy stated: "I would know that my time had come to begin the 'Lord's work' when I would suffer some kind of injury to my left arm. This would serve as a 'sign' to me." Obviously, after my time in the "Midian desert" is completed, I will have spiritual work to do.

In the vision, it was also revealed to me that my mother is not going to initially understand or agree with these things and will, consequently, be upset by them. (And truly, to this day, she doesn't understand or agree and is, consequently, upset about them.) However, God has shown me that in due time she will come to see and understand them and will find peace and comfort, realizing that God is the One who is indeed orchestrating these things. There is one more story that I should relay here regarding my mother. I love her dearly and have the utmost respect and admiration for her, but unfortunately, at this time, she doesn't know me. Yes, she knows me in the flesh, but she doesn't know me in the Spirit. For many years, this has been a great discouragement to me. However, God has assured me that it is clearly biblical, and that I should not be discouraged about it. Many of the family members of the servants of God in the Bible did not understand them at the time—including Jesus Himself. Before He was ultimately glorified, His own family thought that He was nuts and sought to have Him "committed" (Mark 3:21). Joseph, Job, David, and Jeremiah were all misunderstood by members of their immediate family. It is like Jesus said, "A prophet is not without honor except in his own country and in his own house" (Matthew 13:57).

In regard to my beloved mother, let me share with you what the Lord said to me once. One day about six years ago, when my son Evan was born, my mom flew out to Colorado to help me and Teresa. When I was taking her back to the airport, she was telling me about my aunt Emily and how I needed to pray for her because she was going through a rough time in her life. But for the whole month prior to my mom telling me this, the Lord had been revealing to me the fact that He "is not far from each one of us" because we are *all* His beloved children; and that all each of us ever need do at any given time is look to Him and call out to Him for deliverance, and that He would surely hear us and help us. He had been showing me that He loves each and every one of us the same and that He is not a respecter of persons, and does not show favoritism, but would help and rescue *anyone* who looked to Him and put their trust in Him by calling upon His holy name. We do not therefore need anyone else to pray for us or to intercede on our behalf, because He Himself would hear and receive every one of us if we would only put forth the effort and faith to call upon Him. (That is not to say that we shouldn't pray for one another; we should. The Bible clearly supports this. However, for the past month or so earlier, God had really been causing me to focus on the fact that He will answer everybody who calls upon Him in faith and that we don't need any other intercessors doing it for us). So when my mom requested that I pray for my aunt Emily, I was excited to share this truth with her. In addition to agreeing to pray for her, I was going to encourage my mom to tell my aunt Emily to go ahead and pray to God *for herself* because He would definitely help her and rescue her from all of her troubles if she would do so. For God Himself had told me as much! In fact, I was to let my aunt Emily know, by way of my mother, that *now is the time* that He will most certainly hear and rescue all who turn to Him and call upon His holy name (Acts 2:21). (Incidentally, the days are coming when He will *not* hear and when He will *not* answer. Remember the people who banged on the door and clamored to get into the ark when the rains began to fall during Noah's day? God closed His ears to their cries—it was too late. He gave them many years, while Noah was building the ark, to turn to Him and to cry out to Him. But unfortunately they didn't choose to do so until it was too late.)

It was good news that God was commanding me to tell my mom to relay to my aunt Emily. A prophet of the Lord was declaring that God had told him to tell Emily that He would hear and receive her request and to boldly come into His Presence for He Himself said that He would receive her! I received that word directly from the throne of the Living God. But my mom doesn't receive me as a prophet ("a prophet is without honor among his own family"), and therefore, she didn't receive my words that I had received from God ("whosoever receives a prophet in the name of a prophet, shall receive that which the prophet has been given"); and so, she unfortunately became greatly offended at what I tried to tell her. I never even got the chance to relay any of the good news that God had given me to tell her. The only words that I was able to say before she interrupted me were, "I don't need to pray for Aunt Emily, because ..." she immediately cut me off mid-sentence and began scolding me and telling me how self-righteous and uncaring I was. She yelled at me so hard for the next forty-five minutes that I didn't even get a chance to say a single word in my defense. This scolding continued all the rest of the way to the airport, while we were parking, through the airport lobby and check-in, and finally up to the security checkpoint. I was completely demoralized and vanquished. She literally brought me to tears in front of her. The only thing that I could do during this verbal assault was appeal to God in my mind.

While she was still railing on me at the airport, I asked God in my spirit, "Lord, what did I do wrong? Did I sin? Why is she doing this to me?"

Immediately, the Lord answered me, saying, "My mother didn't understand Me either; but I *always* showed her honor." Realizing that I hadn't fully grasp what Jesus was saying to me or understood what He was referring to in the Scriptures, the Holy Spirit immediately brought the verses from the Bible to my mind's eye so that I could clearly see the passages in front of me:

And when they ran out of wine, the mother of Jesus said to Him, "They have no wine." Jesus said to her, "Woman, what does that have to do with Me? My hour has not yet come." His mother said to the servants that were standing by, "Whatever He says to you, do it." Jesus said to them, "Fill the water pots with water." And they filled them up to the brim.

John 2:3–7

The Spirit instantly revealed to me that although Jesus' calling and coming were of much greater importance than His mother had realized, and although He did not come to this earth for the physical comforts and fleeting pleasures of people and for their entertainment and enjoyment, He nonetheless, *out of respect for His mother*, was willing to *honor her* by accommodating her wishes and desires (as long as they didn't conflict with a commandment from God). Jesus let me know, right then and there, at that precise moment, that I had handled the situation with my mother wrongly from the start and that I should have, out of respect for her, been willing to make allowance for her request, and where she spiritually is in her understanding, and that I should have handled the situation differently. I should have readily honored her request when I first began addressing her and then offered what the Lord had given me afterwards. In my initial response to her, I did not show her honor. Therefore, I handled it incorrectly, and it was my fault. Needless to say, I learned a very valuable lesson that day.

HARD LESSONS IN THE DESERT WILDERNESS

The best way to learn something, especially in terms of training for a future assignment, is to have to go through "a type of it" in the mean time. The Bible is replete with examples of this. In order to learn how to properly rule and administer governing authority (in preparation for his future divine assignment as Egypt's prime minister), Joseph first was assigned an administrative position over his fellow slaves in Potiphar's (his master) house. He then was made a warden over his fellow prisoners while he was in prison. David was first a shepherd of sheep, and then he became a "captain" over a small army and band of followers, all in preparation for one day becoming Israel's chief shepherd and king. Likewise, in order to prepare me to help lead His people successfully through some very turbulent and trying times that are soon coming upon the whole world, I have had to help lead a small band of people (some believing and others not so believing) through some very difficult trials in their individual lives. In fact, many of my "assignments" have been doing just that. But before I go any further and relay some of those assignments, I must continue on with what happened to Teresa and me after we were disfellowshipped. As I mentioned above, the Lord gives us our spiritual training and has us learn our lessons through "types" so that we can better understand and truly get a genuine taste of the difficulties that lie ahead and how to properly overcome them.

What better way for me to learn how to deal with His bride (His people) than to make my own bride like His?! It is written that the man who is married has his attentions and his interests (and affections) divided (1 Corinthians 7:32–35). How true that is! The married man is busy trying to please both the Lord and his wife. Sometimes, though, it is not easy or possible to please both parties. As Jesus said, "No man can serve two masters." It is also written that the head of every man is Christ, and that the wife's head is her husband (1 Corinthians 11:3; Ephesians 5:23). In other words, husbands are to obediently follow Christ; and their wives are to submissively follow them. The husbands are to lead and love their wives the same way that Christ leads and loves His bride (His people); and the wives are to faithfully follow their husbands the same way that believers faithfully follow Christ. Our marriages are supposed to be a direct spiritual representation and reflection of Christ working with and leading His wife–His people (Eph. 5:22–33). However, as the Old Testament clearly demonstrates, Israel (the Lord's wife) didn't always have a submissive believing heart that faithfully followed her Husband. As the Bible accurately describes, Moses sometimes had a very difficult time leading and serving the Lord's people. Oftentimes, the Lord's wife would struggle against him, resisting him. As their wilderness journey through the Sinai desert became more difficult and treacherous, and their living conditions more uncomfortable, many Israelites lost their faith, quit believing, became hardhearted, desired to go back to Egypt, sought out and embraced other gods, and came to believe that Moses was nothing but a self-appointed false prophet who was only leading them to death and destruction. Many of them rebelled against God and wanted to stone Moses for "misleading" them. But Moses truly loved the Lord's people; and he obviously personally suffered a great deal in order to serve them and the Lord. This is a common theme throughout the Bible. Many of the Lord's prophets and servants were made to personally suffer in their individual lives and marriages in order to help them better understand and identify with God's feelings and thoughts regarding His own unfaithful rebellious wife, Israel. The prophets Hosea and Ezekiel both had to endure extremely difficult circumstances in their own marriages in order to prophetically illustrate how God's wife had turned her back on her Husband and transgressed her "marriage vows." Hosea was commanded by God to marry a prostitute, and then watch as she sadly returned to her harlotries; and afterwards he was told to accept her back again. The Lord took Ezekiel's wife in death, and then instructed Ezekiel not to cry or to mourn her death as a prophetic sign to the people. The prophet Jeremiah was not allowed to marry or to have children, so that he could experience the loneliness, heartache, and despair that Israel had brought upon the whole land and to prophetically demonstrate how she had completely desecrated and destroyed all the families of Israel with her whoredoms and idolatries. Truly, the Lord's prophets have had to personally suffer a lot in order to serve the Lord and to minister to His people. In keeping with this biblical theme, and to help me better understand His feelings toward His own bride (the church—His worldwide body), and to equip me and train me for my future assignments in dealing with His people, the Lord has made my own wife, Teresa, for a time, a prophetic type of His wife (the church). The following will hopefully give you a clearer picture and a better idea of what kind of personal suffering is involved in order to receive spiritual training and prophetic understanding.

As everyone that we had ever known and loved began to turn their backs on us, as a result of us being disfellowshipped from church, Teresa began to get defensive and bitter against what she perceived to be Christianity and, in turn, me. As the "heat" and the loneliness of the desert wilderness began to surround us, and the seemingly spiritual drought began to overtake us, she increasingly became more and more resentful and disillusioned. Because a lot of "my prophecies" hadn't come to pass as quickly as she would have liked or as any of us had expected (myself included), she has drifted away from the Lord and become pretty hardhearted against me. She has renounced Christianity, denies the authority and veracity of the Bible, and is taking up books that promote and preach atheism, evolution, and agnosticism (false gods). It saddens me very much, especially now that her frustration and disbelief have escalated into outright persecution, but I also realize that God will soon "open her eyes to see Him" because He has told me as much. I pray for her daily and love her with all my heart. But God has shown me that she is a type of His church— that is, His people.

Let me give you an idea of what this means: I have learned a great deal over these ten years that I have been out here alone in this desert wilderness. I have learned to be totally dependent on God for all of my needs. (He has miraculously provided for me and my family in so many ways.) I have learned what it is like to suffer—to suffer for His name's sake and for His truth. I have learned what it is like to be shunned, misunderstood, misquoted, hated, and falsely accused—yet to not strike back. I have experienced what it is like to love and care for somebody deeply, and yet they do not know you or your true feelings for them. They don't see what you see, cannot comprehend what you know, and do not trust your leadership and guidance, although you would gladly give your life for them. You are not able to communicate with them or to reveal yourself to them because they don't believe you and won't accept what you have to say anyway. When you try to draw close to them and interact with them, they spit in your face, hit you, and/or mock you and the very God whom you serve, often misquoting and twisting Scriptures to try and inflame you or reject you altogether. This has been my experience of late with Teresa. But I realize that this is only a type of what is waiting for me yet in the future with the Lord's people. Like Moses, perhaps, this is why I too have had to go to "Midian"—to not only be humbled and become dependent on God, but also to learn how to properly lead and lovingly tend ungrateful and "ignorant" (as in spiritually blind) sheep. I want to share with you what this time out here in the desert wilderness has been like and what it has taught me. Below are some of my diary entries while sojourning in this desert for the past ten years:

> *12/27/00*—Apparently it's been almost a year since I last wrote an entry in this diary. I'm not quite sure why. Today, I feel the need to write down how incredibly lonely I feel! I can't help but feel like I don't have any friends. I feel so misunderstood, misinterpreted, and rejected. It seems like everything I do

and say gets misconstrued by somebody somewhere. I have been asking myself over and over again, "What have I been doing wrong?" I don't understand it. All I ever really wanted was to know God, work for God, and to help teach others about God. Why all of this headache, heartache, loneliness, and rejection?!

Perhaps, this is "part and parcel" with the calling. I guess I'm reminded of the words of Jesus when He said, "The servant is not greater than his master. If they have done it unto Me, they will do it unto you." I sure hope that is what it is. I would hate to be going through all of this for nothing! It's like my dad recently said to me, "Eric, either you have absolutely nothing in this world to worry about if this is truly of God, or you are going to single-handedly destroy your life and your family!" But he also added that "being a servant of God must be truly lonely."

You know, as I sit here and ponder this, I *know* this is from God! Obviously, not every single thing that I have said, done, or suffered is from Him, but rather, some of it (if not most of it) is from my own flesh. But, I do believe that overall, it is from Him. And that He *is* directing my paths. I believe that God is "putting to death my flesh" in order to "raise me up in the Spirit". Surely, this is what's happening!

Hope is a good thing. Perhaps, hope (and faith) is what made the Apostle Paul to write: "For I consider that the sufferings of this present time are not worthy to be compared with the glory which shall be revealed in us" (Romans 8:18). I tell you, it is hard—this Christianity thing! Hardest thing I've ever done or tried to do! But just when I start to think this way, I am reminded of the words written in Hebrews: "You have not yet had to resist unto bloodshed striving against sin." (Hebrews 12:4). Yikes! Apparently, I'm still a babe, and not as spiritually mature as I like to think that I am. God help me!

9/8/06—Lord, I don't want any more of this. I can't take any more. You once said that "a house divided against itself cannot stand." You, in Your wisdom, have chosen not to shed Your Light on my house. You have not opened the eyes of my wife to see Your goodness and Your purposes. She gives me more grief than I can deal with. And yet, I love her. I desire her. I wish I can see her gladness and love for me again. I can't take her belittling anymore. I can't take her meanness. She doesn't know how hard it is to serve You in a world that hates You. Father, it hates You and it hates me. Your people are obstinate and without mercy. My wife cast her lot in with them. She hates me. She is without kindness and respect. She doesn't know my motives for her. At every turn, she mocks me and belittles me. I cannot endure my love for her any longer.

Your people resist You. They are not aware of Your love for them—Your bride. They take Your name in vain, but are not Yours. Why Lord, oh why Lord do You endure so long with us? My God, my God, my heart faints inside me, I cannot go on. My wife has left me. Her heart is turned far from me. She is mine in form only. Her ways have gone from me. Her desire is not for me. She has transgressed Your command. I am as a lonely man. Forgotten and truly sorrowed. My eyes tire with my tears. My heart is far passed. It is burdened with grief. I cannot go on.

Still, my only hope is in You. I have no other god. You sustain me in the midst of my trials. Your purposes shall not fail me. My Father, my God, come to my house and sweep it clean. Purify it in love and let it rejoice in Your Truth. Establish Your House in the Highest.

9/25/06—I am so greatly saddened. As a prophet, I am experiencing a small taste of what Christ must feel about His bride. I love Teresa very much, and yet we have no intimacy in our marriage. In fact, she told me yesterday from her heart that she doesn't know if she even believes in God. This is the God that I serve! This is the God that I love! The One who created heaven and earth! Therefore, she doesn't believe in me also. I am so disheartened and discouraged.

A few years ago, Jesus told me that my wife was a type of the church. I am now beginning to realize what He meant. Jesus' bride, the church, doesn't have any real intimacy with Him. They "serve" Him in name and in form only. They don't really believe in Him to the extent that they put their real trust in Him to lead their lives. They don't surrender to Him and run to His arms to find comfort and security. They don't trust Him.

Like the church, my wife is only going through the motions. Our marriage relationship is only shallow at best and void of any real connection. There is no true intercourse or deep inner "touching." Her love for me is one of convenience and appearance. Oh, how my heart aches inside me! Oh, how I long for true love in spirit and in truth! Hosea must have died inside out of pain and anguish as he watched his wife play the harlot. Instead, I watch my wife find pleasure in emptiness and foolishness. She has traded our love and relationship for mere form and no substance. She doesn't know me. She is misguided and doesn't know. She is consumed with the material and void of any spiritual riches. Her husband has become another "thing" that needs to be "done."

Where is the love? Where is the admiration and the respect? Where is the intimacy between a man and his wife? It has been sold for a lie and traded for convenience' sake. True Christianity and intimacy require work! They require care! They must come first! Like my wife, the church has to love Christ, her husband, before all things. Otherwise, she is empty and without life. She is barren and bears fruit without purpose and brings forth children who are void of understanding. Oh Lord, Your people are cruel and have no merit. They come to Your side in emptiness and act out their "love." They bring no joy, but only sorrow to Your soul. You look into their eyes and see no love. You see no admiration. You feel no respect.

My God, my God, You bear long with us. You endure our vanities and watch us waste away. We throw away all that is precious to You and cast Your affections to the wind. God, my God, restore us to Your favor. Give us hearts that cry out to You and love You intensely; lest we bear Your name in vain.

Lord, You once told me, "How can you show love to My wife (the church), when you don't even show love to your own." God, forgive me. I now know what You meant. My heart aches inside of me. I have been blind. I love my wife. I long to hold my wife. I long for my wife to respond. She is far from me. I see how You love Your wife so dearly. How You care for her, though she hurts You continually. She has turned her affections to the world and its treasures. And yet, You cry out to her to return, and You will forgive her and hold her close. God, I am a fool. I am blind. I am lonely and there is none to comfort me. My heart aches. My body yearns for her, but I am forsaken. Please come to me. Change our wives. Give her a heart to trust. Give her affections in order to love. Let her feel Your love from me.

1/10/07—What can I say, Lord, to make people believe? What can I give to help them understand? We are all accounted sheep unto slaughter. We are all destitute of understanding and knowledge. We can't see, and yet we think we are full. We hunger and lust, and yet, not for the knowledge of You. We cry out for comfort, and yet we find none. Our lives are as miserable as people without water. We are as naked as newborn babes, and yet we brag of wealth. My God, my

God, even my own soul languishes within me. How can a man find eternity? How can a man see the infinite skies and the boundaries of heaven? How can a man number the galaxies, and count the pits on Your face? Your expanse is higher than any mountain. Your countenance is brighter than any sun. Why do we seek emptiness, oh Lord? Who will come at Your beckoning? Who will stand at Your call to attention? Where are my days, oh Lord my God? Where are the healings? Where are the stories of Your miraculous glory? I am confined to the scornings of my brothers. There is no peace. There is no comfort. The masses have forsaken You. They applaud my downfall. But You will restore me for Your own name's sake. You will deliver me according to Your faithfulness and loving kindness.

You have not forsaken me. You will lift me up in the highest. You will strengthen these weak hands. You will guide my arms and hold them up in righteousness. You will create in me a clean heart. For like my brothers, my heart too has turned away from You. It was not found in the Way. Yet, I am humbled. I am broken. Pride has gone from me. Life has become neither a challenge nor a pleasure. I long for the days of sunshine. I long for the rays of light. To behold the dawn of the morning! To see the light of the sun! This is my prayer. This is my hope, oh God. Who else can bring my rescue? Who else is my deliverer? There is no God for me but You.

8/29/07—Lord, I can't do this anymore. I am so lonely and dejected. Not only am I spiritually lonely, but I am emotionally and physically lonely. None of my family understands me. I am heartbroken and all alone. Everyone uses me. There is no comfort, only pain. I am sick to my stomach with grief. I am overtaken with confusion. My tears and my sorrow overwhelm me. They have taken me over. There are no heroes. I am a man of sin. Daily life has become a drudgery and weariness to me. Emptiness consumes me.

Nobody understands. They are all takers and not givers. I have no heroes. Where is the goodness, oh Lord? Where is the righteousness? God, why have You deceived me? I have loved You with a pure honesty. I have sought You and served You with my whole heart. I have been faithful to You since my youth. I have endured much pain and loneliness. And yet, You are quiet to my cause. Is there no one who hears? I follow a fading dream. My hope has become as a distant wind that fades off far away. My God, my God, bring back the simplicity of knowing Your kindness. Bring back the surety of Your word. I am as a lonely man destitute of family, of honor, and of glory. There is no completeness. My wife's feelings for me are a cover. They are as a shallow pool that glistens in the sun. There is no depth. There is no companionship. All of my days are weary, and my sorrows multiplied. Where is the relief You promised me? Where is the deliverance from my adversaries? Where is the vindication that You promised? The whole world laughs at me. They have put me far away from them. They revel in their material gods, and yet, I have not found pleasure in all that You have given me. My God, my God, where are Your miracles? Where is Your visitation? When will the dayspring come forth?

I am empty, and You have made me so. Come forth, oh God! Make me to sing again. Make me laugh. Make me rejoice. You once promised me that we would sing and dance. Where has that gone? Why do You hold out? Come forth and take away my reproach and the disdain that my family has for me. For I am weary, and I am tired, and I can't go on anymore. Your people—my people have hated me without cause. I have spoken Your words to them, and yet I am put forth. I am shamed for no reason at all. God, what happened to my life? I put my trust in You, and yet I am left so barren, so hopeless, and so destitute. There is no pleasure in living anymore. In vain I draw breath.

9/10/07—I believe you, God. Though the world cannot see, yet I hold Your words and my dreams in my heart. I have not forsaken Your ways. Though I am in a quiet place, where You have led me, yet do I still believe. Satan has not destroyed my faith in You. The world hates righteousness, oh God; they have forfeited the knowledge of You for riches that will rust and perish. I have no want for those things. Fame is fleeting, and riches are dishonorable; men of low degree sell out, and justice and equity are perverted by it. Integrity is far from money's door.

You, oh my God, are my hope, my trust. I have placed great hope and trust in You. For Your ways are much higher than man's ways, and Your wisdom is everlasting. I believe in a God who cannot be seen, and yet His intelligence and knowledge are all around me. I believe in Your ways. When found in You, there is no fear. There are no apologies, no regrets. To seek after You is good for my heart. It refreshes my spirit; it renews my soul. You, God, are my salvation. May my eyes see the goodness of my hope—the fulfillment of Your words. Lord God, establish me before my enemies—before the ones who say his God is vain. Let all of my words come to pass which were spoken in You. For in You have I placed my trust, and in You is my belief. For You shall preserve my soul and uphold me in righteousness.

11/1/07—Why, Lord, why? Why have You led me to troubled waters? Why do You desire for my soul to languish as Yours does? You have made my bride as Yours is. She has forsaken her covenant to me. Her love for me is as unstable as the wind, and You have made it so. Why have You taken the wife of my youth? Why have You removed her heart far from me? In vain I lay out my hands and heart before her, only to be rebuked and discarded. Why have You hardened her heart against me? I have only desired to serve You and to know You. Yet You have displaced me. You have removed all that I have loved. My wife is a stranger to me. I have become as a man without a home. Your people have become strangers to me. They hold me with contempt. They have pushed me out of the way, and have discarded me for no reason. Why, oh why, Lord, have You put me here? What evil have I done? My own wife has left me. Her heart has she removed far from me. She serves me in emptiness. She does not know me. She does not know You or the power of Your love. My God, my God, why have You forsaken me? Why have You cast me off from the ones that I love? Why have You placed a wedge between me and my people? Your bride, my bride, has become a stranger to me. They hold me in contempt because I have sought to serve You. They contemplate my death and my demise everyday. They are without natural affection and love. Their service toward me is empty and without intimacy. Oh, how I would long to hold them! Oh, how I long to take them in my arms and show them my goodness! She is beautiful to me. She is wonderful to my heart. And yet, she despises my goodness, and has no pity on my love.

What should be done unto her? Can she repent? Will she repent? Will You make her favorable and grant her mercy? Will You in Your goodness establish her feet and grant her repentance? How long, oh Lord, will You hide Your face? How long, oh Lord, will You remain silent? Will You not hear the cries of Your servants and visit their anguish? Your hand is mighty, and Your cause is right. Therefore, I implore You, to show me a kindness, and take away my reproach. Let my heart sing again. Let me know Your people. Give me an intimacy which can never be taken away. Let me rejoice again. Let me clap hands with the wife of my youth. Give me my heart's desire, for I have served You with all of my being. I have suffered greatly for the cause of Your name. My own house has forsaken me, and I am left desolate.

2/19/08—Without the Spirit of God, I have no knowledge, no understanding. Without God pulsing through my veins, I am an empty vessel; destitute and void; without any leadership or guidance. I am like a small vessel cast about in the wind with no rudder or purpose. My days are vanity and I am lost in hopelessness. God, my God, why have You forsaken me? My sins and my worthless passions consume me; they triumph over me. I am like a forgotten man who is empty and lost. There is none to comfort me. God, why have You made me desolate? I have forgotten the joys of my youth. In solitary confinement You have placed me. I cannot get out. All things have become a bitterness to my soul. I can find no lasting pleasure. Where is Your former love? Where are the promises that You have made to me? Why has it pleased You to leave me empty?

My own people chasten me. They afflict me with their revilings. They persecute my soul and desert me. In weariness I serve them, and yet they despise me. My sins consume me. My flesh lusts after things which are not right. I willingly confess my iniquities. I do not hide my shortcomings. I need Your grace, oh God. I need Your deliverance. Wherefore have You cast me off? My soul is thick with anguish. I have long feared what I deserve. Yet, I know that You are God. I know that Your mercies are everlasting. I know that You deliver in abundance and pardon with great kindness. Oh God, my God, why am I destitute? You once told me that You put Joseph in prison. Yet, he trusted You. He proclaimed Your goodness and Your faithfulness. Still, You showed him severity. You tested him. You tried him before You, and found him favorable. You delivered him and made him steadfast before You. You took away his reproach, and You saved many. My God, my God, please don't forget me! I can't take any more of this. And yet, my heart quietly asks for You. You are my Savior—my Forgiver, my Redeemer. I will ask for You in the morning; I will beseech You late at night. My days are dreary; my life is empty; and yet I will not give up. Where are You, God? Why have I been laid open and filleted?

3/5/08—Although I am still in this prison hidden away, I am nonetheless encouraged. I know that God is with me. He has not abandoned me. He is ever before me. He makes my way. He prepares a table before me in the presence of my enemies. My hope and trust are in Him. He is my God—my salvation. I suffer. But I suffer in patience and in hope. He has not left me desolate. His Word is ever with me. I have promises—His promises. His Word is good with me. My salvation is nearer than I think. He will redeem my soul and bless my name. The days that I have long sought are ever before me. They will bring rain in abundance, and I will be glad.

5/23/08—My Lord, my Lord, You have destined Jerusalem! You have called her and set her above every other woman. You are fond of her, and yet she has polluted Your name and despised You in her heart! She cannot trust You for she knows not Your ways! Turn her heart unto You. Take her to the secret chamber and comfort her soul with Your truths. Let her know Your love. Place within her Your spirit. Give her joy for her mourning, and take away her troubles—her ashes. Show her that You alone are worthy! That You alone are trusted! Deliver her from her destruction and from her desolation. My God, my God have pity on me. Do away with the old Jerusalem and bring forth the new! For she is a weariness to my soul and a blanket to my joy. She tries me all the day long, and scolds me for my faithfulness! Where can I wander? How long can I endure? She casts me off as her lover and rejects my gentle embraces. Wherefore have I done her wrong? For I have been faithful to her and have served her God faithfully. Why does she curse You and yet mingle between two opinions? She mocks all of Your ways and persecutes Your prophets. She claims to be faithful, and yet she blasphemes You all the day, saying, "God will not notice; there is no judgment from heaven!" How long will You be silent, oh God? When will You not answer?

You swear You will change her. You promise to answer her folly. Why have You made me so helpless to deliver her? Gently rebuke her and speak forth Your ways. Open her ears and prick her heart with Your goodness. Her continual groanings and prideful statements are a weariness to my bones and death to my heart! God, my God, will You not intervene? Where are You, my God?

Your heart speaks to me and says, "Is she not My wife? Why has she treated Me thus? Why does she speak so contemptuously? She has hated My love, and put her trust in idols!" Can she be forgiven, oh Lord? Can she be washed clean again? You know, oh Lord! For You have spoken it! You have spoken of a new Jerusalem! You know what is in Your heart, and You have purposed it. You will do all that You have determined. Take me with You, oh God. Let me see her new day! Let me embrace her in her goodness. For she is like a new bride. She is ever in love with her Husband! She has seen His nakedness and rejoices therein. She has been forgiven. Her iniquities are far from her, and she rejoices in the wisdom and faithfulness of her Husband. Take care, oh Husband, and be the Bridegroom, for Your God has made a way for You, and You shall dwell in Jerusalem forever!

6/13/08—Tonight my wife spit in my face! We were arguing about our financial situation, when totally unprovoked, she punched me in the groin as I lay on our bed. And as I tried to restrain her from hitting me some more, she then spit in my face. My first impulse was to smack her, but I didn't. A force held me back from within, as she belittled me and dared me to hit her back. As I was restraining her, she was mocking me and saying, "Now let's see you turn the cheek!" At that moment, I suddenly remembered how they spit in our Lord's face, and I just said, "You know what I am going to do? I am just going to walk away." With that, I just slowly got up, while being mindful of her fists, and went into the bathroom and washed my face, got my clothes, and exited the room. I realize that this is not my wife. It is not my "Sarah." She actually spit in my face! I can hardly believe it! And yet, I am not greater than my Lord. His wife actually spit in His face too! Who am I? I am not anything that they should not spit in my face. My Lord, Jesus, was and is everything, and yet if He didn't strike back, who am I that I should even consider laying that at her charge? Forgive her, Father, for she doesn't know what she is doing. It is so hard for her. Father, if it (this financial situation and the faith issue) is this hard for me, imagine how hard it is for her. Please forgive her, Lord. I have.

7/1/08—My Lord, I sit quietly here and wonder where You are? My breath has gone from me. My meaning, my purpose has dissipated into thin air. I am as a dry man sitting by a forgotten brook which has long since faded away into complete nothingness. Where have You gone, oh Lord? Why have You forgotten me? Behold, You have led me to a dry place, an abandoned hill, a destitute sanctuary. Wherefore have You left me? I cry with no comfort. I languish in desolation. Solitude surrounds me. Companionship escapes me. I have been stricken sore and have been made a reproach and a joke to my people. People scoff at me. My own wife despises me. My mother detests me. I am scorned when I speak of Your goodness, Your faithfulness, and brighter days. My Lord, my Lord, why have You forsaken me? I have obeyed Your word. I have abased myself. I have pleaded for Your revelation. And yet, stillness surrounds me, silence plagues me. My soul wanders aimlessly through this desert. I can find no rest, no pleasure, and no green pastures for my soul. Wherefore have You made me so quiet? Why have You crushed me?

Still, oh my soul, wait in silence for Your God! He will avenge you. He will come to your aid. God will not be angry forever. His silence is wisdom. Love is His decree. What He has purposed, that will He do! He is righteous. He is holy and there is no unrighteousness within Him or before Him. The wicked will not stand. All of their ways are vanity before Him. They will come to nothing. Be still, oh my soul, and wait in silence for God! His ways are perfect, and beyond finding out.

My days are as the wind. Loneliness abounds. I am faint. My eyes are tired with tears. My heart has become a sick captive and I cannot speak. My weariness has overcome me. I have no one to rescue me from my despair. And yet, still I press on. I cannot let my spirit give up. I believe in my God. I have put all of my trust in Him. I will go down trusting in Him. He is all perfect, and there are no apologies in Him. With reckless abandon will I follow Him. He is my Shepherd, and I shall not want. He is able. He is holy. And He is worthy to be praised! His God is my God. And all of His ways are perfect. He will deliver me and all of my people will see it! I shall not lose hope, and I will not relinquish my faith in Him. Oh my soul, trust in Him! Give praise in the dismal hour, and rejoice in the barren place, for He is with you, and you will never be removed.

7/21/08—My Father, I have waited so long for You. My spirit cries out to You, but still I am desolate. I believe in You, Father. I am ignorant of Your ways. I am without understanding of Your timing. I cannot escape the misery and loneliness that You have surrounded me in. In stillness I wait. In silence I endure. In quietness I suffer. Nobody knows me. My life is a lonely walk. My spirit is suppressed all the day. I have been zealous for You all of my life, and yet You will not let me exclaim. I am punished for my love for You. My faithfulness has gone unrewarded. Still my soul waits in silence for God. Still I go on. My neighbors laugh at me. My brothers mock me. My family bereaves me. Oh how my soul languishes within me. There is no peace. There is no love. There is no salvation and deliverance.

Oh God, why have You created me? I have no comfort, I have no friends. Trials and tribulations surround me each day. I am tucked away in a lonely prison. There are no birds to sing; there are no harps to play; there are no minstrels to ease my anguish. Wherefore have You punished me so severely? I have loved You from the bottom of my heart. I have praised You since my youth. Why have You locked me away in this barren cave? My people hate me. My relatives abhor me. And still You do not rescue me. You do not have pity on my situation. I am so sorry that I have failed You. My loneliness and isolation is beyond what my soul can bear. There is no deliverance. There is no excitement. Your people have become an abandoned field whose fruit is contemptible and whom the laborers have long forgotten. I do not understand. I do not know. Your loving kindness I believe in. Your abilities and wisdom I take stock in. Your faithfulness I love. Why have You left me? Why are Your people ravaged by wolves? Why do You not step in? Why has Jezebel been allowed to demolish Your people—to strip them of all dignity and godliness? Behold, You have shut my mouth. You have taken away the Light that is upon me. You have plagued Your people and made Your servants lepers among them. Strange visions circle my memory; strange words encompass my soul. I am not allowed to speak. I am not permitted to leave. Yet, still I witness the vulnerability of Your people! My heart aches for Your people. My love clamors to be released. Your wife, my sister, detest me. She despises my feelings; she mocks my compassion. She harbors hatred against me. Yet, I have loved her with an undying love.

What good are my words? What profit is there in speaking? I have no power; I have no goodness. I have nothing to offer. I have become a desolation to my people. I cannot deliver them. I am without hope. Yet, still I cry out to You! I plead before You. Day and night I lift up my song to You. I long for the days of old when You moved Your right hand; when Your compassion was upon us; the days when we blossomed before You and Your people flourished like little gazelles in the light of Your sun. What happened that You would utterly cast us off? I have no power. I have no defenses or sword. My strength is in a dream. I have no contest left within me. I am in a desolate place, and I have been made dry before all men.

I bemoan my condition, and yet You are not afar off. I can feel Your presence within me. You will not be still forever. I believe in Your goodness. I put trust in Your power. You are higher than any mountain; You are truer than any ray of the sun. There is strength and wisdom in all of Your purposes; calamity is Your tool. Nothing escapes Your thoughts and Your eyes. You can make a road where there is no road. You can deliver when there is no way. All of Your ways are beyond men. Who can speak of it? I shall be happy when I awake. Until then, only dust and sorrow consume me. But I shall wait on the Lord, my Strength. He will surely redeem my soul and deliver all who put their trust in Him.

Although it has been a long and lonely road, as you can gather from reading my diary entries, the Lord has nonetheless been very kind and gracious to me. I can now understand the feelings of anguish that Joseph must have felt and struggled with, having been betrayed and rejected by his brothers, as he "wasted away" and lamented for thirteen years in slavery and in prison, waiting upon God to fulfill His promises to him (Genesis 37–42; Psalm 105:17–19). I can identify with the weariness of soul and the despair that Moses must have felt when he wandered in the desert place looking for an acceptable place to call home. I now understand the questions that must have surely raced through his mind, as he wondered how he had ended up in such a lonely and desolate place having once been so high up in the palaces and courts of Pharaoh. He must have quietly thought to himself, *How could I now be out here suffering in this barren, hot desert wilderness tending my father-in-law Jethro's sheep, when I was at one time a celebrated prince and decorated general in Egypt?* I can now understand and feel the unjust persecution and utter isolation that David felt when he ran from cave to cave trying to find peace and acceptance, all the while, wondering why God had abandoned him and asking Him what evil he had done. I know what it is like to have prayers and psalms pour forth from your soul, in utter anguish and desperation, trying to communicate with God, who seems so far off, and yet, Whom you know is never really far away. Like David before me, I too, now know what it is like to have family members reject you, misunderstand you, and think little of you, and to love a wife who openly belittles and mocks your love for God (2 Samuel 6:16–20). I now feel the loneliness and despair that the prophets felt as they were laughed at, banished, and mistreated by those whom they loved—

their own people, their own countrymen, their own brothers, and their mates. Still they believed, they persevered, and they forgave—never forgetting God or His promises that He made to them. This is what it means to follow Christ! This is truly what it means to be like Him and to walk as He walked, to forgive as He forgave and to love as He loved. This is what Jesus meant when He first said those words to me, years ago, after I was first kicked out of church, as I lay before Him crying, wondering why the elders had disfellowshipped me. He profoundly said to me: "Eric, how can you *show* love to My bride, when you don't even *show* love to your own?" At the time, I took this as an indictment and condemnation against me; however, I have now come to realize that this was the Lord's way of telling me that I can't truly *show love* to His people and properly lead them until He shows me (and trains me by experience) how to *divinely love* and rightly lead as He does—by temporarily making my wife a spiritual type of His church. How ingenious! How marvelous! How wise is the Lord in all of His ways!

> For love *suffers long* and is kind; love does not envy; love does not parade itself, is not puffed up; does not behave rudely, does not seek its own, is not provoked, thinks no evil; does not rejoice in iniquity, but rejoices in the truth; *bears* all things, *believes* all things, *hopes* all things, *endures* all things. Love never fails.
>
> 1 Corinthians 13:4–8, *emphasis mine*

And yes, love also "covers a multitude of offenses" (1 Peter 4:8). This is how God loves us—His people—and how we must learn to love others, the way God does. As He Himself said, there is no righteousness in loving those who love us and treat us well—for even sinners do that (Luke 6:32–35). They love those who love them! This is how the unbelieving world loves. Instead, as believers and as Christians, we are called to love as God loves—*unconditionally*. His love for us is not based on how we treat Him or whether or not we love Him. He loves us regardless—that is, He loves us unconditionally! The Bible says that God clearly demonstrated His love for us by sending His Son to die for us "while we were yet sinners" (Romans 5:8). God loved us even when we hated Him and when we mistreated and falsely accused Him—when we spit in His face! This is how God shows His great love for us—and this is how we must learn to love others as well—unconditionally.

Before I proceed any further, I want to clearly state the following, lest there be any needless misunderstandings or unintended hurt feelings: I truly love my wife and the people of God more than anything else in this life. I want to see God's people grow in faith and become mature in Him. In fact, I would gladly give up my life and do willingly expend it for *her* (both for my own personal wife as well as the Lord's wife—the church). Although she doesn't realize it, my wife, Teresa, has been made (for a time) a prophetic type and a spiritual reflection of His own people—that is, His beloved wife, so that I might come to better understand how great His love and yearning is for His church. Because He used my own wife as an example of His people, I now understand *by firsthand experience* how much God truly loves us, and to what lengths He is willing to go to in order to restore us to Himself and embrace us tightly in His bosom. I now understand how He longs to hold us and to purify us, and to "wash us clean by the water of His Word" (Ephesians 5:26). We are truly the objects of His holy desire, and He longs to have true intimacy and intercourse (interaction and union) with us. His faithfulness and undying love and care for us are beyond human comprehension and understanding, and so to better help me to identify with that Godly love, He took my own bride and made her like His own. He did this to teach me, and to give me a "divine taste" of that profound love and desire and eternal goodness that He has toward each one of us in His body. God longs for true intimacy and oneness with His people. As He prophetically said to us so long ago:

> Husbands, love your wives, *just as* [in the same manner as] *Christ also loved the church and gave Himself for it,* that He might sanctify and cleanse it with the washing of water by the word, that He might present it to Himself a glorious church, not having spot or wrinkle or any such thing, but that it should be holy and without blemish. *So ought husbands to love their own wives as their own bodies;* he who loves his wife loves himself. *For no one ever hated his own body, but nourishes and cherishes it, just as the Lord does the church.* For we are members of His body, of His flesh and of His bones. "For this reason a man shall leave his father and mother and be joined to his wife, and the two shall become one flesh." *This is a great mystery, but I speak concerning Christ and the church.*
>
> Ephesians 5:25–32, *emphasis mine*

Jesus set the example for us on how we husbands should love our wives—that is, *unconditionally* and *sacrificially.* This is what He meant when He said to me prior to my entering my appointed desert wilderness time: "Eric, how can you show love to My bride, when you don't even show [divine] love to your own?!" Lord, according to Your great kindness and mercy, I believe that

I am finally beginning to learn these things. Thank You for Your wisdom, patience, and teachings.

In light of these truths, I do not harbor any ill will for my brothers and sisters in the Worldwide Church of God or for any man or woman for that matter. I greatly love people—especially His beloved bride. They are my brothers and sisters. As it is written: "He who has the bride is the Bridegroom; *but the friend of the Bridegroom, who stands and hears Him, rejoices greatly because of the Bridegroom's voice. Therefore, my joy is fulfilled.*" (John 3:29). I have the utmost love and respect for the Lord's people and for each and every member of His divine body—that is, His bride. But that does not mean that many professing Christians and collective church bodies aren't deceived—or should I rather say—severely spiritually immature! I find that, for the most part, many Christians are blind and deaf to God. They are ignorant of His ways and blind to their own spiritual immaturity. Although many in the church claim to "see and hear," they in actuality don't (John 9:39–41). They are blind and deaf, and do not realize that spiritually they are lacking. It wasn't until I was personally brought to my own knees and began questioning my own spiritual condition and "standing" before Him (as a result of the doctrinal changes that were then taking place within our denomination), that I began to recognize my own spiritual poverty and miserable condition. Prior to this, I thought that I knew God. I thought that I was "all right" with Him. Little did I realize then how spiritually "wretched, miserable, poor, blind, and naked" I truly was before Him (Revelation 3:17). I didn't really know God. I thought that I did! But I really didn't know Him. As a result of this "spiritual awakening" and realization, I became hungry and thirsty, and I longed to get to know Him as He really is. It is from this intense spiritual hunger and searching that I came to "see" and directly hear from God. Brothers and sisters: until we begin to hunger and thirst for God and His righteousness, we will not be filled. Until we begin to realize how spiritually poor we are—that is, how "poor in spirit" we have become—we will not see Him nor enter into His kingdom (Matthew 5:3–8). But God promises us that if we seek Him, we will find Him; if we knock on His door, He will open to us; and if we ask, it will be granted (Luke 11:9–10). For He says whosoever calls upon His name in this hour, and in this day, will be saved (Acts 2:21).

ABRAHAM HAD
TWO WIVES

Recently, the Lord has been speaking to me about Hagar. She was Abraham's second wife, given to him by his first and primary wife, Sarah (Genesis 16:3). After sojourning in the land of Canaan (a type of desert wilderness) for ten years, both Abraham and Sarah were becoming weary in their faith—Sarah more so than Abraham. God had promised them a child, but all of their physical circumstances surrounding this promise seemed now more impossible than ever. Therefore, Sarah began to look to human worldly methods, in order to bring about what God had destined for them. She took her Egyptian handmaid, Hagar, and gave her to Abraham in order to produce an heir. Afterwards, she became angry with Abraham and began to blame him for his part in what they had done (Genesis 16:5). Hagar, being Egyptian, was symbolic of "using the world's wisdom and methods" in order to try and bring about what the Lord had promised. Remember what was written about Moses and how he was "learned in all the wisdom of the Egyptians" (Acts 7:22) before God sentenced him to Midian to have him "de-programmed" through a desert wilderness experience? Well, here is an example of someone (particularly Sarah) who was really struggling to believe God once she had been placed in the desert wilderness for a while (ten years). In fact, it would be another fourteen years of sojourning in this wilderness and of having to trust God, before Isaac would be born to them and the word of God would be fulfilled.

The Lord pointed something out to me recently regarding my wife, Teresa. Both of these wives of Abraham—both Sarah and Hagar—each pictured something, spiritually speaking. Sarah typified a godly wife. She was supportive and submissive to her husband, believed and trusted God, and was incredibly beautiful—both inwardly and outwardly. In fact, the Bible itself clearly described her as such and even holds her up as *the standard* that Christian wives should strive to be like:

> Wives, in the same way be submissive to your husbands so that, if any of them do not believe the Word, they may be won over without words by the behavior of their wives, when they see the purity and reverence of your lives. Your beauty should not come from outward adornment, such as braided hair and the wearing of gold jewelry and fine clothes. Instead, it should be that of your inner self, the unfading beauty of a gentle and quiet spirit, which is of great worth in God's sight. For this is the way the holy women of the past who put their hope in God used to make themselves beautiful. They were submissive to their own husbands, like Sarah, who obeyed Abraham and called him her master. *You are her daughters if you do what is right and do not give way to fear.*
>
> 1 Peter 3:1–6, New International Version, *emphasis mine*

Obviously, Sarah was human and had her faults and shortcomings too. When her faith began to weaken as she saw that her and

Abraham's bodies were getting on in years, she thereby became fearful that God was not able to truly perform what He had promised them regarding having a son, so she began looking to human wisdom and conventionality. This is what Hagar embodied and symbolized—human methods and conventionality! Remember, Scripture says that both women were Abraham's wives—that is, they both formed two halves of one wife, so to speak. When Sarah, who was the free woman and the legitimate wife of Abraham, lacked faith and became fearful, she would consequently introduce "Hagar" into their marriage. Hagar, who pictured bondage (Galatians 4:24–25) and being enslaved to the physical cares and ways of this world, would only bring grief, strife, and contention into their marriage. Hagar was the product of Sarah's waning faith and unbelief. Thankfully, later though, after much infighting and hurt feelings had taken place, Hagar was ultimately cast out. She and "her offspring"—that is, what she "produced" (contention, strife, and hurt feelings)—were permanently cast out and did not inherit the divine promises of God (Galatians 4:30).

But Scripture also says that while Hagar was in the wilderness of Beersheba, "God opened her eyes, so that she saw the wellspring of water" (Genesis 21:19). This is the verse that God quoted to me while I was praying to Him recently regarding my wife, Teresa. As the strife and contention between us has been escalating in our house over the past few years because of the financial and social strains that have come upon us, as a result of me having to obey God and follow His leading and commands, Teresa has been becoming more and more hostile toward me— almost to the point of us needing to separate. However, when I cried to God about this in anguish and despair, He quoted this verse to me—about how in due time He had "opened Hagar's eyes to see the wellspring of water." Believe me, I had never thought of Teresa as being both a type of Sarah and a type of Hagar before. As God showed me, these things are a personal allegory to me right now. Originally when my wife was a believer (that is, "in faith"), she was like Sarah. She respected me, loved me, and trusted me, as well as God who was leading me. But as time has gone by and the "desert wilderness experience" has become more grueling and fearsome, she is becoming like Hagar—that is "of the world," resentful and mocking, and thus is persecuting that which is "born of the Spirit"—just like Hagar and her son did (Galatians 4:29).

You see, this is how God speaks to us. Sometimes, plainly; other times in mysteries and allegories so that we have to search His Word and seek Him for the hidden meanings and the truth. But this is what Scripture says that He does for His glory and for our benefit. His mind and wisdom are so great, and beyond us, that in order for us humans to understand, we have to learn "one step at a time" like a little child does. For it is written:

> Whom will He teach knowledge? And whom will He make to understand His message? Those weaned from milk and those drawn from the breasts [that is, those who are maturing and are no longer infants]. For precept must be upon precept, precept upon precept. Line upon line, line upon line. Here a little, there a little.
>
> Isaiah 28:9–10

And again, it is written: "It is the glory of God to conceal a matter; but the glory of kings to search it out" (Proverbs 25:2).

This is the meaning of what God prophetically said to me earlier regarding Teresa (who is a prophetic type of the church) and how He will open "Hagar's" eyes to see the "wellspring of water." The "wellspring of water" represents Jesus Christ and the Holy Spirit. For Jesus said, "If anyone thirsts, let him come to Me and drink. He who believes in Me, as the Scripture has said, 'out of his heart will flow rivers of living water.' For this He spoke concerning the Spirit, whom those believing in Him would receive" (John 7:37–39). He also said, "He who believes in Me shall never thirst." (John 6:35). Because of what God said, it is evident to me that God will sometime in the near future open Teresa's eyes so that she will be my "Sarah" once again; and then that bondwoman, "Hagar," will be permanently cast out of her. For she (Hagar) is the product of fear and unbelief, and fear and unbelief have no part in the kingdom of God. But rather, they have their part in the lake of fire (Revelation 21:8)—for God has spoken it. Yet, a little while, and these things will be so.

Lest anyone gets the wrong idea and incorrectly thinks that I have been "blameless" through this wilderness ordeal and that Teresa is the only one who needs to change and overcome, I want to relay the following story to show just how difficult "overcoming ourselves and our human way of thinking" really is. Yes, it has been difficult for Teresa to keep believing and to exercise true faith in God, but I have had a hard time overcoming and putting to death my flesh and its carnal way of thinking as well. I want to share a quick story here that hopefully helps illustrate just how hard it is sometimes living in the flesh and yet trying to "walk in the Spirit" (Galatians 5:16–17). One day, after a few months of desperately trying to keep peace at home and trying to draw closer to my wife in patience and understanding, I was feeling pretty good about myself regarding the idea of "demonstrating Christ's love" to her in order to "overcome evil with good." I had been striving very hard in the preceding weeks and months to become more Christlike in responding to her and to follow His loving examples in dealing with His disbelieving bride.

A friend of mine had mentioned to me earlier that whenever Teresa becomes angry and contentious, I should try to do something positive for her—in other words, learn to "overcome evil with good." He suggested that the next time that she got angry at me (for a spiritual reason), I should immediately go to her and put my arms around her and hug her and tell her how much I love her. Thinking that this was good sound advice, and "words of wisdom to live by," I happily agreed to do so. A couple of days later, Teresa became angry with me, and so I remembered this man's advice. As she was leaning over the bed making it, I came up behind her and put my arms around her to hug her and started to tell her that I loved her, when she suddenly turned around and punched me squarely in the face! I was so stunned and horrified that I stepped back and yelled, "What are you doing?! I was only trying to hug you and to show you Christ's love. I can't believe you just did that! I can't believe that you would dare hit your husband!" As I held my nose in pain, the thought that she would disrespectfully hit me, with me being much bigger and stronger than her infuriated me the more that I stood there in front of her thinking about it. Now visibly angry but wanting to also show her that I wasn't going to severely hurt her back but certainly wanting her to know that "I could if I wanted to," *I hit her three times* (not very hard) on her upper arm to make my point and self-righteously said, "I was just trying to be like Jesus to you. I can't believe you would punch me!"

Her face and countenance immediately changed, and she smiled and sneered with an evil laugh, "Ha! You were trying to be like Jesus? Ha! Why didn't you turn the cheek then?!"

At that very moment, Jesus then spoke in my ear, and said, "Eric, *you* just denied Me three times!"

Totally stunned by His convicting words, I stumbled back and suddenly realized what I had done and what I had become. I had become like Peter *before* he was converted! Jesus was now saying the exact same words to me that He had spoken to Peter two thousand years ago. When Peter erroneously and self-righteously thought that he was on the same spiritual footing as Jesus and was therefore "prepared" to join Him in spiritual battle, he proudly proclaimed, "I am ready, even now, to go and to die with You, Lord. I will not deny You. Although everyone else may forsake You, yet, I will never be made to stumble!" (Matthew 26:33–35). However, Jesus turned and informed him that before that very night would end and the rooster would crow the following morning, Peter would deny Him three times. And he did. And so did I! I learned a very valuable lesson at that moment. I came to suddenly realize that it doesn't matter how much you "put on" Jesus or study about Him, or *try* to be like Him—it doesn't work. Unless you die and Jesus comes to live in you (that is, in place of you), you will never be like Him! You will never be "a new creation in Him"—that is, you will never be a *new person* with a new mind and a different spirit. Jesus Christ has to come into us bringing a new spirit—His Spirit, the Holy Spirit, the Spirit of Christ and His mind, which "melds" with our spirit and our mind to create a whole new person, so that the "old man" and his way of doing things can be put away (Romans 6:6; Colossians 3:9–10). Yes, we still live in the flesh—that is, we live in a fleshly body at this time—as a "son of man"; yet when we have His Spirit in us, we are also a "son of God"—that is, we are now born of the Spirit also. Like Jesus, we are now fully man and fully God—that is, if we have His Spirit residing in us. This is what Paul meant when he wrote: "I have been crucified with Christ; *it is no longer I who live, but Christ lives in me*; and the life which I now live in the flesh I live by faith in the Son of God, who loved me and gave Himself for me" (Galatians 2:20). And again, it is written: "But as many as received Him, *to them He gave the right to become children of God*, even to those who believe in His name; *who were born, not of blood, nor of the will of the flesh, nor of the will of man, but of God*" (John 1:12–13). The book of Hebrews further states:

> For it was fitting for Him, for whom are all things and by whom are all things, *in bringing many sons to glory*, to make the author of their salvation perfect through sufferings. For both He who sanctifies and those who are being sanctified *are all of one Father, for which reason He is not ashamed to call them brethren*, saying: "I will declare Your name to My brethren; in the midst of the congregation I will sing praise to You"…and again: "Here am I and the children whom God has given Me."
>
> Hebrews 2:10–13, emphasis mine

The Apostle John writes:

> Behold what manner of love the Father has bestowed on us, *that we should be called children of God*! Therefore the world does not know us, because it did not know Him. Beloved, *now we*

are children of God; and it has not yet been revealed what we shall be, but we know that when He is revealed, we shall be like Him, for we shall see Him as He is. And everyone who has this hope in him purifies himself, just as He is pure.

1 John 3:1–3, *emphasis mine*

And again, the Apostle John says, "And by this we know that He abides in us, by the Spirit whom He has given us" (1 John 3:24).

Like the disciples, I too had erroneously thought that just because Jesus was working with me, and I had been walking around with Him and communicating with Him that I was ready to "do spiritual battle" with Him. I felt that if I "acted" like Him, then I could "be" like Him. But as I quickly found out, when Satan entered my wife that day and confronted me, I quickly crumbled and denied Him entirely. I wasn't as spiritually strong and vigilant as I thought that I was! By "striking back" and being self-righteous, I wasn't truly in Christ, and He wasn't truly in me. Although I thought that I was "acting in divine love," I was really only *reacting* carnally and humanly. I guess to a certain degree that is exactly what I *was* doing—acting! *Acting* like a Christian is not the same as *being* a Christian—that is, acting like Christ, is not necessarily being like Christ. To be like Christ, you have to *become* Christ. Let me explain: the Greek word for *christ* means "anointed." Being "anointed" means having a "God-given commission and supernatural ordination" to do something or to be something. This is what the Holy Spirit is—a God-given supernatural ordination. It enables you to be Christlike! In other words, it is impossible to be Christlike or to be as Christ without the baptism of the Holy Spirit. You can try all you want to, but without the Holy Spirit transforming your mind and spirit, you can't be like Christ, walk like Christ, follow Christ, do the works of Christ, or become Christlike at all! Peter (and the other disciples) tried and failed miserably. And so did I. That is why Jesus later said to Peter: "Peter, *when you are converted* [changed by the power of the Holy Spirit when the Holy Spirit is given to you], strengthen your brethren" (Luke 22:32). In other words, before Peter was given the Holy Spirit, he couldn't make a difference in his life or in the lives of his spiritual brothers and sisters either. This is why the Scripture says, "Apart from Me, you can do nothing" (John 15:5). The disciples all had to learn this same valuable lesson as well. Thinking that they were *reacting* righteously toward a Samaritan village that had rejected them, John and James asked Jesus if they should "call down fire from heaven to consume those people just as Elijah had done" (Luke 9:54). Jesus immediately rebuked them, telling them that they "didn't know what manner of spirit they were of" (Luke 9:55). In other words, they were not acting in the Holy Spirit because it had not yet descended upon them—but rather they were acting in some other fallen spirit—demonic, human, or otherwise. Sadly, this is what I was doing in regard to Teresa as well—working in my own human efforts and not in the power of the Holy Spirit.

BAPTISM OF THE HOLY SPIRIT

This brings me to a supernatural occurrence that happened a couple of years ago that my wife personally witnessed. Most of the miraculous things that had happened to me over the years, Teresa was not an eyewitness to. In this case, however, she was. One afternoon, I was speaking to my dad on the telephone, sharing with him some of the amazing things that were happening. My dad is not a professing Christian, per se, so I was excited that he was actually listening to me talk about the wonderful things that God was doing among us. After I hung up the phone, I was literally leaping for joy at the rare opportunity to be able to witness to my dad. I was so overcome with joy that I began praising God. I got down on my face in my bedroom and was joyfully professing my love for Him and praising Him for His goodness. The more and more I praised Him from my heart, apparently the closer He drew to me. Because a few moments later, I began to hear what sounded like thundering horse hooves coming toward me from a great distance away, fast approaching me. It sounded like a great army, a cavalry of horses coming closer and closer. As I lay there listening, the thundering hooves formed a distinct cadence that grew louder as it quickly approached. I found myself bobbing my head in unison to its beat. Pretty soon, my mouth began slowly moving in a strange way as my head followed the distant beat. All of a sudden, as it approached, I realized that it wasn't the sound of thundering horse hooves at all, but rather the praises of many different languages all being spoken individually, yet forming one voice in unison to God. And then all of a sudden, *boom!* It entered my mouth! My tongue began moving faster than is humanly possible, and although I had never learned or spoken a foreign language before (except limited French in high school), my mouth began professing the praises and goodness of God in many different languages! I couldn't stop it, nor did I want to. I heard hundreds of languages, many of which were coming out of my mouth—both human languages and angelic ones (1 Corinthians 13:1). Some of them I recognized, but many of them I didn't, although, I could tell in some cases what dialect they were. They were all praising God and proclaiming His wonderful works. I was astonished! The power of the Holy Spirit had come over me and had literally taken over my tongue. And now my mouth and tongue were moving faster than was humanly possible.

Absolutely astonished at what was happening to me but also recognizing that what was happening was biblical, I sat up in excitement (I had been down on my face praying). Immediately, the Lord said to me, "Show yourself unto your wife." By this time, the languages were just pouring forth out of my mouth; I couldn't control it. Dozens of them! I opened the sliding door to our master bathroom from our bedroom where I had been praying, and at that very moment, Teresa was stepping out of the shower. She saw me standing there with all of these "foreign languages" coming out of my mouth and my tongue rushing at an incredible speed. Her eyes flew open in shock and amazement wondering what in the world was going on. Within a few seconds the "speaking in tongues" was gone, and the electrifying power that had consumed my mouth vanished, leaving me on my butt without any strength and one very tired tongue. As my wife stood there staring at me, I couldn't do anything but laugh. I laughed so hard rejoicing at the incredible mercy and kindness that God had just shown me by granting me a taste of His incredible power, and for being able to experience firsthand something so amazing and of biblical proportions. All of my life, I had read and heard about the "gift of tongues" and of "speaking in tongues" and/or the "baptism of tongues," but I never really knew what it was. I realized that the Pentecostal churches believed in it, and some even claimed to regularly practice it, but I had always thought of them (and in some cases, found them) to be fraudulent. But now here I was experiencing it for myself firsthand—totally unexpectedly and without looking for it. I was completely blown away by this experience!

I realize that to most of my readers, this miracle is going to be completely outside their paradigm, their comfort zone, and their realm of personal experience and reality. The truth is, until it happened to me, I would have definitely sided with you. I had read about it occurring in the Bible a few times, but as far as it happening in today's modern world and age, well, forget it! I would never have accepted it. In fact, if I had witnessed it happening to someone else, as my wife was seeing it happen to me, I would have slowly backed away, believing it to be somehow demonic, or maybe involving a mental illness—or as the Bible says that some of those who witnessed it in the first century said, "Those people are full of new wine!" (Acts 2:13). When it comes to supernatural occurrences, I am an admitted skeptic, and apparently not very perceptive. In fact, I once asked the Lord why He speaks to me so clearly, and why I can hear Him so plainly, and yet, He doesn't apparently speak to very many others in this same way, and He answered me, by saying, "Because you wouldn't get it otherwise. You have to be hit by a two-by-four to the forehead before you will believe or get something." Obviously, the Scripture is true then that God "chooses the weak and foolish people of the world" to work with, and not the mighty and the brightest (1 Corinthians 1:26–29).

Perhaps, I should explain why this "speaking in tongues" or baptism of tongues occurred. There are a few reasons: First of all, for *confirmation*. Second, for *education*. And third, for *realization* (as a witness). Let me explain.

For confirmation: The Bible shows that on a number of occasions the baptism of tongues or "speaking in tongues" was granted as a special sign of confirmation that the Holy Spirit had been given to an individual or to a group of individuals. Notice these verses:

> Now when the Day of Pentecost had fully come, they were all with one accord in one place. And suddenly there came a sound from heaven, as of a rushing mighty wind, and it filled the whole house where they were sitting. Then there appeared to them divided tongues, as of fire, and one sat upon each of them. *And they were all filled with the Holy Spirit and began to speak with other tongues, as the Spirit gave them utterance.*
>
> Acts 2:1–4, *emphasis mine*

> While Peter was still speaking these words, *the Holy Spirit fell upon all those who heard the word.* And those of the circumcision [the Jews] who believed were astonished, as many as came with Peter, because the gift of the Holy Spirit

had been poured out on the Gentiles also. *For they heard them speak with tongues and magnify God.*

Acts 10:44–46, emphasis mine

When they heard this, they were baptized in the name of the Lord Jesus. And when Paul had laid hands on them, *the Holy Spirit came upon them, and they spoke with tongues and prophesied.* Now the men were about twelve in all.

Acts 19:5–7, emphasis mine

And He said to them, "Go into all the world and preach the gospel to every creature. He who believes and is baptized will be saved; but he who does not believe will be condemned. And these signs will follow those who believe: in My name they will cast out demons; *they will speak with new tongues;*"

Mark 16:15–17, emphasis mine

For education: This happened to me so that I could understand it biblically and know what it was like. The Holy Spirit leads a believer into all truth, so that he or she can begin to understand all the words of God; yes, even the deep things and great mysteries of God (John 14:26; 16:13; 1 Corinthians 2:6–10). As I mentioned before, I was very skeptical of people claiming to "speak in tongues" or of "the gift of tongues" in general. I had never personally done it or experienced it before; and furthermore, those that I had witnessed doing it, on TV, or in Pentecostal/Charismatic churches and meetings seemed to me, to be at best, insincere, fraudulent, and/or just for show. I had never seen or witnessed a person exercising this gift in a genuine, humble, and spiritually edifying way. Therefore, it was foreign to me and a biblical concept that I couldn't identify with or be edified by. But now, I understand differently. I am better able to understand certain Scriptures and see the God-intended purposes for "tongues." Incidentally, the baptism of tongues or speaking in tongues is different than the "gift of tongues." I do not have the gift of tongues. That is, I do not regularly exercise that spiritual gift. It is not an ongoing tool that I use to edify the church, myself, or anybody else for that matter. There are some in the universal body of believers that do have that gift (I personally know of a few of them), and they use it accordingly to edify and strengthen themselves and others in the church as the Spirit wills and imparts that ability to them. However, I did have the "baptism of tongues" (speaking in tongues) supernaturally happen to me as was mentioned above. This is usually a one-time event, or may occur at very infrequent and special times to illustrate a great move of God being done in the midst of people. I tell you the truth; you will see this occur more often in the near future as the Holy Spirit once again begins to be poured out upon people in these last days as a witness (Acts 2:17–19).

For realization: This is why God told me "to show myself unto my wife"—as a witness and testimony to her. Remember what was said earlier about how "prophesying is for the believers, but signs are for the unbelievers"? Well, tongues are given as a sign for the unbelievers. Notice this in Scripture; the Apostle Paul writes: "Tongues are for a sign, not to those who believe, but to unbelievers; but prophesying is not for unbelievers, but for those who believe" (1 Corinthians 14:22). Teresa does not believe. And yet, she was witnessed to on that very day that God had me stand before her and speak in tongues. To this very day, she is still scratching her head, trying to figure out what in the world she had witnessed and how and why it happened. Isn't this the same reaction that those who were at Jerusalem during the Feast of Pentecost had when they witnessed the apostles and disciples receiving the gift of the Holy Spirit and begin speaking in tongues? Looking at one another amazed and perplexed, they asked among themselves, "What do these things mean?" (Acts 2:12). Peter and the other apostles were then given the opportunity to be able to witness and speak to them about Jesus Christ, and the Bible says that about three thousand people were saved that very day (Acts 2:41).

I tell you the truth, all these things that were written about long ago will happen again very shortly on a worldwide scale!

GO ALL IN—NO MATTER
WHAT THE COST!

Do you want to know what it will cost you to be a follower of God? It will cost you everything. It will literally cost you your reputation, your name, your possessions, your family, your friends, yes, even your own life and will. Even as I write this, I am in tears. My own wife has left me. She has decided that she can no longer follow me or be with me. I am so sad. Still, I hear the words of Jesus running through my spirit: "If anyone comes to Me and does not hate [love less by comparison] his father and mother, wife and children, brothers and sisters, yes, and his own life also, he cannot be My disciple" (Luke 14:26). Jesus further said:

> Do not think that I came to bring peace on earth. I did not come to bring peace but a sword and division. For from now on five in one house will be divided: three against two, and two against three. Father will be divided against son and son against father, mother against daughter and daughter against mother, mother-in-law against her daughter-in-law and daughter-in-law against her mother-in-law. A man's foes will be those of his own household. He who loves father or mother more than Me is not worthy of Me. And he who

loves son or daughter more than Me is not worthy of Me. And he who does not take up his cross and follow after Me is not worthy of Me. He who finds his life will lose it, and he who loses his life for My sake will find it.

Matthew 10:34–39; Luke 12:51–53

My readers, I have given up everything I have to follow Him. I have given up my job, my riches, my good name, my family's respect and honor, even my wife's love to follow God. My soul—the human part of me—cries out and aches in bitter sorrow and anguish at being crucified. Still, I believe Him. I trust Him. I won't let go. I will go the distance with Him even if it kills me. This is what it will cost you too in order to follow Him. You cannot truly serve Him if anything comes between you and God. You must put all of your "Isaacs" on the altar of God. And I tell you the truth, He will require it of you and make it happen in order to see what is truly in your heart and whether or not you will do so.

There are two kinds of Christians, even as there are two types of Jews. The Bible describes two contrasting Jews within its pages. The "fleshly" or physical Jew is the one who is born after the natural—that is, he looks like a Jew, acts like a Jew, is circumcised in the privates of his flesh, keeps the Jewish laws and customs, and persecutes that which is born of the Spirit (Galatians 4:29; Acts 7:51). The spiritual Jew or the one who is born of the Spirit is the direct opposite of the physical Jew. In most cases, he doesn't look like a Jew—that is, he does not look "religious." He doesn't act like a Jew—that is, he doesn't feel compelled to observe religious customs and traditions in order to draw close to God. He is circumcised in the "privates" of his heart and not necessarily in his flesh (Romans 2:28–29). And he is always being persecuted, mistreated, and misunderstood by the fleshly Jews whom he thought were his brothers. This is the "Jew" that God commends in His Word and to whom He gives His promises (Revelation 3:9–10; Zechariah 8:23).

Likewise, there are two kinds of Christians today. On the one hand, you have the "fleshly" Christians. Like their Jewish counterparts, they outwardly appear religious. They go to church or church-related meetings weekly. They readily identify themselves as being "Christian." They absorb themselves in reading Christian-related materials (many times, in place of the Bible) and reciting and displaying "Christian" monikers, symbols, and slogans. They closely associate themselves with and have membership in a Christian church or organization. Although they may read the Bible occasionally, they put more credence in what the pastors and elders teach or what tradition dictates than in what the Living God says and reveals. They are not open to the idea of, *nor do they believe in*, "continuing and on-going revelation from God" through His Holy Spirit and, consequently, are not led by Him (Romans 8:14). This unbelief therefore renders them spiritually useless, and this lack of open-mindedness automatically disables them from growing or becoming productive and fruitful. Theirs is a dead religion that keeps them perpetually in religious bondage having no life—"having a form of godliness, but denying the power thereof" (2 Timothy 3:5). *Jesus Christ is more real to them as a past figure of history than as a present reality.* They believe that all knowledge of God has already been revealed, and therefore they rest in the fervent belief that all they need do now is wait for the kingdom of God to come to them (either through the physical return of Jesus or by death). In them is fulfilled the Scripture that Jesus prophesied to the Jews of His day: "In vain you worship Me, teaching for doctrines the commandments and traditions of men. Search the Scriptures for in them you think you have eternal life. These words testify of Me. But you are not willing to come to Me that you may have life!" (Mark 7:7; John 5:39–40).

In order to be a fruitful and profitable servant—that is, one who is useful and productive on the job—a worker has to first be able to *hear* his boss's commands and then *do* them. (For it is "not the hearers who are justified, but the doers" [Romans 2:13]). Likewise, in order for a Christian to be profitable and productive, he (or she) has to first be able to *hear* his Master's voice speaking to him and then obediently *do* what his Master has commanded him to do. It's that simple. But what if a person doesn't "hear" God speaking to them in the first place? This *is* the problem for "fleshly Christians"—they don't *hear* God speaking! Jesus said, "My sheep hear My voice" (John 10:27). He also said, "He who is of God, hears God's words; therefore you do not hear, because you are not of God" (John 8:47). Scripture warns in a number of places, "Today, *if you will hear His voice*, do not harden your hearts" (Hebrews 3:7, 15, 4:7). Some of Jesus' final words recorded in the Bible is the following admonition to His people:

> Behold, I stand at the door and knock. *If anyone hears My voice* and opens the door, I will come in to him and dine with him, and he with Me. To him who overcomes I will grant to sit with Me on My throne, as I also overcame and sat down with My Father on His throne. He who has an ear, *let him hear what the Spirit says* to the churches.
>
> Revelation 3:20–22, *emphasis mine*

Many people have asked me, "Eric, what do you mean by 'hearing God's voice'? Does He actually talk to you?" The answer to this question is a resounding, yes! Yes, He actually does specifically speak to me. I hear His voice. Jesus said, "My sheep hear My voice, and I know them, and they follow Me. They know My voice, and they will by no means follow a stranger, but will flee from him, for they do not know the voice of strangers" (John 10:4–5, 27). He also said to His followers before His death and ascension:

> I will not leave you orphans; *I will come to you.* A little while longer and the world will see Me no more, *but you will see Me.* Because I live, you will live also. At that day you will know that I am in My Father, and you in Me, and I in you. He who has My commands and keeps them, it is he who loves Me. And he who loves Me will be loved by My Father, and I will love him *and manifest [reveal] Myself to him.*
>
> John 14:18–21, emphasis mine

I want to clarify something here to my readers lest anyone become discouraged because they don't hear God speaking to them as I do. I am a prophet. That is my job in the Lord. It is my assignment from Him. It is how I serve Him and His body—the church—the body of believers (Ephesians 4:11–12). Not all people are called to serve in this function. Just as Paul said: "Are all apostles? Are all prophets? Are all teachers? Are all workers of miracles? Do all have gifts of healings? Do all speak with tongues? Do all interpret?" (1 Corinthians 12:29–30). The answer is clearly, no! Not everyone in the church is an apostle. Not everyone is a prophet. Not everyone is a teacher, etc. Not everybody in the church has the same function—any more than any part of the body has the same function. Else as Paul said, "Where would the body be?"—without the eyes, the ears, the hands, the feet, the mouth, etc.? (1 Corinthians 12:12–30). Therefore, because I am a prophet, I have been given the gift of prophecy by the Spirit in order to fulfill my God-given responsibilities to the church—that is, to His people. The gift of prophecy is the ability to hear God speaking directly and clearly regarding a matter and then relaying that message on to its intended recipient or recipients. It is being a messenger of God. In today's modern vernacular it is sort of like being a postman or a deliveryman. It is not the prophet's job to interpret a message (although interpreting dreams, visions, and tongues can sometimes accompany a prophet's special giftings), nor is it the prophet's responsibility to "open and read another's mail." Let me explain. As a prophet, I am not allowed to add to or take away from the original message that the Lord commands me to speak to a person. Many times the natural part of me wonders at what the Lord is having me specifically tell a person. A lot of times I don't even understand what the Lord means when He has me tell a certain person something that pertains only to them. But either way, I am not allowed to question it, add to it, or try to put my own interpretation or spin on it. I am just to deliver the divine message "as is" to them and then go my way. In the Bible, there is a true story written about a prophet of the Lord who was sent to give a message to the king from God and that prophet was warned by the Lord to not meander or be delayed, neither to greet anyone nor socially visit with anyone going to and from his divine assignment. He wasn't to eat or drink with anyone, and he wasn't supposed to hang around and socialize. Unfortunately, the prophet didn't obey the Lord's clear directions to him, and he consequently was attacked and killed by a lion (1 Kings 13:1–32). Delivering the Lord's messages is serious business! A prophet is not allowed to taint nor flavor the Lord's perfect holy wine.

Having said this, I want to clarify and demonstrate what the Bible means by "hearing His voice." Yes, it is true that as a prophet I hear God directly speak to me. He has clearly spoken to me many times in the English language—that is, *in a language and in a tongue that I understand*. Many times, I hear Him as plainly and concisely as a man would hear another person speaking to him. I have even seen Him—that is, Jesus, on a couple of occasions—in visions. However, I realize that this is not the case for most people. They are not prophets, and this is not their job to directly hear from Him and pass it on to other people. To do the job of a prophet, one has to clearly hear from Him what is to be relayed so that the prophet is not guilty of "speaking from his own heart" (Jeremiah 23:16–26) and thus would be in danger of blaspheming by saying "thus says the Lord" when the Lord did not truly say it. But you don't have to be a prophet to hear God speaking. *God clearly speaks in some way to all of His people.* Jesus said, "My sheep hear My voice" (John 10:27). "Hearing Jesus' voice" actually means *receiving some form of communication from the Lord.* This could be in the form of receiving "a revelation" from the Lord by way of a vision, a dream, a word from another, a Bible verse that "hits home" so to speak, a quickening thought or inspiration that you know is from God, or an answered prayer. God speaks to His people in ways and in languages that they can receive and understand. Although God's "voice"—that is His communications—might be broadcast and manifested in many different "languages" (different "forms"), He nonetheless gives spiritual "ears to hear" to His intended recipients. In other words, He "speaks" in a language that *they* can understand and receive! This is clearly illustrated in the following biblical example:

> When the Day of Pentecost had fully come, they were all with one accord in one place. And suddenly there came a sound from heaven, as of a rushing mighty wind, and it filled the whole house where they were sitting. Then there appeared to them divided tongues, as of fire, and one sat upon each of them. And they were all filled with the Holy Spirit and began to speak with other tongues, as the Spirit gave them utterance. And there were dwelling in Jerusalem, Jews, devout men, from every nation under heaven. And when this sound occurred, the multitude came together, and were confused, *because everyone heard them speak in his own language.* Then they were all amazed and marveled, saying to one another, "Look, are not all these who speak Galileans? And how is it that *we hear, each in our own language* in which we were born? Parthians and Medes and Elamites; those dwelling in Mesopotamia, Judea and Cappadocia, Pontus and Asia; Phrygia and Pamphylia; Egypt and the parts of Libya adjoining Cyrene; visitors from Rome, both Jews and proselytes; Cretans and Arabs—*we hear them speaking in our own tongues the wonderful works of God.*" So they were all amazed and perplexed, saying to one another, "Whatever could this mean?"
>
> Acts 2:1–12, *emphasis mine*

Notice that it was only one Spirit that was giving the many different utterances being spoken! Each man and woman was hearing God speaking to them in a specific language that they, and *they* only, could understand. Although it was coming from (and through) another person divinely and directly inspired by the Spirit of God Himself, it nonetheless was relayed in such a way and in a language that the recipient could "hear" and identify with. At first, being new to hearing from God, they were a little puzzled and confused, but as they listened to what was being communicated by the Holy Spirit—that is "the wonderful works of God" as well as receiving Peter and the other apostles' follow-up biblical explanation for what was happening, they were all consequently converted. They had "ears to hear" what the Spirit was saying.

The same is still true today. God speaks to us in a language that we can understand. To illustrate further, I want to share a true story that happened to me about four or five years ago. One day I was just walking along, minding my own business, when the Lord suddenly spoke to me. Apparently, I wasn't getting something that the Lord had been trying to show me. Obviously frustrated by my lack of perception and my mental dullness, the Lord suddenly declared in a somewhat exasperated and annoyed-sounding groan, "I will speak to you in a language that *you* understand!" Immediately, I fell into a vision where I found myself sitting at a poker table playing poker. (Incidentally, I really enjoy playing poker—so this was definitely a language that *I* understood!) I was sitting in first position to the left of the dealer who was wearing a dealer's cap that was pulled-down low over his eyes so that I couldn't see his face. There were four other players seated at the table with me who were playing against me. The poker game that was being dealt was seven-card stud.

For those of you who don't know what seven-card stud is, it is a card game where each player gets seven cards. The first two are dealt face down (where only the player receiving them can see them), and the third card is dealt face up so that all of the other players can see it. After these first three cards are dealt, each player is then given the choice to either bet, fold, or "check" (pass the bet) depending on the strength of their developing hand. As the game continues, three more cards are dealt face up one at a time with the opportunity to check, fold, or bet as each card is dealt. Then a last card (called the "river card" or "seventh street" card) is dealt face down so that each player now has seven cards with which to make their best five-card poker hand. Whoever has the best five-card hand wins. The betting strategy is based on the strength of a player's developing hand and the probability that his hand will win—that is, that his hand will ultimately survive all seven cards being dealt out to each player at the table.

When the vision began, we were in the middle of receiving our fifth card (also known as "fifth street") from the dealer. This card is dealt face up so that the other players at the table can see it. Keep in mind, with this card we now have three cards facing up, and two cards facing down. Nobody but me could see the two cards that were face down in my hand. This fifth card that I received was another club. I now had five cards that were clubs— all the same suit—I had a flush! This is a pretty strong hand in seven-card stud. I was pretty sure that my hand was going to hold up and be the winning hand. As I looked around the table at the other players' face-up cards, I was suddenly made supernaturally aware of what all of their hands were—meaning that I could "see" everybody's cards, including their facedown cards. Nobody had a hand that was even close to mine with the exception of one player who was sitting across from me. He had two pair. With a flush, my hand was still better than his; however, there were still two more cards that needed to be dealt out, so there was a chance that he could still receive another card that matched one of his pairs—thus giving him a full house, which would have beaten my flush. At that moment, the Lord suddenly asked me, "Eric, what would you do? How would you bet your hand?"

Well, I said as I thought to myself. *I have a pretty good hand—the strongest one so far, but that guy over there could still beat me; therefore I would probably make a pretty sizeable bet hoping that he would fold (give up and quit) his hand. I probably would bet half of my chips (money). That way, if he did "catch me" (make his full house), I would not be out all of my money. But if he didn't catch me, and I was to win, then I would still have made a pretty good profit on my bet.*

"That's right," the Lord said. "You would hedge your bet, wouldn't you?"

"Yes, Lord, I would. That way, if I won, I would still win a sizable pot; but if I lost I wouldn't be totally out of chips."

Immediately, the tone of the Lord's voice changed, and He became angry. The dealer—whom I didn't realize was actually the Lord and the One that had been speaking to me all along—raised His cap that had been covering His eyes and protecting His identity, and turned to me, and glared, and angrily said, "You don't hedge your bet with Me! Not if I'm the One dealing your cards to you, you don't! You don't stick your toe in the water with Me in order to test the waters when I'm involved. *You go all in!*" With that, I saw a ghostly spiritual hand suddenly move all of my poker chips into the middle of the table, and then the vision ended.

I stood there speechless, weighing in my mind the magnitude of what the Lord had just said to me. I knew in my spirit that all of those stacks of poker chips that He had just taken from me and pushed into the middle of His poker table represented my whole life and my entire livelihood. I panicked as I saw the Lord move all of my "life's chips" into His "poker pot," jeopardizing my very existence! It suddenly became very clear to me that following Him was going to require everything that I owned, that I was, and that I valued and treasured in my life. I suddenly realized then that from my perspective His calling on my life was still a "gamble" to me and not a "sure bet," and that the Lord was saying to me that I needed to "go all in" on Him and not hold anything back. I hadn't realized it before until then, but I apparently was still holding back—"hedging my bet" as the Lord put it, in not fully jeopardizing my life and all of my possessions in completely following and trusting Him. That is, I wasn't completely betting on Him—putting my complete trust in the Lord for everything and believing that He would take care of me and sustain me and my family. Truly following God requires no less. You cannot withhold *anything* from God—believe me! This is where I am now, still struggling to totally rely on Him—but growing in faith day by day, even as I write this. I have turned everything over to Him. Being human, I still struggle with my carnality and lack of faith sometimes as everybody does. But yet, the Lord has caused me to "risk" everything that I have and everything that I own, including my family, my possessions, my reputation, and my name. Daily, I am learning to place "all of my bets" on Him. For the last fourteen years (since 1995 to the present) I am learning "to lose everything" that I have and everything that I am. My trust is in Him, for He alone will deliver us (that is, me and my family). To me, I will either live in the Lord or die in the Lord (Romans 14:8); either way, His will be done. So be it.

It is not what you *say* that shows what you believe; it is what you *do* that truly reveals what you believe. Many people *say* that they believe God exists and is real, but what they do (or don't do) *really shows* what they believe. Let me clearly illustrate this point: At the turn of the last century, there was a high-wire walker pushing a wheelbarrow on a high wire suspended between two tall buildings. He was way up high successfully pushing this wheelbarrow back and forth from building to building. Each time he reached the destined building that he was headed toward, he would stop, turn around, and proceed back to the other building. On one particular trip across, he noticed that a man had been watching him. Apparently, the man had witnessed him make the successful trip many times before and was once again curiously watching him. As the high-wire walker approached with his wheelbarrow toward the building ledge that the man was watching from, and as he prepared to turn back around and proceed to the other building for another trip across, he called out to the man who had been watching him: "Sir, do you believe that I can successfully cross again?" the high-wire walker asked.

"Sure," the man answered.

"Do you *really* believe it?" the walker asked again.

"Yes, I believe that you can do it." The man firmly nodded.

The high-wire walker looked deeply at his inquisitive witness one last time and asked, "Are you really sure that I can successfully do it again? Do you really *believe* it?"

Obviously, a bit dismayed at the walker's redundant and persistent questioning, the man flatly exclaimed, "Yes! I *really* believe it!"

"Okay," the high-wire walker said, "then get in the wheelbarrow!"

This is the problem with many people today—especially professing Christians. They say they believe. They think they believe.

They have even convinced themselves that they believe. But until they are willing to *act on those beliefs*—they really don't believe! Until there is risk involved and a person is willing to lose something of value because of those beliefs, that person doesn't truly believe. We can say we believe all we want, but until that belief is tried and tested by putting something of value in jeopardy, it is nothing more than lip service. Jesus continually preached about this. He said that a person cannot be His follower unless he or she is willing to lose his or her house, possessions, lands, wife, husband, mother, father, brothers, sisters, children, and/or life. Abraham demonstrated the authenticity of his beliefs by his willingness to sacrifice his son Isaac—because as the Scripture says, he *believed* that God was even able to raise Isaac from the dead if need be in order for God to fulfill His promises that He had made (Hebrews 11:17–19).

I am reminded of a divine appointment and message that I had to give to someone once. A couple of years ago, I had to go to a hospital to have ear surgery done. I had been suffering significant hearing loss in my left ear for some time, and the doctor wanted to reconstruct my eardrum. After consulting with the Lord about it and telling Him that He could certainly heal my ear if He wanted to, I was strangely convinced that I had to go through with having the surgery. Realizing that God wasn't choosing to heal me through "miraculous" means (although some things that doctors are gifted by God to do are certainly miraculous!), I proceeded to go to the hospital for my appointed operation. While I was lying on the preparation table in the prep room getting ready to be wheeled into surgery, one of the nurses asked me what I did (presumably, for a living). Because she and another nurse and I had been previously joking, I said to her that she wouldn't believe me if I told her. As she was busily filling out paperwork on my examination chart, she straightway replied, "Try me."

I said, "Okay. I am a servant of the Most High God. I give messages to people that the Lord specifically sends me to."

"Are you a pastor, then?" she further inquired.

"No," I replied. "I am a messenger. I only speak to those to whom the Lord sends me and tells me what to say." Expecting her to now drop the conversation out of embarrassment and discomfort, she instead dropped the pen she was writing with and turned around and stared at me with her mouth wide open in a visible state of shock!

As she gathered her thoughts together, she immediately launched into the following discourse: "Let me ask you a question then. Why when I go to church do the pastors preach about how a person will be so blessed materialistically speaking if he or she follows God, when I read in the Scriptures how Jesus talks about that if you choose to follow Him, it will cost you everything? Jesus said, 'If you want to be My disciple, then you must pick up your cross and follow after Me.' But instead, the preachers don't talk about that! They just talk about how good and how easy it will be for you if you choose to follow God. Why is that? And another thing: What did David know that Jesus obviously commended him for knowing that none of the other people living during David's time knew? For instance, why did Jesus hold David up as a good example, as opposed to a bad example, for eating the showbread that wasn't lawful for him to eat in the first place? What is it that David obviously knew in his heart that the other Jews and Israelites didn't? Instead of condemning David for eating the showbread, Jesus instead seemingly held him up as an example for the rest of us to follow. What is it that David knew and understood that no one else apparently did or does today? Whatever it is, I want that! Can you please tell me, sir, what David knew, and how do I get it? I want that so bad!" She pleaded with me with her eyes, constraining me to answer her if I could.

Not expecting this assignment from the Lord at all and being completely caught off guard, I then quickly realized why I was there—I was sent there to this hospital for her! I immediately inquired of the Lord in my mind, asking Him what, if anything, He wanted me to tell her. He immediately filled my mouth with His words. He had me say to her: "Dear daughter, thus says the Lord God of Israel unto you: 'Because you seek to know Me and because you have asked, I will give you that which you seek. But it will cost you. It will cost you dearly. My servant David knew Me, and you will know Me also, but it will come at a great price. Behold, you will lose a dear relationship because of it. But that is the price you will pay in order to know Me.'"

Without hesitation, or without even pausing to consider what that great price might be, or what dear relationship the Lord was speaking about, she immediately exclaimed, "Then so be it! Let all that the Lord has said to me come to pass!" She grabbed my hand and squeezed it and smiled broadly as tears of joy streamed down her face. I lay there stunned marveling at this lady's faith. I had not witnessed such great faith anywhere like this before. She didn't even care what the "price tag" was or what "relationship" would be required of her. It could have been her marriage, her relationship with her church, her relationship with her parents, her children, her boss, etc., that the Lord was referring to—I don't know. The Lord did not reveal that to me. But either way, this woman simply did not care! Nothing was more important to her or of greater value to her than knowing the Lord. It was as if she "hated" all of her other relationships in comparison to her relationship with the Lord, just as Jesus said that it had to be for His followers (Luke 14:26). I was then wheeled away to the surgery room, thinking to myself, *Indeed, this woman is truly worthy of You, Lord! She is worthy just as You said in Your holy Word* (Matthew 10:37).

I can't tell you, my dear readers, how many people I have been sent to over the years who just don't "get it" and who continually prove themselves unworthy of Him. They are nothing like this dear lady. I preach to them until I am blue in the face, and they just don't get it. They are absolutely blind and deaf to His indescribable priceless value. It is as if I am offering them solid gold bars and free unspeakable riches and treasure and/or a wad of free cash, and they are absolutely blind to it; they don't even see me freely handing it out to them! They can't comprehend the incredible eternal value that is in it. It is like Jesus said:

> The kingdom of heaven is like treasure hidden in a field. When a man found it, he hid it again, and then in his joy went and sold all that he had and bought that field. Again, the kingdom of heaven is like a merchant looking for fine pearls. When he found one of great value, he went away and sold everything he had and bought it.
>
> Matthew 13:44–46

This is how that nurse reacted, but sadly I have found few like her since. Many people that I am sent to talk a good talk, but by their actions—or should I rather say, by their inactions—they show what they truly believe. They do not grasp the kingdom of God and the knowledge of Him for all that it is worth! I tell you the truth—like the rich young ruler who refused to give up what temporal things he had in order to follow Christ during His day—these people too have shown themselves unworthy to follow Him as well. If you don't value Christ and the knowledge of Him far above everything else, then you, my dear reader, are not worthy of Him either. He will try you to see if you are like Jacob, who was willing to wrestle and struggle all night long in order to be able to know Him and to be blessed by Him, or whether you are more like his brother, Esau, who traded the blessings of God for a mere bowl of lentil soup. In comparison to knowing God, everything else in this world is just that—a mere temporal bowl of worthless soup!

If you hear my voice, or shall I rather say, His voice, speaking to you today, because you have been given "ears to hear" by Him, and you are "pricked in your heart" by this testimony that He has caused me to write, then repent! Repent of your unbelief and spiritual complacency and be baptized, every one of you, my readers, for the remission of your sins. Believe and receive the gift of the Holy Spirit that you might be able to know Him and to be able to stand in the day of judgment that is quickly coming upon the whole earth. I tell you the truth; do not delay! For the time of God is at hand, and the kingdom of God shall not be trampled upon under the careless and carefree feet of men any longer. For the mouth of the Lord has spoken it!

EMBRACED AND LOVED
BY STRANGERS

Shortly before Teresa and I were disfellowshipped, a man called me out of the blue one day and informed me that he had "volunteered me" to help out and minister to the underage inmates who were incarcerated at Dahlia Youth Center in Denver. Apparently, these inmates were all between the ages of thirteen and eighteen. Curiously, the man, whose name was Mike, was also the same man who had prophesied to me a couple of years earlier that a man named Tucker and I were "sent to the Jews." I agreed to help out, not really knowing why I was chosen to help minister in this youth prison or what it was exactly that I was going to be doing, but no less glad for the opportunity to serve. My responsibilities at the youth center included teaching, giving short sermon messages, leading praise and worship, hosting small Bible studies, and helping facilitate Bible-related discussions. I was usually in charge of leading one Sunday church service and two weekday Bible studies a month. There was such constant inmate turnover that I hardly ever saw the same teenager twice. Their criminal offenses ranged from such minor infractions as trespassing and running away to serious felonies such as armed robbery and murder. It literally was a prison for teenagers. Because church services and Bible studies were optional activities for the inmates, as you can imagine, attendance was usually pretty low. At church services on Sundays, we usually only got anywhere from five to fifteen kids who showed up, and only about four to eight for the weekday Bible studies.

I remember one particular Bible study. A teenager came up to me and said, "Mister, I came to one of your church services a number of weeks ago, and I heard what you said. I believed you. You even hugged me; do you remember? Well, ever since you said those things, I have been trying to straighten out my life and do things right. I've been praying, reading my Bible, and trying to help other people out in this place. Why heck, I even helped stop a kid from committing suicide a couple of days ago; he was going to drink a bottle of bleach, and I took it away from him. Why then, mister, won't God let me out of this place? I was supposed to have been released a number of weeks ago, but every time my hearing date comes up, the judge postpones it, and I am stuck here! I don't understand it. I am trying to do things right. And you even said that if you put God first in your life, He will be with you and help you. Why does this keep happening to me? Why, Pastor? Tell me!" By now, he had tears forming in his eyes. He was about fifteen years old.

I looked at him, not recognizing him because the turnover was so great in that place, but nonetheless, I felt compassion for him and was moved by his genuine faith. Immediately, I appealed to God in my mind for the answer. The Lord said to tell him, "Yes, you have indeed tried to follow Me, and have made some changes. But there is one thing that you have held back and have not chosen to give up and surrender to Me. Therefore, until the day you do, you will remain here, and no man will let you go. But know this: in the very hour that you give it up and surrender it, I will send word to you immediately that you will be released!"

I told him exactly what the Lord had said. He looked at me puzzled and asked, "What is it that I am holding back?"

I said, "I don't know. The Lord has not revealed that to me. But you go and ask Him, and I am sure that if you *really* want to know so that you can obey Him, He will bring it to your mind." I then felt compelled to walk away. The bottom line being that the "ball was now in his court." If he *truly* wanted to please God and to follow Him, then that young man would need to take some action himself and pursue God on his own—seeking Him out and searching for the right answers from Him. The question was: was this young man willing to put forth the required effort that was necessary in order to follow God?

Three days later, I was asked to fill in for another minister who was scheduled to lead the church service at the prison that Sunday but who was unable to make it. When I walked into the room, this same young man ran over to me all excited and exclaimed, "Hey, Pastor, remember me? Guess what?!"

"What?" I replied.

"After you said that to me a couple of days ago, I went back to my cell real sad and confused. I didn't know what you were talking about. I kept praying about it and wondering to myself what I was holding back from God. Then as I was lying on my bed, it suddenly hit me! You see, Pastor..." He paused for a moment and looked down, a bit embarrassed at what he was about to tell me. He regained his courage and excitement and continued,

"You see, Pastor, ever since a few weeks ago when I was originally scheduled to be released, I have been hiding a bag of marijuana in my backpack, intending to sell it on the street just as soon as I got out. I had forgotten about it though. However, the other day, after I spoke to you, and I went and prayed about it, God reminded me of it, and so, I immediately went and got it and threw it in the dumpster. And as I was returning back to my cell, a guard came up to me in the hallway and said that the judge had just called and that I am to be released first thing tomorrow morning!" Truly, God never misses.

I will share with you another true story that happened shortly after this at Dahlia Youth Center. I believe that this happened in 2000 or in 2001. I am absolutely positive of the calendar date though, just not the year, because it happened on my birthday, April 9th. Once again, I was asked to fill in for church services for someone who couldn't make it because he was sick. It was a Sunday afternoon, and I really didn't want to because it was my birthday and I wanted to be home with my family on that day. Realizing that I had to because I was feeling pressured by the Spirit that this was "an assignment," I reluctantly started driving toward the youth center. On the way, I asked God in my car what He was going to have me speak on that day.

He said, "Today, I am going to do something different. I am going to fill the room with people!"

I asked, "Really?" thinking that that would be highly unusual because we at most only had twelve to fifteen kids ever show up for church services. He didn't respond to my question, nor did He give me any indication what I was going to speak about. When

I arrived, I met Gail Schwindt and a couple of other volunteer helpers (whom I didn't know) in the parking lot.

As we were entering the prison, Gail leaned over to me and said, "So what is God going to do today?"

"I don't know," I said. "He told me that He was going to do something different today, and that He was going to fill the room with people."

"Really?" she asked, looking at me puzzled.

As we entered the front lobby, where you sign in at the guard desk, the lady receptionist (who was also a guard) asked us if we were there to host the church service. As she asked this, she sort of disrespectfully rolled her eyes at us, as if to say, "You Christians! Why do you bother?! No one in this prison is interested in hearing what you have to say." She got on her radio and called to one of the prison guards inside and snidely asked, "How many of the prisoners are interested in going to church today?"

A voice on the other end sharply answered: "All of them."

"Come again?" she asked.

"All of them, I said!" the prison director angrily answered.

"Okay. Yes, sir," she replied. Turning to us, clearly surprised, she said, "Well, it looks like you are going to be having a bigger than usual church service today. Go down to the large recreation room at the end of the hallway. A guard will be waiting for you there."

Gail and I looked at each other in amazement, wondering what the Lord had in store for us.

When we got to the end of the hallway, it opened up into a very large recreation room. There was a big burly black man (whom I recognized as the prison director) standing between two groups of inmates from two different cellblocks. He was angrily standing between them with his arms folded as if he were there separating them, just daring them to try and approach each other again. One group of inmates, representing one cellblock, was dressed in orange prison garb; and the other group, representing a different cellblock, was clothed in green. When we first entered the room, you could feel a very contentious and aggressive spirit in the air, as each group of young men were eyeing each other just waiting for the opportunity to kill the other. Angry and disgusted, the prison director yelled at them: "All you guys want to do is fight and kill each other! This kid said something about this guy's mother; and then this one said something about what he was going to do to him in return. And then these three guys over here joined in, and then you all over there started threatening back! I am sick and tired of all of you guys and all of your fighting. Therefore, everybody is going to church now. Free time is canceled. The whole place is in lockdown. Get busy setting up chairs for church!"

At that moment, he looked at me and said, "Pastor, how do you want the chairs set up for church?" Never having been put into a situation like this before, I didn't know how I wanted the chairs to be arranged. Usually, we only have a handful of people in a small room, but now it looked like we were going to have about a hundred or so! I told them to set the chairs up in a big circle around me, so that we could all see each other. After they did so, I started to address those sitting there.

"Uh, wait a minute, Pastor!" the director said, interrupting me. "This is only half of the prison. We need to wait for the rest of the inmates." At that moment, rows and rows of other inmates began filing in, each dressed in their corresponding cellblock's colors—red, yellow, and white. When the room was entirely filled to capacity, with standing room only, and with a number of guards posted all the way around the room, the director then said to me, "Okay, Pastor, we're ready now." I had never in my life been in such a dreadful situation like this one before. I had over two hundred sets of eyes staring at me all the way around—just glaring at me with hate and disgust in their eyes. There were blacks and whites, Hispanics, and Asians. I could tell that many of them were gang members, and that if given the chance, they would knife me in a minute. A lot of them had dreadlocks and big, bulging muscles, and although I was a lot older than them, they could easily crush me like a tomato. It was incredibly intimidating, especially knowing the fact that I was their punishment! I could tell that they didn't want me to be there and that they despised the fact that the warden was making them listen to me. Talk about a "captive" audience—literally!

Realizing that I had nothing to say to this angry group of young men, but that God had sent me there for His purposes, I then told them all as much. I sternly said, "Listen! I know you guys don't want me here. And to be perfectly honest with you, I don't want to be here either. Today is my birthday, and I would much rather be home with my family than to be here with you. I don't have anything to say to any one of you. But God, my Father and your Father, sent me here to give you a message from Him, and so therefore, I will give it to you from Him, and then after that, I am out of here! And I don't care what you think about me; I am here only because He sent me here to you. I don't know what that message is yet that I am supposed to give to you from Him, but as soon as I find out, I will tell you, and then I will leave. So if you don't mind, I am just going to take a few seconds here to kneel down and ask Him what it is that I am supposed to tell you from Him. So excuse me for a second, while I find out from Him what that message is."

As I said this, I turned around and knelt down on the ground and put my face in my hands upon my chair and began asking God to tell me what it was that I was supposed to tell them. As I was praying, I could hear them saying to one another, mocking and laughing, "This dude is crazy! Man, he is loco! What is he doing?"

All of a sudden, as I got up, the Lord opened my mouth, and I began speaking and preaching to them like nobody's business. I have no idea what I said that day, and I can't remember a single word that I said. Apparently, I spoke to them for a solid hour and a half, and when I got done, many of them were in tears and openly repenting and confessing their sins! They began hugging each other and crying and asking God for His forgiveness. To this day, I have no idea what the Lord had me say to them, but whatever it was, it was incredibly powerful; because when I finished, they all gathered around me and began thanking me and trying to hug me.

When the Spirit left me—that is, when the Word of the Lord finished speaking through my mouth, and I got my own human mind back—I remember looking around the room at their faces and seeing the tears streaming down their cheeks. I remember wondering, *What happened? And what did I say?* As they all stared at me, trying to hug me, I didn't know how to finish. So I simply ended with, "So that is it! That is the message." Not knowing what to say or how to dismiss everyone, I sheepishly suggested, "Well, maybe we should close in prayer. Would anybody like to join me in giving thanks to God?" Feeling a bit embarrassed and out of place, especially since I didn't know what I had said or what had transpired during that hour and a half, I didn't know what else to say or do.

At that moment, everybody huddled around me in the center of the room, with their arms around each other—the blacks hugging the whites, and the whites hugging the Latinos, and the Latinos with their arms around the Asians, etc. It became one big football-type huddle in the middle of the room. I couldn't believe what I was witnessing! At that moment, many of them began praying out loud and saying, "Dear Lord, our Father, thank You for sending this man to us; even on his birthday he was willing to come and give us the message of how You love us and how You want us to change and begin living for You. We are so sorry for how we have lived and for all the evil things we have done and said. Thank You, thank You, so much for forgiving us, Father, and for calling us back to Yourself!" (It was upon hearing them pray this that I began to realize some of what God had said to them through me.)

With tears in their eyes, I saw rival gang members embracing and apologizing for wronging each other, and for trying to harm one another. The biggest and oldest inmate in the room, who had arm muscles the size of my thighs and dreadlocks down to his shoulders and who was obviously the leader of a prison gang, began praying out loud for his rivals right there in the room. He grabbed a Hispanic rival gang member and hugged him tightly, openly asking him for his forgiveness. I heard the Hispanic rival do the same—both men with tears unashamedly streaming down their faces. The guards and all of us volunteers were speechless! And I looked over at the prison director, and he was smiling from ear to ear. The whole room was rejoicing with tears of joy and praise, and many were praying together along the walls and holding hands with their fellow inmates. Truth, love, forgiveness, and mercy were everywhere.

After a little while, the director announced that he had called the cafeteria and had the dinner hour extended because we had literally worshiped and rejoiced right through dinner! As the last of the inmates lined up to leave the room and head to the cafeteria, Gail and I finally got our first chance to look at each other. All of us (the other volunteers included) were all so busy afterwards praying with the inmates, counseling them, and answering their questions that we didn't even have time to consult each other. Gail and I made our way to the parking lot and sat down on the ground, both of us incredibly excited but emotionally exhausted and drained.

A few minutes later, a black woman who looked to be in her midsixties approached us carrying the garbage from the cafeteria to throw into the dumpster. She said, "Excuse me, but can you please tell me what is going on in there?"

Gail and I looked at her and asked, "What do you mean?"

She said, "I have worked here for almost thirty years, and I have never seen anything like this before! I just saw rival gang members and inmates from different cellblocks and races hugging each other and praying for each other right there in the cafeteria. I can't believe what I am seeing! Can you please tell me what happened? I heard that a man of God had come here and given them a message from the Lord, and now I am witnessing some things in that cafeteria that I had never thought I would ever see—no, not in a hundred years! Are you that man? Please tell me, sir, are you he?"

Not quite sure how I should answer her, I smiled and said, "The Lord said that He was going to do something different today."

At that instant, she grabbed my hand and said, "Glory be to God! I have prayed for this day to come for a long time. Please, please, sir, will you come home with me and speak to me and my family? I get off of work in fifteen minutes; would you be willing to come to my house and visit with us? Please, please. I have waited so long for this!" Totally surprised by her reaction and request, I immediately appealed to God in my mind to see whether or not I should go with her. When the Spirit bid me go, I gladly accepted her gracious invitation, all the while marveling at her wonderful childlike faith. I followed her home and was warmly received by her husband, her children, her grandchildren, some in-laws, and some of her extended family—there were probably fifteen to twenty people there. They sat me at their table and all gathered around me asking me different questions and telling me about their individual lives and sharing what they had with me. I had never been shown such kindness and honor before—especially from complete strangers! I was amazed at their faith. I remembered thinking about how I had been so poorly treated by my own people (especially in the church), and yet here were complete and total strangers who seemingly loved me, and yet they didn't even know me (in the flesh, that is). The woman, who had brought me there, then came over to me, bringing her four-year old grandson, who had some kind of terrible skin disease and rash all over his body, and asked me to pray for him. I did so, and consequently told her afterwards that he would be all right, and that he would be healed of it. Although, I didn't recognize it then (I told you that I wasn't too perceptive), but what was beginning to happen and what I was getting a spiritual taste of was what God had told me was going to come to pass. I have cited that prophecy here from the first page of my diary:

My Spiritual Diary

Preface (9/8/98)—Since this is the first time that I have actually begun to keep a record of my spiritual life, I feel it is necessary to give a backdrop of the events that have occurred over the past few years. About 3 years ago, after praying for understanding and the Holy Spirit, I had a series of visions and supernatural revelations that astonished me! I didn't understand them then, nor could I recall them in specific detail when they occurred, but now as each day passes, I can both recall and interpret them more and more. Some of the messages were that God would begin speaking through me, and would astound and confound many that profess that they are His people. Some would have "ears to hear" and receive the message with "tears of joy" and praise God, but many would not. Many of those who wouldn't believe would try to discredit me, and would become offended, and greatly persecute those that believed, and me. I saw great numbers of people come from all walks of life believing and coming forward to be fed, and wholeheartedly drinking in the waters that flowed from my mouth. They began to be strengthened, and some bore much fruit as their Father worked with them.

I saw people that I had long-embraced as family and friends turn and begin to hate me. But those that I recognized as strangers to me, reached out to me as though they knew me and loved me. I saw that my main message was that God lives, and that He is real. I was told to tell His people *to believe*! In the visions, God directly told me what to say, and He never abandoned me. Early on, He would speak and then I repeated what He said in my ear. Later on in my ministry, I would simply open my mouth and He would fill it. In all the cases, I too, was astonished at both what I heard and what came out of my mouth. I saw scores of people coming forward to be fed. But strangely though, as I began to open my mouth and God began to speak, the multitude of people all had different reactions on their faces. Some were crying tears of joy; others were dumbfounded; some were indifferent; others were whispering as though they were conspiring. The whole assembly though was gathered there to hear me speak. When I asked God why the mixed reactions, a great Voice declared, "Behold, the believers will weep!" There are many more things to write, however I don't feel particularly motivated to record them now.

Clearly, what God had told me many years before that I had recorded in my diary was now truly coming to pass!

A FULL-TIME MESSENGER
FOR THE LORD

One day, about four years after Teresa and I had been disfellow-shipped, I was driving my daughters to their new school. It was a small private Christian elementary school that was founded by a lady named Nancy. I did not know much about the school or anything about its history, financial situation, teaching staff, or cur-riculum. Quite frankly, I didn't know anything about the school other than the fact that my children went there. (Apparently, my wife had found the place after praying about where we should send them to school. She told me that she felt the Lord had led her to this school.) As I was driving them to school one day, I felt this overwhelming feeling that I had to give a message from the Lord to Nancy Thurston, the school's founder and director. I didn't know Nancy at all, other than the fact that she was my kids' school principal. I tried like mad to shake this feeling from the Lord. I dropped the kids off and quickly headed out of the parking lot, refusing to park. As I pulled out onto the street and began heading around the block, my steering wheel literally made a sharp left turn in my hands and pulled me right back into the school's parking lot! Still refusing to give in, I tried once more to exit the parking lot, but again, my car turned itself left after going around the block and re-entered the school's lot again. Realizing that it was no use fighting Him, I parked my car and sat there pouting, telling God that I didn't want to give a message to somebody whom I didn't know and who was obviously going to think that I was crazy. I didn't need another "church-going Christian" rejecting me and rolling their eyes at me—especially my kids' school principal! God ignored my complaint and ordered me into the school.

I remember when I entered the school's main office, the receptionist, Nancy's secretary, was sitting at her desk. When I walked in, I was a bit agitated and annoyed—admittedly at God for making me do this! I asked her if Mrs. Thurston was available. She graciously said yes and showed me to her office. Nancy's office was incredibly small. In fact, every office and classroom in that entire school was small. (It actually was an old Safeway grocery store which had been recently converted into a large church. The kids' school was leasing a very small part of the building from the church that owned the property. However, I didn't know any of this until after my meeting with Nancy.) Nancy kindly invited me to sit down and asked me what she could do for me. After looking around the room intently and listening for God to tell me why I was there, I then said, "Nancy, tell me, what have you been praying about?"

A bit taken aback at my forwardness and brash question, she reservedly answered, "Well, I pray about a lot of things. I pray for our school, for our teachers, and for our students—"

"No, I'm sorry, that is not what I mean." I interrupted. "What is on your heart? What have you been asking God for?" I quickly clarified.

She looked at me puzzled and said, "I don't know what you mean. I ask God for a lot of things."

"No, Nancy. This is a very specific thing that you have been asking God for. You have been crying out to Him from your heart. And it is something that you really want. Please, tell me what that is." I flatly stated encouraging her to dig deep inside and to let her heart's cry come forth and confess what it really was that she wanted and desired.

At that moment, she burst forth in exasperation and shouted, "Okay, yes, we need a new school! This place is not working for us, and the children have nowhere to play or to eat their lunch. And the people that we are renting from here are threatening to raise the rent and kick us out. And I have been praying to God about it, and I don't know what to do!" She put her head in her hands in anguish.

At that precise moment, the Lord filled my mouth with what to say.

"Dear Nancy, the Lord has heard your cry and has sent me to tell you to not fear. For the Lord your God will give you a place of your own. And He will give you that which you seek. It will not be a closet like this place, but you will have room to grow and to move. You will have a cafeteria and even, in due time, a gymnasium. Behold, the Lord has made you as a Moses among these teachers to lead them, to encourage them to put their faith in Him, and to trust Him. He is pleased with you and, therefore, will bless you with a place of your own—away from this closet!"

Tears began to form in Nancy's eyes, and she said, "I believe you." And then she came around to my side of her desk and hugged me and thanked me. I then quickly left. I couldn't believe that she had accepted me and, furthermore, that she believed me! I got into my car and began to drive home praising God and rejoicing greatly. It had been a long time since anyone—especially a church-going Christian—had believed me!

I was so excited; I began thanking God and telling Him how great it was to be sent to someone who actually believed me. He then clearly spoke to me and said, "You will give messages to My people—both good and bad [messages]. That was a good message and good news. And now I am sending you to give bad news to someone. Go home and tell your employee Rick, 'Thus says the Lord God Almighty: "I am against you, and you have no part in this inheritance, for your heart is not right before Me."' Go, tell him now!" I was shocked and, needless to say, very afraid and apprehensive. How was I going to say that to him? Rick was my employee after all. Surely, there are laws against seemingly threatening a person's job for having a different religious point of view. I was stuck in a real quandary. I clearly heard what God had commanded me to do, and He didn't leave me much time or wiggle room to figure out how I was going to casually present it to Rick either. He told me to "go tell him now" and I was only about ten minutes from home (Rick worked in my basement at the time).

When I got home, I immediately called Rick into my office. I said, "Hey, buddy, I don't exactly know how to tell you this, but I have to. This has no bearing on our friendship or your job. I am not coming to you as your employer, but rather, as your friend. So please don't get the wrong impression or take this as a threat to your job. But on my way home just a few minutes ago this is what happened and what God said to me." I then shared the entire story with him.

He sat back in his chair and said, "Wow! What does that mean? What should I do, Eric?"

"I don't know, Rick. That is between you and God. I don't know what that means, but God commanded me to tell you that, so I did. If I were you, though, I would get on my face before the Lord and ask for His forgiveness and to show me the error of my ways. One thing I know about the Lord, Rick, He loves His children, and He doesn't tell you these things for no reason. He wants you to repent, and He is very forgiving. If you turn to Him with all of your heart, He will forgive you and bless you; but if you don't, beware because the Lord is very serious, and you don't want to be in trouble with Him. Take it for what it is worth, Rick. I have told you what the Lord commanded me to tell you."

About this time, Tony Dopp re-entered my life. I hadn't seen him in years. (As I had mentioned earlier, Tony had been my beloved boss at VU Videos for a number of years, until he moved back to California to care for his dying mother.) Apparently, Jim Howe, the owner of VU Videos whom we had both previously worked for, had recently called Tony in California and made him an offer to begin a new business venture together, so Tony relocated back to Denver. Tony called me a few weeks later after arriving in Denver and asked me if I wanted to invest in their new deal. I didn't feel led to, so I politely declined but asked Tony if he wanted to get together and go golfing sometime. We quickly became "golfing buddies" and started spending a lot of recreational time together. Tony's business deal with Jim fell through because of a lack of financing, and so Tony began looking for work. Having difficulty finding steady work and sharing his employment woes with me one day out on the golf course, I half-heartedly mentioned to Tony that "maybe we should try and do something together, and maybe you should come and work with me." I was really only kidding, not thinking much about it. First of all, I never in a million years would have expected that Tony, a man whom I highly respected in business and a man who had made millions, would ever come and work with me—after all, I was still working out of the basement of my house at the time.

To my utter surprise, Tony called me that night and said, "Okay, I will take you up on your offer!"

I said, "What offer?"

And he said, "Remember what you proposed this morning on the golf course—the offer to come and work for you?"

I was dumbfounded. I wasn't really serious. In fact, I proposed it at the time to be a bit ridiculous. Nevertheless, because of how things were unfolding on the phone, I began to perceive that all of this might be a "God-thing." Therefore, I agreed to hire him on as a sales person but indicated that because there wasn't much room left in the main part of my basement, he would have to sit at a little desk in a small little room (ironically, next to my water heater and furnace—a.k.a. "the boiler room")! My, how things had changed and come full circle between us!

I can't begin to tell you how astonishing and humbling it was for me to see the man that I had worked for and admired for so long, now ten years later, working for me—in my basement, sitting at a little kid's desk, between the toilet and the furnace. The last time that I saw Tony in a working environment, he was sitting behind a big expensive cherry wood desk with thirty-some employees (including me) all gathered around him obeying his every order and command. And now, here he was—my employee, taking orders from me. I was so humbled by that realization that I knew that only God could have done this thing! In fact, I remember sitting in my car in my driveway one day with tears in my eyes as I considered this miracle that had happened. I asked, "Lord, who am I that Tony Dopp should come and work for me? He has always been like a father to me. Who am I, Lord that he should work for me? Indeed, I am nothing."

The Lord then answered me, saying, "Eric, I made Joseph work for Potiphar for awhile; and then in due time, I made Potiphar work for Joseph." I was astonished at the Lord's response, wondering what in the world the Lord was doing among us. *What is going on here?* I asked myself. *And why is the Lord seemingly taking an interest in my company and its employees?* I wondered.

Soon after Tony began working for me, I noticed that he was asking a lot of questions about God. This was strange, because Tony was never a religious person by any stretch of the imagination. Nevertheless, I answered his questions as best as I could. He just seemed so spiritually hungry. "It was as if I could see and feel God peering at me from behind every tree." he would later confess to me.

Late one evening on a Thursday night in April of 2004, I was standing at my kitchen sink washing dishes, when all of a sudden I heard the Lord say to me, "You better clean out your hot tub because you are going to baptize Tony."

I said, "What?! Baptize Tony?! Who am I to baptize anybody? I am not a minister or a priest. I can't baptize somebody! And, furthermore, Tony? Him, Lord? He's a believer? He is going to be baptized? What, Lord?" I stood there in total disbelief, truly wondering if I had heard what I thought I heard. I decided that it was my own imagination speaking to me and that I was "just hearing things"; therefore, I shook it off as nonsense. A few minutes later, Teresa asked me to go to the grocery store to get some things for the children's sack lunches that they were going to need for school the next day.

As I was driving back home from the grocery store, the Lord said to me a second time: "You better scrub out the hot tub; you are going to be baptizing Tony soon!" He said this rather forcibly. I was afraid not knowing what to do or how to react.

I still couldn't believe it. *Me? Baptize Tony? Who am I to baptize anybody?* I kept thinking. When I got home, I said to Teresa (who was lying in bed sick), "Dear, can I ask you something? When I was downstairs washing dishes earlier, I heard a voice that said to me, 'You better wash out the hot tub because you are going to baptize Tony.' I heard that same voice say to me again those same words in the car just now as I was returning home from the grocery store. I don't know what to do. What should I do?"

She answered, "It sounds to me like you better get busy and scrub out the hot tub!" Ironically, the weather on that following Sunday was perfect; it was warm and sunny (earlier in the week, it had been snowy and cold), and so I cleaned out the hot tub.

The next day on Monday, Tony and I went to lunch somewhere, and as we were returning back to the office (my house), he turned to me and out of the blue asked, "Hey, Eric, have you ever baptized anybody?" I almost fell onto the floor of the car. In fact, I think I almost puked. I couldn't believe he just asked me that! I hadn't said anything to him about what the Lord had said to me earlier. The next morning, as I went downstairs to my office, Tony came up to me and said, "I need to get baptized, and I want *you* to baptize me!" I could hardly believe what was happening; but obviously, it was the Lord's will, so I baptized him.

About a month later, Teresa and I bought a building so that we could move our business out of our house. By this time, we had five employees working down in our basement, not counting me and Teresa. I was sitting in my office one day when all of a sudden, I had a vision. It was of a man whom I had known from my previous days back in the Denver South Congregation of the Worldwide Church of God, whose name was Dwight Lewellen. It was now May of 2004, and I had been away from the Worldwide Church of God for almost five years. In fact, I hadn't had hardly any contact with anybody from that church except for just a very small handful of people. The vision that I saw was basically this: I was standing in the parking lot of our new building, in front of a small baptismal tank with a long line of people coming to me that I didn't know. I was baptizing them one by one as quickly as I could. I didn't have time to get to know anything about any of them; I only had time to ask them what their names were and whether or not they had repented of their sins as they were stepping into my baptismal tank. One by one, I baptized them and sent them on their way, reaching for the next convert as they were beginning to step into my tank. Dwight was there reluctantly assisting me, somewhat fearful of what he was doing. He was actually just there adding more water to the tank as it was needed. A few seconds later, the vision fast-forwarded to a scene where Dwight was in the warehouse of my building busily trying to manage, inventory, and distribute the "Lord's resources" that were pouring in. People were sending in baskets full of offerings, such as wheat, corn, jewelry, rice, barley, and such, and Dwight was very busy just trying to keep up with it all. After the vision ended, I sat there and pondered what it might mean. I seemed to recall that Dwight had had a hard time in the past finding a job, and I wondered if he still needed employment. Later in the week, when I saw his son, Mark, who played on my recreational basketball team, I asked him if his dad was still looking for a job. He answered, "Yes!" I asked him for his dad's phone number.

When Dwight answered the phone, I said, "Hi, Dwight. This is Eric Wheeler."

There was a brief silence, and then he gingerly said, "Hello, Eric Wheeler. What can I do for you?" I could tell that he was a bit apprehensive to speak to me—keep in mind, I had been "disfellowshipped" from his church, and its rules "unofficially" stated that its members weren't to be talking or fellowshipping with me.

"Dwight, let me ask you a question—do you believe in God?" I asked.

"Of course, I do" was his immediate response.

"No, Dwight, I don't mean in an academic sense. I mean, in a literal and *real* sense. Do you *really* believe in God?"

"Yes, Eric. I do." he replied a little more firmly.

"Dwight, I need to ask you, one more time: Do you really believe in God in the sense that He talks with us and communicates with us and that He is more real than most people think He is?" I asked.

"Yes, Eric, I do!" he exclaimed strongly. "Why are you asking me this?" he demanded, obviously a bit irritated by my repetitive questioning.

"Because, Dwight, the Lord just told me to offer you a job as my shipping warehouse manager." I flatly replied.

He immediately rushed over to my house and gladly accepted the position.

A few months after we moved into the building and things were getting settled in, I was driving to work one morning, listening to the Bible on tape. As I pulled into my parking lot, the tape ended at the part where the Apostle Paul said:

> I wrote to you in my epistle not to keep company with sexually immoral people. Yet I certainly did not mean with the sexually immoral people of this world, or with the covetous, or extortioners, or idolaters, since then you would need to go out of the world. But now I have written to you *not to keep company with anyone named a brother, who is a fornicator,* or covetous, or an idolater, or a reviler, or a drunkard, or an extortioner—*not even to eat with such a person.*
>
> 1 Corinthians 5:9–11, *emphasis mine*

For some reason, when I turned off my car engine and the tape shut off at this particular verse, the Holy Spirit quickened these words in my mind. Unlike the other passages that I had just heard while driving to work that day, these words just "jumped out at me" and rang in my ears. As my mind quickly raced back and forth, weighing the Word of God against my conscience judging myself, I quickly felt relieved as I realized that I wasn't aware of any violations on my part that transgressed this commandment. But as soon as I had finished examining myself, the Holy Spirit whispered to me, "Dean Sargent—an adulterer!"

I paused, and questioned, "Dean Sargent?"

That was a name that I hadn't heard in a long time. He was a guy that I had known in college and a kid that I had grown up with in the Worldwide Church of God long ago, whose dad was our pastor when I was a child. I hadn't seen him in a long time, never really fellowshipped with him, and although I knew that he now lived in the Denver area, I really wasn't in close contact with him. Therefore, I shrugged it off, thinking, *I don't get together with him anyway, so I don't need to worry about it; I haven't violated the Lord's Word*, and so I dismissed it in my mind and went to my office. About five minutes later, as I was sitting at my desk, my secretary called me and said, "I have Dean Sargent on the phone for you." Needless to say, I almost fell out of my chair!

Panicking, I didn't know whether or not to take Dean's call. I didn't know what to do. So very reluctantly, I hesitantly answered the phone. "Hello?" I said.

"Hey, Eric, old buddy. This is Dean Sargent!" he excitedly said. "How are you?" he asked.

"I'm okay. How are you?" I sheepishly answered.

"Hey, I was wondering if we could get together and visit for a while for old time's sake. It would be fun to catch up. How about we meet for lunch today?" he excitedly asked.

My heart sank when he said, "Let's meet for lunch." I remembered the last words of the Apostle Paul's statement that I had just heard—*"do not even eat with such a person!"* I was really stuck as to what to do right at that moment. Immediately, I appealed to God in my mind. Upon doing so, I felt that it was His will that I should meet with Dean; therefore I agreed to meet him for lunch at the golf course restaurant next door to my building. When Dean and I met a couple of hours later, we both sat down at a table. The waitress came over and took our drink orders; however, curiously, she forgot to bring them to us. As we sat there waiting for our drinks to arrive, Dean began talking about how wonderful things were for him. He talked about his new wife, all the money that he was making at his mortgage company, how well his kids were doing, his new truck, how happy he was, etc.

But as he was talking, I kept hearing the Holy Spirit behind me making comments in my ear such as, "He is a liar. He's a fake. He's plastic and not real. Don't believe him!" It was weird and surreal. All the while as Dean was talking and bragging on and on about his successes, I could hear him, but it sounded like he was actually saying, "Blah, blah, blah," in slow motion. As he carried on, the Holy Spirit was speaking in my ear and contradicting everything he said. At that moment, the Holy Spirit said to me, "Don't eat with him! But get out of here and go and take your Bible with you and take him to a place that I will show you." I immediately obeyed.

I got up and said, "Dean, let's skip lunch and go take a walk."

At that moment the waitress came over and said, "I'm sorry, gentlemen, but I forgot to get your drinks. Let me go and get them right now for you."

I said, "No problem; forget them. We changed our minds. We actually need to leave right now anyway."

We went outside, and I stopped at my car and retrieved my pocket Bible as the Lord had commanded me, and immediately the Holy Spirit let me know which direction we were to walk. We walked down the golf course cart path, which was completely abandoned. All the while, Dean continued to tell me all about how wonderful everything was and how successful he had become. I was not allowed to say a word, but the Holy Spirit kept contradicting in my ear everything he said, calling him a liar and a fake. When we walked part way down the path, where it became private, the Holy Spirit had me stop. As Dean faced me, still talking, the Holy Spirit then said to me, "Behold, the rich young ruler!"—referring to the young man in the Bible who came up to Jesus, wanting to appear righteous and wanting to "*do*" the right thing, but he wasn't "*being*" the right thing. He was a fake.

At that moment, the word of the Lord came upon me, and I said: "Dean, stop lying! For I know what you are and what you have done. You do not fool Me, but you are a liar and a pretender. For I hear the crying and the wailing of your children in My ears even now for the wickedness you have done against them and against their mother. For you have sinned against Me and have dealt treacherously with the wife of your youth!"

Dean looked at me stunned. When he was able to speak, he said, "What? What are you talking about?"

I then reached into my pocket and pulled out the Bible. The Lord had me turn to the following passage and begin reading out loud to him: "Whosoever divorces his wife, and marries another commits adultery." (Matthew 19:9). As Dean looked at me completely shocked, the Lord had me quickly turn to another passage and continue reading out loud:

> You cover the altar of the Lord with tears, with weeping and crying; but He does not regard your offering anymore, nor does He receive it with good will from your hands. Yet you say, "For what reason?" Because the Lord has been witness between you and the wife of your youth, with whom you have dealt treacherously. Yet she is your companion and your wife by covenant ... For the Lord God of Israel says that He hates divorce; for it covers one's garment with violence.
>
> Malachi 2:13–16

The Lord had me continue: "You, Dean, have treated your family with violence! And I, the Lord, have seen it. Yet, you dare come before Me and pretend that you are right with Me? Behold, I have seen how you have put away your wife and have married another and have committed adultery. I have seen how you have done wickedness against those—your wife and children—whom I have put in your care. Your little ones, even now, cry in their beds against you for how you have treated them, and dealt treacherously with their mother! You are an adulterer and a liar! And I, the Lord, therefore, am against you."

Dean stood there speechless, not able to say a word. I could tell that he was stuck between two worlds and two reactions; he didn't know whether to get angry and try to resist me or to be afraid and humbled because he had been found out. I could see that one part of him was beginning to ball up his fist in anger in order to hit me, and the other part of him was afraid of me because there was absolutely no way that any human being could possibly know what I was telling him. Nobody knew that he had had numerous affairs while he was married and that he had actually left his wife and kids to marry one of his mistresses. Nobody knew that he had also recently been trying to re-establish a relationship with God that he had abandoned long ago and that he had recently been privately praying to God seeking to know Him. Nobody knew that Dean had been living a "double life" for many years and wanted to appear righteous and successful to men, and yet inside he was empty and void of any integrity or truth. As Dean stood there frozen, unable to move or to speak, God told me to go over to him and hug him, and then quickly leave. He didn't want Dean to begin focusing on the "messenger" and not on the message and the One who was sending it.

As I hugged Dean, he started to mumble in shock, "Who … what … ah … how did … um …"

I quickly whispered in his ear, "You need to go to God and speak to Him." I immediately pulled away from him and quickly walked away, not looking back.

As I walked away, I didn't know what to do or where to go. I hadn't eaten lunch yet, but I felt too overwhelmed and nervous to eat. I really just wanted to get away from there—the "air" was way too heavy and uncomfortable. I asked the Lord, "Do I just go back to work? Do I leave him there in the woods? Lord, what do I do now?"

The Lord said, "Go up there [on the hill next to the clubhouse] where you can see the parking lot, and wait for him there."

"Lord, is he going to hit me?" I asked.

"He might," God flatly replied.

"Or is he going to repent?" I further inquired, obviously hoping for the latter.

"We'll see. Wait for him up there," the Lord responded.

I remember gulping at the prospect that Dean might hit me and the Lord was telling me that I needed to wait around for him to possibly do so. After about ten to fifteen minutes, Dean emerged from the woods, slowly walking up the path toward his truck. I watched him get into his truck, and as he started to drive toward me, the Lord said to me, "Go to where he will see you." I started walking toward Dean, as he was driving toward me, and I was glad to see that he wasn't "stepping on the gas" in order to run me over! That was a good sign. He pulled up alongside me and humbly asked me if we could talk.

I said, "Sure." I got into his truck, and we parked at the far end of the golf course parking lot.

I just sat there and listened as Dean began to cry. He poured out all that had been wearing on his conscience and confessed all that he had done and been doing. In tears, he spoke about his children, his ex-wife, his new wife, all the mistresses and strippers, the lies, and all the garbage and sins that had consumed his life the past ten years and what he had become. He "spiritually vomited" and confessed all the evil things that he had been hiding and acknowledged how he had been running from God for so long. For the first time in a long time, Dean became *real*, both with himself and with God.

With tears streaming down his face, Dean said, "You know, this feels good. As strange as it seems, even though I am so ashamed, for the first time in a long time, I actually feel clean and free again." As I sat with him, I didn't say a word, I just listened. After a long while, he humbly asked, "Eric, do I need to leave my new wife and return to Amy? Is this what the Lord wants me to do?"

Not knowing how to answer Dean, I immediately appealed to the Lord in my mind for His answer. The Lord had me say to Dean: "It is written: 'Let every one remain in the same state in which he was called. Was anyone called while circumcised? Let him not become uncircumcised. Was anyone called while uncircumcised? Let him not be circumcised … Were you called while a slave? Do not be concerned about it … Are you currently bound to a wife? Do not seek to be loosed. Are you loosed from a wife? Do not seek a wife. Let each one remain with God in that calling in which he was called'" (1 Corinthians 7:17–27). The Lord had me continue: "For God knows what He is doing, and He knows in what state you are in when He chooses to call you and to open your eyes and to grant you repentance. Therefore, do not seek to return, Dean, to your former wife, for the Lord has now forgiven you of your sins. But now you must consider, like Jacob, that you have two wives. You must now take care of both of them, as well as the children. Obviously, you will not have a sexual relationship with the one, but you must always provide for her until if and when she marries another. You must treat her as a sister and a wife—caring for her and providing for her. It will be hard for you to do this, but this will be the just recompense for what you have done. You must now provide for two households and be willing to justly endure all of the grief, anger, and hurt that you have caused them. This is what the Lord has determined, and it is His righteous justice and judgment. He has heard your prayer and forgiven you, Dean. Be of good cheer, and go forward now." I baptized Dean a few days later.

A couple of weeks later, Dean and his new wife invited me to their house up in the mountains for dinner. I remember getting ready for work that morning and wondering to myself what the day had in store. Suddenly, I then remembered, *Oh yeah, I am going to Dean and Jen's house for dinner tonight.*

Just then, the Lord said to me, "I am sending you up there for her." I remember being startled at this because I didn't know Jen (short for Jennifer) at all. When I got to their house that night (I was late because of car trouble), all three of us sat down to a really nice meal that Jen had prepared. As I was eating, the Lord suddenly said to me, "You will baptize *her* this night!"

I remember being shocked at this statement, and I almost choked on the piece of meat that I was swallowing at the time. In my mind, I said, *What Lord? But I don't know her!*

He answered, "You don't need to. I know her."

Again I protested, *But, Lord, she doesn't go to church; she doesn't know the Bible; I don't know if she has even heard the gospel message; she hasn't read any booklets or been counseled; she doesn't...*

Immediately, the Lord's anger was kindled against me. He angrily said, "You men! Of a truth did I not say about you that you set aside the commandment of God to keep your own vain traditions?! For I said, 'Go and make disciples of all the nations, baptizing them, and teaching them to observe all things that I have commanded you,' but you men instead say, 'Nay, but let them *first* go to our churches and be taught, and make sure that they pay their tithes and read all of our booklets and take our correspondence courses *first*, and thereby qualify themselves, and *then* let them come and be baptized!' You religious fools—you set aside the commandments of God to keep your own vain traditions. Now, you go and do what I told you to do!"

With that sharp rebuke, I lowered my head and tried to muster up the courage to say what the Lord's intentions were to Jen and Dean. I did not know how she was going to receive what I was about to say: "Uh, Jen?" I inquired hesitantly.

"Yes?" she replied.

"I don't know how to say this, but the Lord just said to me to tell you that I was sent here by Him to baptize you this night. And that *if you are willing*, I am to do so."

She looked at me in complete shock and awe and said, "So He *did* hear me, didn't He!?"

I was amazed as tears filled her eyes as she said these words, smiling.

After an initial few seconds of inspiring joy, I watched as fear and doubt began to immediately set in on her face. Lowering her eyes and her head, she said, "But I am not good enough; I have so many sins. What if I fail Him?" she humbly and meekly protested.

Immediately, the Lord told me to put my right hand gently on the side of her face and to say these words to her: "Jen, could your young son, Brody, ever fail you?"

She shook her head, no.

"'Neither could you fail Me,' says the Lord."

Suddenly, with these words, her face lit up, she grinned from ear to ear with joy, and she stood up and said, "All right, let's do it!"

"Now?" I asked somewhat surprised at her sense of urgency.

"Right now!" she demanded.

"Well, don't you want to change into a bathing suit or something else first?" I asked.

"Nope, let's do it right now!" she insisted.

"Okay," I said, shrugging my shoulders in agreement, "As the Lord wills then."

We immediately went into their master bathroom where there was an unusually large bathtub that was deep enough for someone to be completely submerged. As she was sitting in it, fully clothed in her nice dinner outfit, waiting for me to dunk her under, Dean and I looked at each other in complete disbelief at what was happening! Seeing our incredulous looks, she began to explain to us what had happened over the last day or so. She told us that she had been praying to God over the last couple of days, really crying out to Him, wanting to know Him. She said that the night before, she had asked God if He really loved her and that if He did, to please reveal Himself to her. When she heard what the Lord had commanded me to say to her while we were eating, she knew that God had heard her prayer the night before and was now answering her request. She admitted that she became afraid for a few seconds about being baptized, feeling unworthy, but when the Lord had me make that comment about her son Brody and how he could never "fail her," she knew that God was calling her and wanting her to be baptized. Therefore she said, "Let's do it now," realizing that it was the Lord's will. (Incidentally, I did not even know at the time that Jen had a five-year old son named Brody from a previous marriage. I just said to her what the Lord had instructed me to say.)

Having now moved into a new building and taking on more new employees, our company was really growing and expanding. Curiously, however, Tony wasn't really having any success at selling. This was really surprising to all of us because Tony had originally taught me and trained me in how to sell. In fact, he was the best salesperson that I had ever met! Teresa and I couldn't figure it out, and apparently, neither could he. But I had this strange sense deep down inside of me that I was not "allowed" to fire him. So I just waited on God to provide the answers.

On another note, as the weeks and months went by, I personally was becoming more and more depressed. I was finding myself overseeing a rapidly growing company and having to manage a number of employees, while still maintaining and servicing all of my own personal accounts. I was feeling very overwhelmed and out of place. My individual talents and abilities are in sales, not in managing a company and its employees. One particular Monday morning in October of 2004, I got so depressed about my distressing situation that I got down on my knees and poured out my heart to God in prayer. "Father," I prayed, "I am not gifted to manage and oversee a company. I feel like a square peg in a round hole, and a fish out of water. But Lord, if this is the cross that You have given me to carry, then I will certainly do so, but You will need to gift me differently. I do not currently have the gifts and abilities to successfully manage this company and to do this job. Please help me."

As soon as I sat up from praying, the word of the Lord immediately came to me: "This is why I have brought Tony here. You are to turn everything over to him except for two accounts. [He specifically mentioned those two accounts by name.] Just as a professional football team has its owner with a head coach that answers to him; and that head coach has his own coaching staff and administration and way of doing things; so I am removing you and your administration from overseeing this team. And I am bringing in a new head coach. He will have his own way of doing things and his own administration, and you are not to interfere. If he acknowledges Me in all of his decisions and does not turn to his right hand nor to his left hand without first consulting Me, I will guide him, and so it will flourish under his hand. Turn it over to him quickly because I have work for *you* to do."

Totally amazed by the Lord's revelation and wisdom and foresight, I eagerly got up and began heading toward the office before anything or anybody could distract me from doing what the Lord had commanded me. As I was pulling out of my driveway, my wife was returning from dropping off the kids at school. She stopped me and asked, "Where are you headed? And what's wrong?" She could see that I had been crying (in prayer) only minutes before. Not really sure if I should share with her what the Lord had directed me to do, in case she tried to dissuade me from obeying His command, I tried to downplay it. She begged, "Please tell me! If it truly *is* of God, don't you think that He would have prepared my heart ahead of time for it to be okay with me too?" she asked. She had a good point. Being reassured by the Spirit that it was okay for me to do so, I turned back around and shared with her all that had happened. After everything was said and discussed between us, she happily concluded, "Yes, this seems good to my spirit also. Do it!"

As I drove down to our building, I excitedly and nervously wondered how I was going to address this with Tony. The last time that the subject of managing another company was brought up with Tony in a casual conversation with him many months earlier, while we were playing pool and he had had too much to drink (before his conversion to Christ), he drunkenly stated, "You couldn't pay me a half a million dollars to manage another company!" They say that the words of a drunken man are usually the truth of how he really feels. These heartfelt words of his kept ringing in my ears as I headed toward the office.

On the way there, I asked the Lord, "So how is Tony going to receive this news?"

God responded, "I've already told him."

"What!?" I exclaimed. "You mean that he already knows? You mean that when I tell him that this company is now being turned over to him and that I am being removed as its head, he is going to say, 'Well, it's about time! I have been waiting for this all along!'?"

"No," the Lord responded, "he's much too humble for that. Go to your office and call him in, and say nothing about this, and I will show you how much he loves you and how loyal he is to you."

I did exactly as the Lord commanded. I called Tony into my office and asked, "Tony, what has the Lord told you?" He sat back in his chair and took a deep breath (probably thinking that I was going to fire him for his lack of sales), and he said in a somewhat exasperated tone, "Eric, I don't know why I am here. I keep wondering that myself. I am trying very hard to sell, and to be profitable to you and to this company, but for some strange reason, nothing is materializing. I don't get it. But I know this much, I want to help you with all of this. I want to repay you somehow for all that you have given me and done for me. I don't care if I make any money for myself or not! I just want to help you and to give back to you and Teresa in some way for all that you have done for me and Jill [his wife]."

Immediately, the Lord said to me, "See how he loves you and how loyal he is to you." His demeanor and attitude were so humble and meek as he said all of this that I was blown away. At that moment, the Lord opened my mouth and filled it, and I said, "Thus says the Lord God: 'Because you have been willing to humble yourself before Me and because you have been faithful with little, you shall therefore now be entrusted with much.' As of this moment, all that I have shall be entrusted to your care. This company, with all of its employees and accounts, including my own personal livelihood, and the financial welfare of my entire family has now been given and entrusted to you. You are to faithfully manage it as you best see fit. You shall do all that the Lord God shall place on your heart to do, and you shall lead as He directs you; you shall neither turn to the right hand nor to the left without first consulting Him. And the Lord God swears that under your hand and direction this company will flourish!"

With that, Tony lowered his head, as humble tears filled his eyes, and after a few seconds, he quietly confessed, "I know; the Lord has already told me this."

After a few minutes, Tony then humbly asked me, "Eric, can I take off for a while? I need to go and talk to the Lord."

I said, "Of course, take as much time as you need."

About three hours later Tony returned. He confidently and excitedly entered my office and declared, "I will do it. I will do all that the Lord commands!" It was both amazing and reassuring.

We hugged, both of us very excited at what the Lord was working out in our midst. I asked Tony, "When shall we tell the employees? And when shall I turn all of my many accounts over to you? I don't want to overwhelm you or pile too much on you right away."

He replied, "The Lord will let us know." I happily agreed.

Two days later on Wednesday, I was absolutely swamped with orders. It almost seemed like all of my clients were ordering on the same day. I only had time to write down what my clients wanted in note form, but I didn't have enough time between fielding calls to even write up their orders or to process them. Later that afternoon, when my phone finally quit ringing, I pulled the notes together on my first order and began trying to write it up. Just as my pen hit the paper, the Lord sternly asked me: "What are *you* doing? I told you to turn everything over to Tony, and to do it quickly because I've got work for you to do. Do it now, and do it quickly, for I've got people coming!"

You've got people coming? I thought to myself. *What does that mean?* I wondered.

Nevertheless, I grabbed all of my pending orders that I hadn't written up yet, and all of my job folders, client notes, and customer files, and I carried them down the hall and plopped them down on Tony's desk. "Well, Tony," I said, "I guess it's time. The Lord just told me to hand everything over to you right now! I am sorry if I am overloading you with all of this, but God just told me to do it, so I am doing it."

Tony graciously said, "No problem; as the Lord wills."

I headed back to my office and began cleaning out my desk. No sooner than I had gotten rid of all of my files and accounts (except for the two that the Lord had specifically told me to keep) and cleaned out my desk, did my secretary call me and say, "Eric, I have a Virginia here to see you."

I asked, "Who?"

And she said, "Virginia Shobe."

I thought to myself, *Virginia Shobe? Wow, I haven't seen her in a long time.* (She was a friend that I knew from the Denver South Congregation.)

"By all means send her in," I said. When Virginia entered my office doorway, I gladly greeted her and jokingly said, "Boy, the Lord told me that He had people coming, but I didn't think He meant you!" I was only kidding and trying to break the ice.

She looked at me seriously and said, "I'm glad to hear you say that, so now you won't think that what I am about to tell you is so crazy." Intrigued, I pulled my chair from around my desk beside her so that I could sit next to her. She continued, "I was just on my way to the grocery store and to run some errands, and while I was driving, I heard a Voice tell me, 'Go see Eric!' You are the only Eric I know. So that is why I am here."

Realizing that this was definitely an appointment from God, I immediately asked Him what to say or do. He said, "Just listen to her." So I just started listening to her as she described all the things that were going awry in her life. It was obvious that she was greatly stressed and heavy burdened and that she was deeply concerned about many things in her life. She described how she had been earnestly praying to God about all of her worries and concerns, and that she didn't know what to do about her seemingly mounting problems.

At that point, the Lord then said to me, "Ask her if I told her something."

I said, "Virginia, has the Lord told you anything?"

She answered, "Yes, He told me that He loved me."

The Lord then said, "Ask her if I told her to do something, yet she has not done it. At first she will deny it, but then I will remind her of it."

"Virginia," I asked, "is there something that the Lord has told you to do that you have left undone?"

At first she adamantly shook her head no, and then she gradually slowed down, as her eyes began to widen, until she began shaking her head yes. "Yes," she slowly admitted, "yes, the Lord did tell me to do something, and I didn't do it."

"What is it, Virginia?" I asked. "What did the Lord tell you to do that you haven't done?"

"He told me to drive up into the mountains, to a place that He would show me, and that He would speak to me there," she reluctantly confessed.

"And so why haven't you done it?" I inquired.

"Because I'm just too busy!" she exclaimed in exasperation. "I have too much to take care of. I have to buy groceries, do the laundry, pick up the dry cleaning, help the kids, clean the house …" As she was speaking and naming off all of her long list of concerns and worries, she slowly began to smile. The answer to all of her problems was now becoming obvious to her—obey God and He will take care of all of your problems and concerns for you. For He says, "Come to Me, all you who are weary and burdened, and I will give you rest." (Matthew 11:28, NIV).

As she came to this conclusion on her own, I gently said, "Virginia, go and do what the Lord has commanded you to do." She smiled, hugged me, and walked out relieved, and headed toward the mountains to obey God. As a side note, she came back to my office the next day all excited and told me about how God had spoken to her up in the mountains. She told me that when she got up there, He explained to her how He was going to fix everything for her and that she didn't need to worry about her finances, her sons, her health or any of those things—but that all she needed to do was be focused on Him and that He would take care of everything else for her. For Jesus said, "Seek you first the kingdom of God and His righteousness, and all these things [that the unbelievers are concerned about and worry over] will be added to you [freely taken care of for you by God]" (Matthew 6:33). And again, God promises: "Cast all of your cares upon Him, for He cares for you" (1 Peter 5:7).

"A BROKEN AND A CONTRITE HEART, I WILL NOT DESPISE"

Ever since the day that the Lord first called me into full-time unpaid ministry back in October of 2004, it has been very difficult. It requires a great deal of faith to walk this road. I have since lost my house; the company that we own is in dire financial straits (close to bankruptcy); we are having a very difficult time selling the building and getting out from underneath its huge mortgage in this bad economy; and to top it all off, my wife told me this morning (December 18, 2008) that she doesn't trust me or respect me anymore and wants a divorce. I can't say that things are all bad though; I still have my health, and my kids are fine (thank God!). Sometimes, it is hard to hold-up under all of this pressure. And I really can't blame Teresa—after all, I am the one who is hearing from God, not her. If things were reversed, I really don't know if I could have faithfully stayed with her this long. God bless her for her faithfulness and loyalty to me all of these many years. I remember a long time ago when my dad unknowingly prophesied to me saying, "Eric, you have nothing to worry about if these things truly are of God; for if they are of Him, then you are a man greatly blessed, and everything will work out fine. But if they are not of Him, then you will most certainly single-handedly destroy not only yourself, but your entire family as well!" These words often ring in my ears, especially at times like these when I have bet everything that I have on what God is telling me to be true, and I have put all of my trust and faith in Him. In addition, I have bet my own personal health on Him too because, a number of years ago, my doctor told me that I needed to be on cholesterol-reducing medication. But after I tried taking some, it just didn't feel right with my spirit, and so I quit taking it. I also remembered what the Lord had said to me years before: "Eric, am I your Healer—your physician? . . . I am either all of these things to you or none of these things—now which is it?"

Walking and living by faith can be a very hard thing sometimes. But the key is never take your eyes off God! Peter had to learn this valuable lesson too when he was trying to walk on the water. He did well when he first stepped out of the boat in faith, but he quickly began to sink when he started to focus on the blowing wind and roaring waves all around him (Matthew 14:28–31). Looking at the physical circumstances surrounding you only causes you to lose your spiritual footing and to slip—allowing the world's physical cares and concerns to "take you under" and potentially drown you. Jesus reminded Peter to keep his head up and to not take his eyes off Him through doubt and fear. If you keep your head up and your eyes focused on Jesus instead of on the cares and elements of this world, you can literally "walk on water"—that is, you can walk above it all. This is what Paul meant when he speaks about "walking in the Spirit" and "living in the Spirit" and not in the flesh (Romans 8:1–14).

I realize that I stand to lose everything in this world. But isn't this what Jesus meant when He said that anyone who wants to follow Him and be His disciple, must forsake all that he has, deny himself, and remove and forsake anybody or anything that hinders him from following after Him? He also told us that even if our own right eye or right hand causes us to stumble from following Him, then we should pluck that eye out and/or cut that hand off, so that it doesn't prohibit us from pursuing the kingdom of God and entering into it (Matthew 5:29–30). He concluded that it is better that we enter into His kingdom with only one eye or with only one hand than to not enter into His kingdom at all (Matthew 18:8–9). This is what Jesus meant when He personally told me to "go all in" with the poker chips of my life and to not hold *anything* back, but to go ahead and bet it all—especially since He is the One who is dealing my cards to me! I am not afraid, therefore, to lose it all in order to gain it all. "For he who finds his life will lose it; and he who loses his life for My sake will find it." Jesus said (Matthew 10:39; 16:25). I have done everything that God has told me to do; therefore, I will wait on Him for my reward. This is what I truly believe—therefore this is what I have done.

One day about four years ago, Cindy, our accountant, left our company. As we were saying our good-byes, the Holy Spirit said to me that someone else would be leaving us soon as well. I suspected it to be a different person in our company, so when Rick called me and asked if we could meet, I didn't put "two and two together." I was completely caught off guard when he came into my office and sat down and announced to me and Tony that he was leaving. He told us that he wanted to go out on his own and start his own competing company. Tony and I were shocked to say the least! At first I was angry, but suddenly the Holy Spirit said to me, "See, I told you someone else was going to be leaving soon." When I heard the Holy Spirit say this, I quickly realized that I shouldn't resist his departure and that I was to let him go. I told Rick that I was his friend and that I would support him and help him get started in business. But I also said, "Rick, I am your friend and brother, so please don't betray me and hurt our company as you go off and start your own. Please give me your word that you won't betray me, brother."

He said, "I give you my word that I won't betray you."

Immediately, my mouth unwittingly opened and the following unintended oath came rolling out: "Although you betray me, Rick, yet will I not betray you." I was shocked at what the Holy Spirit had just made me promise. I didn't mean to say that! I did not mean to give Rick my word that I wouldn't take any action against him if I had learned that he was harming us as a company. Immediately, I asked God in my mind, *Lord, why did You make me promise him that?*

God answered, "Eric, I knew beforehand who was going to betray Me, yet I *still* washed his feet."—obviously a reference to Judas Iscariot. At that moment, I realized that Rick was going to betray me and that he probably already had, and yet the Lord was letting me know right then and there that I was not to return evil for evil or avenge myself—but that I was to do good to those who spitefully use me and mistreat me (Matthew 5:44). Therefore, to Tony's surprise, I blessed Rick and hugged him and assured him that he would have our company's genuine support and goodwill.

It wasn't long after we threw Rick a farewell party and he left that we began to realize the full scope of how he had been betraying us all along. Little by little, Rick had been contacting our clients beforehand in preparation of his leaving and informing them that he was going to be going into business for himself. After his departure, despite having signed a "noncompete/confidentiality agreement" with us when I first hired him, he took over a million dollars worth of business from us, stealing our clients. We soon discovered this because one of our vendors "accidentally" sent us one of our regular client's proofs erroneously made out to Rick's new company. I use quotes around the word "accidentally" here because I knew that God had made it happen so that we would know what Rick had been doing and how he had been betraying us all along. I also realized that God was testing me to see what I would do with the information and whether or not I would seek vengeance or threaten him. Instead, I sent Rick a kind e-mail requesting that he please stop what he was doing and to please honor our "noncompete/confidentiality agreement." He refused and denied any wrongdoing, as I knew that he would. Rick had worked for me long enough to know that I wouldn't sue him but that I would instead "turn the cheek" and allow myself to be defrauded and wronged according to the Scriptures (Matthew 5:39; 1 Corinthians 6:7). But sadly, what I think Rick didn't realize is that God said that vengeance was His and that He would repay all evildoing (Hebrews 10:30). I don't need to fight my own battles because God promised that He would fight them for me. Again, I remembered what the Lord had said to me that day in the hot tub: "Eric, am I your Shield—your defense? Am I your Sword—your offense? I am either all of these things to you, or I am none of these things—now which is it?" I believe God; therefore, I chose to do nothing but bless Rick and wish him and his family the best.

Rick knows what is right and what is wrong. In fact, he had already witnessed how the Lord repays. He saw what God had done to another couple who had wronged me. Some might even say that God is severe—and the truth be told, sometimes He is (Romans 11:22). When Teresa and I first bought our office building, soon after we closed, the basement began flooding when it rained. Water started pouring in from around the office-level window seals and was leaking inside the walls continuing all the way down to the basement warehouse. The basement concrete walls also began cracking and water started spewing in from the outside, completely flooding the basement warehouse. The previous owners, who had sold us the building, did not disclose the water-leakage problems or the previous water damage, although they were clearly aware of them. We know that they were aware of the water problems because after we closed on the building, their own warehouse employees later warned Dwight, our warehouse manager, "not to store boxes in certain places in the warehouse because when it rained the whole basement would leak." The previous owners clearly defrauded us by not disclosing these things prior to our closing on the building.

I called the previous owners four times asking them to please help me with the growing costs of the repairs (which were rapidly approaching $250,000 to fix). I told them that I wanted to work something out between us, apart from the courts having to get involved, and that I was just asking for them to financially work with me in "good faith" to amicably resolve the distressing situation. I assured them that I would be "more than fair" in dealing with them and that we just needed to stop and fix the growing problem. I tried unsuccessfully to give them the opportunity to "step up and do the right thing" since we knew that they had prior knowledge of the continual leakage but hadn't disclosed it up front, as is required by Colorado law. Each time, they said that they would meet me to discuss it but never bothered to show up or even call. Teresa and I paid the whole expense of the repairs ourselves and never called them again. Somehow, I knew that God was going to "judge" the situation. I knew in my spirit that they would be bankrupt within a year because when they were given the opportunity (four times) to do the right thing, they instead mocked what was right and just, and consequently, God exacted "His justice" upon them. I found out a year later—again, quite by "accident" through a business associate of theirs—that they indeed went bankrupt within a year of our closing. Sadly, I also am aware of what is going to happen to Rick and his family in the near future, because of his sin, but I am not going to disclose it. I pray to God for His great mercy upon them. I love Rick and his family, and I forgive him. Hopefully, God will forgive him too (Romans 9:15).

I realize that some of these things that I have shared and stated here might seem to some to be harsh, self-righteous, or even vengeful. But one thing that God has shown me is that we must take into account the whole Word of God and pay particular attention to what God reveals about His eternal and sovereign, immutable (unchanging) character. He is the same yesterday, today, and forever (Hebrews 13:8; Malachi 3:6). In the New Testament, He struck two people dead (a husband and wife team) who had conspired to lie to one of God's servants (Acts 5:1–11). He struck a man blind for trying to hinder the apostles as they were preaching and teaching the gospel (Acts 13:6–12). And the angel of the Lord smote a Gentile man for being too haughty and for not giving due glory to God (Acts 12:20–23). All of these occurrences happened in the New Testament, not to mention the familiar and true Old Testament stories of Sodom and Gomorrah, Noah's flood, and the destruction of the Canaanites. The point is God is to be respected and feared. He judges all men regardless if they know Him or not. Because due justice and retribution aren't necessarily meted out immediately, some people erroneously think that there is no God, and that if there is, He isn't really involved with us directly anyway. I am here to tell you that there *is* a God and that He is fully aware of everything and that nothing escapes His eyes or His knowledge! He knows all of our thoughts—before we ourselves even think them.

But even as I write all of the above truth, I am still greatly mindful and appreciative of His incredible limitless mercy upon all of us. He is very quick to forgive and strongly desires to reward His children instead of having to "spank" them. I know Him, and He loves all of us very much, and there isn't anything that He wouldn't do for us—up to and including giving us the life of His very own beloved Son—in order to be able to gather us all together "under His wings as a mother hen gathers her chicks" (Matthew 23:37). He loves us that much! However, the problem lies with us—for the most part, *we simply don't believe.* We refuse to see and hear Him as He really is. We would rather embrace *our images* of Him, instead of allowing Him to reveal Himself to us. We refuse to believe Him and to take Him at His word. I am mindful of the great lengths to which He goes to in order to reveal Himself to us and to get our attention. But still we don't listen and we don't believe. Using Rick as an example, I want to relay the following true story: between the time that God had me first tell Rick and warn him that "his heart was not right with the Lord" and that he needed to repent, and the time that God then ultimately led him away some two years later, God "visited" Rick and "touched him" (in order to get his attention) in such a way that few have ever experienced—but still, sadly, Rick refused to listen and to change.

Keep in mind, I didn't realize at the time that God was making me say it, but the day after 9/11 happened, during the time when Rick's wife was pregnant with their first child, Rick came to me emotionally shaken up and wanted to talk. He was completely freaked out about what had tragically taken place in New York City the day before (as I'm sure that we all were). In our deeply spiritual discussion that followed, Rick and I were mutually talking about in what or in Whom a person puts their confidence and what strengthens a person during a time of personal crisis and tragedy. We were discussing how there are "no guarantees in this life," and so how does a person who doesn't believe in God keep from totally falling apart when catastrophes and tragedies occur? I then said, "Take for instance, you. What would you do, Rick, if your baby was born deformed or severely handicapped? Who or what would you turn to?" I don't even know why I said this. It just came out of my mouth! He looked at me a bit angry and asked, "Why would you say that?! Why would you even ask me that?!" At the time, I honestly didn't know why I had said it. I was just trying to make a relevant point in our discussion regarding what do we humans do or who do we run to in times of need or in times of trouble. Little did I realize then, but the Lord had just had me prophesy to him. I assure you, my reader, I had no idea at the time that that was what I had just done.

Thankfully, his firstborn son was born just fine. However, approximately four years later, his wife became pregnant again with their second child. We were all so happy for them. It seemed that life couldn't have been any better for Rick and his wife. He was making lots of money with our company—more than he had ever dreamed of—and he was very well liked. His wife, "Susan" (not her real name), was very beautiful, and his son was everything you'd want a firstborn son to be. However, after he and Susan went in for their scheduled inducement-delivery of their second child, surprisingly no one heard from Rick for three days. He didn't call in to the office or e-mail us or anything. It was like he had just disappeared. Then my wife accidentally intercepted an e-mail discussion that Rick had been having with his parents. Apparently, Rick's mom had inadvertently sent an e-mail to Rick's work e-mail address instead of sending it to his private one. My wife read the e-mail and described to me Rick's disheartening situation. Apparently, Rick and Susan's newborn daughter had unfortunately been born with a number of birth defects. She was missing her right hand just above the wrist and her left foot just below the knee. Sadly, in addition to these severe deformities, I believe that she also had some other "more minor" birth defects as well. Teresa and I were crushed for them, our hearts ached for them, and we certainly shared in the pain and sorrow they must have been feeling during this time.

I remember stepping into the shower that weekend (we still hadn't heard from Rick or Susan), feeling very sorrowful and discouraged for them because of their situation, when all of a sudden, the Lord asked me, "Why are you so downcast and disheartened?"

In anguish, I answered, "Because of Rick's baby!"

Immediately, the Lord's overall tone changed. He sternly said to me, "It is written that children are a gift from Me and that I give good gifts unto My people. Why then do you therefore call My good gift evil?! I gave Rick and Susan this daughter for good. This child can either become Rick's greatest blessing or his biggest curse, depending upon what he does and how he reacts to the situation. Remember that it is written, Eric, that the fear of the Lord is the *beginning* of wisdom" (Proverbs 9:10).

Rick called me the next day. I didn't let him know that Teresa and I already knew about their situation. I wanted to hear it all from his own mouth; I wanted to hear his true thoughts and feelings. He talked about how crushed and devastated he was at first, and how completely caught off guard he and Susan were, but as he continued speaking, I could tell that he had hope. Apparently, a number of doctors and specialists had stepped forward to offer their help and advice. Rick also began talking about the Lord. He mentioned how he had been trying to pray about it some but that Susan didn't believe in God. Trying to encourage him, I then mentioned that Teresa and I had accidentally intercepted an e-mail between he and his mother and that we already knew about their situation. I expressed our love and support for him and Susan, and I also told him how God had rebuked me for being down about his situation, telling me that this was a great opportunity and tremendous blessing for him depending upon how he looked at it. However, I did not mention anything about how God had said to me that "the fear of the Lord is the beginning of wisdom."

All of a sudden Rick said, "Hey, Eric, I think that I am going to name her Sophie."

"Really?" I asked. "That's a pretty name" I said.

"Yeah," he commented, "the name means *wisdom*." I was really taken aback when he said this. He then continued, "I thought that the name would be very fitting because she has taught me so much already, and she has only been with us for three days." I was very proud of Rick that day—it seemed like he was starting to get the message.

God's intention for each of us is for us to repent and to turn to Him with our whole heart and start *believing* in Him and calling out to Him to save us! The whole intent of this creation (that is, this physical world that we live in right now) and our existence in it, is so that we human beings can come to the realization and understanding that apart from God we can't survive–that is, we have no control over anything. Of ourselves, we can do nothing. We can't control our circumstances (either personally or collectively); we can't heal our infirmities (ours or anyone else's); we can't tame nature or prevent natural disasters; we can't control the weather; we can't survive without certain necessary provisions; we can't extend our lives or the lives of our loved ones; and we certainly can't, and won't, live forever. God has given us this world to demonstrate these eternal facts and truths to us. Specifically stated, we are a deficient and vulnerable race. That is, apart from God's divine intervention, we are as good as dead. And creation itself (the physical world that we now live in) is here to clearly teach us that sobering fact! But still, many refuse to humbly and honestly acknowledge this glaring truth.

Let's go back to the garden of Eden for a moment to help identify Rick's problem (which is really every human being's problem). Our problem, as human beings, is that most of us are still running from God in pride and in disbelief. Through Adam and Eve, we

"A Broken and a Contrite Heart, I Will Not Despise"

have all collectively eaten from the tree of the knowledge of good and evil and consequently, "our spiritual eyes have been opened" to the knowledge of the truth (Genesis 3:6–7). That truth being, we now *know* that we are "naked." That is, as a human race, we are vulnerable, susceptible, and lack a "covering." Both collectively, as well as individually speaking, we realize that we, as human beings, are truly powerless and vulnerable when it comes to defending ourselves against adversaries and opponents such as nature, illness, tragedies, aging, natural catastrophes, sinful impulses, addictions, temptations, demons, and death. But instead of honestly admitting our human frailties and weaknesses and, consequently, running to God and asking Him to help us and to deliver us—most of us instead just chose to ignore the plain truth of our circumstances and our mortality and simply "run away and hide." By "running away," I mean we either completely now ignore the truth, pretend that it doesn't exist, make up "fairy tales" to try and minimize it, or simply choose not to think about it or deal with it at this time. In doing so, we are effectively just trying to "hide from God" (who is the Truth) just like Adam and Eve did when *their* "spiritual eyes were opened" and they became self-aware, recognizing their own "nakedness"—that is, their vulnerable human state and frail condition. In their initial embarrassment and shame, instead of running *to* God and asking Him to clothe (cover) them, Adam and Eve ran *from* God and vainly sought to "clothe themselves." In other words, they tried to cover up and "conceal" their vulnerability when they spiritually recognized their own human inadequacies and frailties. Likewise, when we today also refuse to face the truth of our circumstances and recognize and admit our own human vulnerabilities and shortcomings (sins), we too are just trying to do the same thing that our parents, Adam and Eve, did when they ran from God and "sewed fig leaves together" in which to cover themselves (Genesis 3:7). But when God confronted them, He quickly took away their "man-made coverings" and gave them clothes of "animal skin" which He Himself had made for them; thus signifying the truth that God has already prepared a "covering" for us if and when we look to Him and begin trusting Him to clothe us and to protect us. For Jesus Christ is that "animal skin" (that sacrifice) that God had originally provided and intended human beings to be clothed with (Genesis 3:21; 22:8). This is why God removed Adam and Eve's fig leaf clothing *that they had made for themselves*, and replaced it with the animal skin that He Himself had provided long ago—picturing Jesus Christ and His redeeming sacrifice for us (Genesis 3:7, 21; John 1:29). For it is written that Jesus is that Lamb of God "who was slain from the foundation of the world" (Revelation 13:8). We do not need to "clothe" ourselves therefore, for God has already prepared a spiritual covering for us.

Spiritually speaking, "clothing" pictures two things: First, it pictures we humans trying to run from God and not choosing to live in the truth—that is, not living openly and honestly ("naked") before Him and before each other. It represents our futile human attempts at trying to "cover ourselves up" and hide what we *know* to be the truth—in this case, denying our own human vulnerabilities and our spiritual inadequacies (our "nakedness"). A good example of this is our use of the English word *cloak*. A "cloak" is not only a garment we wear, but the word itself also means "to hide and to conceal something." In other words, to try and spiritually "clothe" ourselves is just a poor attempt by us at trying to "hide" and "conceal" our sins and shortcomings, instead of openly admitting them and outright confessing them. The second thing that "clothing" spiritually pictures and represents is our need to be covered. That is, because we are so vulnerable (both physically and spiritually), we need a protective covering over us. As was mentioned above, God has already provided that covering for us in the form of Jesus Christ. For Jesus' blood was freely shed for us by Him in order to be our spiritual covering. This truth is clearly illustrated in the true story of the Exodus where the Israelites were led out of Egypt by Moses. On the very night that the Jews now call Passover, when God was first calling His people out of bondage in Egypt (which spiritually pictures God calling us out of this world and its sinful enslaving ways), God instructed the Israelites to put "lamb's blood" over the doorposts of their houses to keep the Death Angel from entering in and exacting "justice" upon them for their sins. For just like their Egyptian neighbors and taskmasters, the Israelites too deserved judgment and death. However, God had made a way for them (through the lamb's blood) to be "passed over" from judgment, and subsequent, certain death; God Himself providing this "covering" for them in the prophetic form of a "sacrificial lamb." He did this so that His people Israel could have a chance to be free, and to live and grow, and to continue on in faith, learning how to trust God and rely upon Him to personally lead them and be their sovereign Lord. The Bible states that all of this happened to them as a prophetic type for us, and for *our* learning, so that we might learn to trust Him and to believe Him, and realize that God truly has a plan for all of us, and that He has made a way for us to be restored back to Him, so that we can dwell and abide with Him once again forever in paradise (1 Corinthians 10:6–13; Hebrews 3:7–19; 4:1–13). He is calling to us, even now, and wants us to wholeheartedly come out of this "barren desert world" which the Bible spiritually likens to both Sodom and Egypt to inherit the true promised land of God which is His glorious kingdom. But just like the Israelites, we too first need the Lamb's blood over our "houses" (our lives), so that we too can be "passed over" by the Death Angel and can escape judgment and (eternal) death and live. This "great pardon" and miraculous deliverance by God is available to everyone; and yet, it is only granted to those who call out to Him from a sincere, contrite, broken heart and spirit; to those who truly want to know Him and seek to faithfully follow Him as they pass through this "Sinai desert wilderness" that we now call home, and refer to as planet earth.

Sadly though, most people don't believe. In fact, many of them even *choose not* to believe. They don't want to have to submit and surrender their lives to God, and have to acknowledge a greater Power and Authority other than themselves, or admit that there is a divine purpose and meaning to life. To do so, would automatically entail and impose personal responsibility and accountability—things they don't want. Instead, they would rather just ignore and neglect what little truth they have been given, and what spiritual knowledge they have acquired through living, as well as what has been supernaturally and divinely revealed to all of us through the pages of history and Scripture. For every human being has been given some spiritual truth and/or knowledge and enlightenment. For all of creation itself was given by God to reveal spiritual truth to us (Romans 1:18–32). You don't have to be a rocket scientist to realize that you are one day going to die, or that you, as a human being have no control over nature or your circumstances; you don't need an Ivy-league education to realize that you are vulnerable as a human being and assailable to almost everything in creation. Why do we continue then to bury our heads in the sand, pretending that we are invincible, and thereby, deny what we *know* to be the truth? The truth being that apart from God's help and intervention (Jesus' sacrifice), we are not going to live; but rather, we are all going to die (eternally). Both the natural world ("nature"—that is, creation itself) and our own sinful human nature are quickly moving us all toward death. That is, left to ourselves, we human beings cannot control, nor are we going to survive, what "nature" (speaking here of both the physical world and our own human nature) is going to do to us; we, *by nature*, are going to die! There is no stopping it; nature itself is going to consume us. It is inevitable. Left to ourselves, apart from God, we are all simply going to waste away on this earth and die—for dust returns unto dust.

My friends, it all comes down to *believing*! It all comes down to individually realizing and believing that God can and will save us if we call upon Him to. If we stop trying to "do it" (survive) *our own way*, by trying to sustain ourselves and choose for ourselves how to live, and realize and admit that we can't survive on our own, either physically or spiritually, and humbly cry out to God for His help and deliverance, He will definitely save us! Remember, collectively speaking, we were originally kicked out of paradise (pictured by the garden of Eden) and banished to this "desert wilderness" (the earth as we now know it) because we collectively didn't *believe*. Our original progenitors (Adam and Eve) didn't believe God or trust Him; so as a consequence, God took paradise away from them (and us). In paradise (that is, in the garden of Eden) everything that we needed (and wanted) was freely given and provided to us. But when we collectively decided as a race (in and through our original parents) that we didn't need God and that we could "make it on our own" (thus, desiring "to become our own gods"), God in His infinite patience and wisdom kicked us out of paradise and sentenced us to this "desert wilderness" to collectively learn the hard and steadfast truth *that man cannot survive without Him*! But sadly, still true to this day, collectively speaking, we human beings, in our obstinate and foolish pride and perpetual unbelief still refuse to admit that truth—even after sixty centuries of continual suffering and dying. For the most part, we humans still don't *believe* God and are still choosing to "do it" *our* own way living according to our own means and by our own judgments and decisions; ever-searching for lasting happiness, complete and total fulfillment, contentment, and immortality, but never finding any. I tell you the truth; if we would only learn, as individuals, and as families, to believe God and to put our trust in Him, and truly learn the lessons of "this life" (that we can't survive on our own without Him), then we would soon be able to leave this desert wilderness and find true life, and happiness, and prosperity in God. He Himself would change our personal circumstances! We don't have to continue aimlessly wandering and wasting away in this desert place with no eternal purpose and abiding hope. We don't have to end up like the disbelieving Israelites whose "carcasses fell in the desert wilderness" and who never entered into the promised land because they refused to believe God (Hebrews 3:17–19). We don't have to die! We can live. It really only comes down to our own individual choice and belief. Each man and woman has to choose for themselves what they will do and Who they will believe. But

I tell you the truth, if we stop and repent (renounce our way) and turn around and start *believing* God (believe what He says and live by what He says), then we will be accepted back into paradise once again and truly find life and live forever. It is that simple! It is all about believing—that is, *believing what God says*.

Notice that I did not say that "we will start going to church." I said that if we start *believing* God and living by what He says, then we will find true life and live forever, and we shall not die. Some people erroneously think that going to church is the way to eternal life. Going to church never saved anybody! In fact, if anything, in a lot of cases, "going to church" has only hindered people from entering the kingdom of God (Matthew 23:13). I already explained how they kicked *me* out. In most cases, they did the very same to every servant of God that He has ever sent to them—including Jesus Christ Himself (Acts 7:51–52; Matthew 23:34; Luke 4:28–29). Jesus never told anybody to go to church. Instead, He told the people to *follow Him*! If going to church were so important, He certainly had every opportunity to tell the people to go there—for the "capital" and "headquarters" of all the churches existed during His lifetime—that was the very Temple itself! Instead of telling the people to go to the Temple, He told the believers to *follow Him* because He was going to tear down that whole church system (the Temple system)—stone by stone anyway (Matthew 24:1–2; Luke 19:41–44). In a lot of cases, "going to church" only hinders people from following the Lord. It can give them a false sense of security. Serving the Temple of the Lord is not the same as serving the Lord of the Temple! Ask any Jew who lived in the first century. While some Jews were faithfully attending weekly "church services" at the Lord's Temple, they were completely missing out on the actual Lord of the Temple's coming. I realize that some Christians who are reading this may be saying to themselves, "Hey, wait a minute. Doesn't the Bible command us to go to church?" The answer is no. There is no Scripture in the Bible that requires regular weekly church attendance or commanded corporate worship. The only Scripture that churches use to support their case for requiring regular weekly church attendance is the following Scripture:

> Let us hold fast the confession of our hope without wavering, for He who promised is faithful. And let us consider one another in order to stir up love and good works, not forsaking the assembly of ourselves together, as is the manner of some, but exhorting one another, and so much the more as you see the Day [of Christ] approaching.
>
> Hebrews 10: 23–25

This Scripture doesn't require regular weekly church attendance or demand corporate worship. But rather, it encourages us believers to not become reclusive in our faith, but instead to get out and let our lights shine by fellowshipping and intermingling with one another in order to encourage and strengthen each other in the faith. It is not so that a "hired professional theologian" can regularly preach at us as if *we* ourselves are unbelievers!

Getting back to Rick, Rick's problem is the same one that every *nonbeliever* has: they don't want to submit their lives and their decisions to a higher authority—God! They refuse to surrender. They just can't give up "the reins of their life." Like little disobedient children, they believe that they can "go about it" and "do it their own way." So, God the Father wisely says, "Okay, then go ahead and try."

So each man and woman then vainly goes through "life" trying to survive by doing it "their way," only to find out that it is futile and that they are going to eventually die anyway having accomplished absolutely nothing eternal. It is like aimlessly floating around in the ocean, continually flapping your arms and earnestly treading water, trying to stay afloat and keep your head above water, all the while refusing out of stubbornness to call upon God who is just standing nearby watching and waiting for you to call upon Him to save you. Eventually, "nature" itself is going to overtake you and you are going to drown. This is what Rick and I were first addressing a long time ago after 9/11 happened.

"Where are you going to turn, Rick, when your circumstances and surroundings—that is, when nature itself, are too much for you to handle on your own? Are you going to continue relying on your own mind and on your own judgments—that is, are you going to continue 'being your own god'? Or maybe like some do, you are instead going to run to others—to self-help books and worldly counselors [other gods] to help you and to rescue you from all your troubles? Or are you going to finally submit and look to the One and Only true God [your heavenly Parent] who is just waiting patiently by to help you, and for you to finally start listening to Him?" This is what God meant when He said to me in regards to Rick that "the fear of the Lord is the *beginning* of wisdom" (Proverbs 9:10). The word "fear" used here refers to *having a healthy respect for someone or something.* In other words, unless a child or student respects what his or her parent or teacher knows, and views that parent or teacher as a legitimate authority in their life, then that child or student will never listen to and learn from that parent or teacher. Likewise, unless a person views

God as *the* Authority of their life, they will never listen to God and learn from Him, and will consequently, never have *life* and will ultimately die.

You see, God gave Rick that deformed and handicapped daughter to teach him, and to show him that he really doesn't have control over anything in his life; and that apart from God, he can do nothing. She was specifically given to him as a blessing to help demonstrate the fact that without God's protection and covering and involvement in his life, nature itself is going to control Rick and his circumstances, and Rick is powerless to do anything about it. At the same time God was also making Himself known to Rick and calling him, by presenting Rick with an incredible opportunity to get to personally know Him and His awesome power. During this time it was said to Rick that if he would turn to God with his whole heart, and would seek after Him diligently, then he wouldn't have to worry about a thing regarding Sophie or anything else in his life for that matter; for God is able to make all things right. He is able to straighten the crooked, heal the lame, make a way when there is no way, and "have limbs suddenly appear where there were no limbs." I know this was said to Rick, because God had me say it to him—soon after Sophie was born! Just as God had said to me when He first gave Sophie to them, that He was presenting Rick with a unique opportunity, and letting him know, that if he turned to the Lord with all of his heart then the Lord *his* God was going to personally deliver him from all adversity including deformities and death. That is why God told me years earlier that He is going to heal Eddie Benavides and Paul Thornton—both of whom are deformed and handicapped; because both of their fathers put their trust and hope in God and believe Him. "For all things are possible to those who believe" (Mark 9:23). Nature wasn't, and isn't, supposed to be ruling over us and having dominion over us; but rather, we humans were originally supposed to be ruling over nature and having dominion over it. For in the beginning, God said this to Adam and Eve (Genesis 1:26–28). However, because we—the human race, didn't collectively believe Him, in and through the form of our original parents, we have all consequently lost our divine rights and privileges as children of God. We have lost "our divine birthright," as it were—the godly rights and privileges that were originally given to us by our Father. We were created by Him "in His image" to be His children and to rule with Him—and thankfully, that destiny has never changed. But while we "children" are in our current state of rebellion, our destiny to rule with our Father has been "put on hold" so to speak. God *will* certainly accomplish in us all that He has purposed for us. Yet, the first step we have to take in fulfilling our destiny in Him is to *believe* Him. In one sense, this is the "Basics of the Kingdom of God 101"—using today's modern vernacular. But as long as we choose to remain in our arrogant state of disbelief and rebellion, we will just continue being "runaway spiritually-estranged" children who no longer reside at home with our heavenly Father or are members of His great glorious kingdom. Let us change therefore, and start believing Him, that we may be accounted worthy to enter into His House once again! For it is written that Jesus is now "giving *those who believe* in His name, the right [the right by birth or *birthright*] to be the children of God; who are born, not of blood, nor of the will of flesh, nor of the will of man, but of God" (John 1:12–13).

For what good does it do to live for a moment on this earth, earnestly building and growing, and working diligently, only to ultimately die and be forgotten? With all of our works and our efforts (and growth) completely lost and ultimately coming to nothing? Indeed, it is a vain and futile existence. That is why we need to humbly return to God and start believing in Him in order to truly find life. Now, I realize that the scientific and academic atheist naysayer will put forth some silly argument like, "Well, all of my research hasn't been in vain. There is such a thing as 'collective knowledge'; that is, when I die my research and ideas will continue on and survive me and will benefit those who come after me. Therefore, I have not lived in vain!" To this I reply, not I, but God: "All of your wonderful accumulative knowledge is going to lead mankind to one place—that is death. For it is written that 'there is a way which *seems* right to a man, but its end is the way of death'" (Proverbs 14:12; 16:25). In the Bible God foretells what the end of man's days are going to be like; he is literally going to come to a place where he is about to wipe himself (and all flesh) completely out of existence—except that God in His infinite mercy is going to step in at the last minute to save us all from doing so (Matthew 24:21–22). All of our "superior" collective knowledge therefore is going to lead us to one place—complete annihilation of ourselves off this planet—which is *death*!

It is all just a matter of time. Sooner or later, "every knee will bow and every tongue will confess" that He is God, and every person will have to give an account of himself or herself to God (Romans 14:11–12). It is inevitable. Right now, everybody can choose to ignore God and pretend that God isn't real. You can also pretend that you don't have cancer or that you are not dying and that you are healthy. You can bury your head in the sand as much as you want to and convince yourself that you aren't getting any older either. But sooner or later, you are going to have to face reality—whether now or as soon as you close your eyes to take your long-appointed "winter's nap." In the "spring," when you wake up, I tell you the truth, you will sorely regret your willful ignorance and spiritual complacency. Lip service is not enough. Pretending that you weren't "aware" will not work for a defense either (for God reads your thoughts and He already knows what you know and what you don't know). He says that He is not mocked but that you *will* reap what you have sown in this life (Galatians 6:7). I guarantee you, after years of working for Him and knowing Him firsthand, I *know* that no man or woman is going to get away with anything! You cannot and will not be able to "pull the wool over His eyes." And if you say in your heart, even now, "I don't need to worry about that—that is a long way off." I tell you the truth; your appointment with Him is not as far off as you think! God never promised you tomorrow or guaranteed that you are going to wake up in the morning. But He did promise you this: You will wake up in front of Him, and He knows you better than you know yourself.

This is why Rick is in trouble: he is responsible for what he knows (as we all are). He knows it is wrong to steal; he knows that God is calling him and trying to get his attention; he knows that he took advantage of a brother; and he knows that he hasn't fully submitted himself and his will to God's will. This is very dangerous territory! At one point, Rick knew that God had given him his daughter Sophie to open his eyes and to begin to realize that God is sovereign over his life and his circumstances and that he needed to turn to God with his whole heart. He was starting to get that message, but somewhere down the line, Rick forgot or chose to ignore the fact that God is always watching him, and he quit fearing God or caring what God thinks. Therefore, he will answer to God for his willful disobedience. God knows how to get someone's attention—I assure you. What we might think is cruel and severe—God does for our own good. He knows how to "touch" every one of us in a way that we won't forget. As Scripture attests: it is a good thing to fear the Almighty (Hebrews 10:31).

God is also very merciful to those who call upon Him and ask for forgiveness. I remember one time when I was getting kind of proud and haughty when things were going financially well for me. I hadn't realized that it was "going to my head" so to speak, but it was. One morning I was driving across town to meet with a client of mine. It was about a forty-five-minute drive one way, but to my disappointment, the meeting only lasted about five minutes at most. I thought to myself, *Boy, that sure was a waste of my time! I could have done that over the telephone.* As I was driving back to my office, the Holy Spirit suddenly began instructing me on where to turn. It soon became apparent that I wasn't going back to my office any time soon. I kept driving where the Holy Spirit was leading me.

Eventually, I pulled up at Tucker's house. I had only been to his house once or twice before at the most. When I knocked on the door, his dear wife let me in. As I entered, Tucker arose from the couch where he had been sleeping and said, "When I was asleep, I knew in my spirit that you would soon be showing up."

I said, "Tucker, I am not sure why I am here, but we must leave now and take a walk together." (Somehow, I knew that this was the Lord's will.) He agreed, and so we walked out the front door and down the sidewalk. After going about three hundred yards, I sat down on the curb, and said that we must wait here. After about three or four minutes, a mutual friend of ours, Jerry Olson, came walking down the sidewalk toward us. He said that he had also been led there by the Holy Spirit. I assure you, my reader, that none of us had "compared any notes" or discussed it at all beforehand to meet there on the sidewalk. Therefore, I knew that this meeting was of the Lord.

As soon as Jerry arrived, the Holy Spirit came upon both Jerry and Tucker, and they both began prophesying to me at the same time: "Thus says the Lord God Almighty: 'Behold, you have begun to put your trust in your riches and in your wealth that I have given you. You are not to do this, but you are to be humble before Me knowing that I have given you these things and that I can surely take them away. Be zealous therefore and repent, lest I come upon you and remind you that you are but poor, blind, and naked. Put your trust in Me, and not in your riches!" Both men said this in agreement as the word of the Lord came upon them. I knew that it was from the Lord because His own Word says, "By the mouth of two or three witnesses will every word be established." (Deuteronomy 19:15; Matthew 18:16). This came as a great surprise to me; I hadn't realized that my heart and attitude were becoming prideful and sinful before God. Although I was truly sorrowful and ashamed, I was extremely grateful to God (and these two men) for spiritually keeping me on a short leash, not allowing my feet to slip from His paths of righteousness (Psalm 66:9; Proverbs 4:10–13). For the next three days, however, I was so remorseful; I felt so badly regarding what I had unknowingly become in my heart. Every time I was alone, I would start crying, asking God to please forgive me and to change me. On the third day, Teresa asked me to go to the grocery store to get something for her. Being alone, once again I started praying to God in tears while in the parking lot of the grocery store.

Immediately, the Lord spoke to me, saying: "Eric, it is written that *'a broken and a contrite heart, I will not despise'* (Psalm 51:17). You are forgiven; therefore, get up and go your way." I can't begin to tell you the relief and forgiveness I felt at that moment. I have never forgotten those gracious words that the Lord spoke to me that day. He is both forgiving and kind, if you turn to Him with your whole heart.

I remember another man that the Lord sent me to a while back. I was invited to a friendly poker tournament at his house one evening. I didn't know him, but I was invited because he was a friend of a friend. As I was standing there in his house among all of these strangers, before the tournament began, I remember thinking to myself, *How is it that I am standing here? I don't know anybody, and it is not like I have anything in common with any of these people.* (I don't like to drink because I am somewhat allergic to alcohol, I don't sleep around, and I don't do drugs or smoke pot—not that any of them were doing drugs; it just seemed like a little rougher crowd than I usually would hang out with.) I went to the bathroom with these thoughts on my mind, when all of a sudden the Lord spoke to me: "I sent you here to heal somebody."

Immediately, my mind began racing. *What, Lord? You mean You are going to have me heal somebody? Here? Is somebody going to have a heart attack or something?* He didn't answer me a word. A few minutes later, the tournament started. I played all night and nothing happened. I was beginning to think that I must have just thought that I had heard the Lord speaking to me, and that He really didn't. I made it to the final table of the tournament and then got knocked out. I basically won my "buy-in money" back. As the tournament host came over to me to give me my money, he introduced himself. Apparently, he worked for a company that sold industrial light bulbs and had been wanting to meet me to ask if he could supply light bulbs to my building. I told him, yes, but that he would need to contact my warehouse manager to make all of the arrangements because I didn't work at my building anymore. (This happened after the Lord had me quit my job and hand everything over to Tony to manage.)

He then asked, "Really? What do *you* do then?" I told him that I work for the Lord full-time.

Immediately, he grabbed my arm and dragged me outside onto his porch privately away from everyone else. He began pouring his heart out to me: "Why is God killing my little sister? Why, oh why is He taking her from us?" Tears began flowing down his face. He continued: "I don't understand it. We don't deserve this— maybe I do, but my parents certainly don't! They have already lost my older sister to cancer, and now my younger sister has it too. Why would God do this to us? I have been crying out to Him night and day. I sit in that garage there late into the night just crying and crying, asking God why He would do this to us. My parents go to church and Mass three to four times a week; I try to go to church when I can. I am not always able to go because of work, but I try to go when I am able. Is He punishing me for not going to church enough? Why then is He punishing my parents also? Please, sir, tell me. Tell me why the Lord is punishing us and taking my little sister away. She has three little children that she is going to be leaving behind! Why would He do this to us?!"

I stood there speechless, totally taken off guard! This man was sobbing. His heart was broken, and he desperately wanted to hear from God. (My eyes are even welling up with tears right now as I recall this man's poor broken spirit. He was so humble and contrite before the Lord.) I immediately appealed to God in my mind for the answers. He told me to tell the man this: "Do not be afraid. I, the Lord, have heard your cry from the very first day that you called upon Me regarding this matter. Behold, your sister shall not die, but I will give her thirty more years. I will not do this because of your church attendance or because of your lack of church attendance. That has nothing to do with anything to Me. But I will do this because you turned your heart toward Me and cried out to Me in faith. This is what pleases Me—your faith. Therefore, tell your sister and your parents that she will surely not die, for the mouth of the Lord has spoken it." We both wept together, hugging and rejoicing at the gracious words and promise that the Lord had just spoken. [Incidentally, the man later told me that his younger sister was forty years old, which means that she will live to at least seventy! Praise God!]

EVERYTHING SHALL BE PROVIDED FOR YOU—GO FORWARD IN FAITH!

As I have tried to clearly demonstrate in this book, serving God is never easy, but always rewarding. You have to *believe*—no matter what the costs. When God first called me to quit my job and to go into the full-time unpaid ministry, He had to show me some things to help quiet my nerves and my anxiety. I didn't get the chance to say goodbye to my long-held accounts and loyal clients. When my "call" came to serve and follow the Lord, I was sitting at my desk trying to write up orders that both my family and I relied upon for our income and sustenance. It was hard to get up, without saying good-bye, and to just walk away from it all—not looking back. Remember the words of Jesus: "No one, having put his hand to the plow, and looking back, is fit for the kingdom of God" (Luke 9:62). I struggle with this even now. It is hard to live by faith sometimes, trusting God each day to provide, especially when I am continually berated and mocked by family and friends. The constant belittling from family members and so called "Christian brothers and sisters" is sometimes more than I can stand. I hear comments and whisperings from people who consider me to be a deadbeat, lazy, foolish, manipulative, a deceiver, mentally ill, bi-polar, demonic, etc. I wouldn't so much care if it were my enemies saying these things. But it really hurts to hear these things coming from close relatives and companions. I remember recently crying out to God about this persecution from my family and friends, and He pointed me to the following verse in the Bible:

> Do not trust in a friend; do not put your confidence in a companion; guard the doors of your mouth from her who lies in your bosom. For son dishonors father, daughter rises against her mother, daughter-in-law against her mother-in-law; a man's enemies are those of his own house.
>
> Micah 7:5–6

It wasn't so bad initially when things were going well financially for us. But now that the "lean years" are here, and God is requiring our family to solely look to Him for our daily sustenance and provision, the fears and the doubts of those among us who live according to the flesh are causing them to get particularly nasty and adversarial. It is like David once wrote:

> For it is not an enemy who reproaches me; then I could bear it. Nor is it one who hates me who has magnified himself against me; then I could hide from him. But it was you, a person my equal, my companion and my acquaintance. We took sweet counsel together, and walked to the house of God in the throng.
>
> Psalm 55:12–14

So far, this has been the hardest thing for me to bear. But Jesus warned His servants that in the last days "the love of many would grow cold" and that family members and friends would betray one another on account of Him (Matthew 24:12; Luke 21:16).

When I first left my job to go into His full-time unpaid service, the Lord had to help encourage me by giving me Scriptures to show that what I was doing was clearly biblical. Requiring that I step out and follow Him in faith first, He didn't reveal these to me until after I had left my job, turned everything over to Tony as He had commanded, and walked away from all of my beloved clients without saying good-bye. Afterwards, He pointed out the following Scriptures to me:

> And as He walked by the Sea of Galilee, He saw Simon and Andrew his brother casting a net into the sea; for they were fishermen. Then Jesus said to them, "Come after Me, and I will make you become fishers of men." And immediately they left their nets and followed Him. When He had gone a little farther from there, He saw James the son of Zebedee, and John his brother, who also were in the boat mending their nets. And immediately He called them, and they left their father Zebedee in the boat with the hired servants, and went after Him.
>
> Mark 1:16–20

> Then as Jesus passed on from there, He saw a man named Matthew sitting at the tax office. And He said to him, "Follow Me." And he arose and followed Him.
>
> Matthew 9:9

After He showed me these Scriptures in my mind's eye, the Lord then asked me the following rhetorical questions: "Tell me, Eric. Don't you think that Simon and Andrew, and James and John, and Matthew all had long-standing accounts and clients that they walked away from without saying good-bye to? Don't you think that Matthew, as part of his accounting business, had clients that he had developed relationships and friendships with through the years? According to the Scriptures, he just got up from his accounting table and walked away from his stacks and stacks of client folders and files. And what about Simon Peter and Andrew his brother, don't you think that they had vendors and customers that they regularly supplied fish to in the market place? And what about James and John his brother? When I called them, they literally just dropped their nets where they were standing and walked away from their father's business—leaving their father, their employees, and their customers behind. Don't you think that like you, they too all had wives and children to feed and to provide for at home? Don't you think that they too had mortgages and car (chariot) payments to make? Am I not able to provide for My own and for their families also? You are an employer. You care not only about your employees, but their families also, don't you? That is why you provide insurance benefits, 401(k) plans and give them holidays and sick days off. If you, being a fallible human being, rightly do these things, how much more shall not I, being righteous, also provide for My employees and their families? Is it not written that 'a laborer is worthy of their hire' (Luke 10:7)? When I sent My servants out, didn't I instruct them to not even so much as bring an extra coat or a purse or a staff or money or a suitcase or an extra change of clothes with them (Matthew 10:9–10)? Because I told them that *all* would be provided to them as they needed it on their journey and on their assignment. And when they returned, how did they answer Me when I asked them if any of them lacked for anything on their trip? Did they not all answer Me, saying, 'No, Lord, we didn't lack for anything!' (Luke 22:35)? Why then do you worry, Eric? Am I not able to take care of My own? What employer sends out an employee to do a job on his own dime? You are an employer; do you send your employees out of town or on a job assignment at their own expense? If you being a fallible human being don't do this, then why would you think that I would?" These are some of the questions and statements that the Lord posed to me soon after He had me quit my job five years ago to serve Him and His people full-time without pay.

The Lord soon began miraculously backing up what He had been teaching and telling me. He soon sent me on an assignment to Las Vegas. About four weeks beforehand, a friend of mine, named Bob, who liked to play poker, invited me to go to Las Vegas with him. When he asked, I remember saying to him, "Right now, I don't have any extra money. But if the Lord wills, then He will provide the means and the way for me at the last minute if that is okay with you." He said that that was fine because he was going to be going either way. About a week or so out, I suddenly won a bunch of money playing in a friendly poker game (I was part of a regular poker club at the time; we played twice a month.) To my surprise, I won an uncommonly huge amount! I called my friend and happily said that "my Boss had made a way for me to go." My airfare was free (because I had accumulated enough frequent flier miles), and so I gladly joined my friend on his trip to Las Vegas.

On the plane trip there, however, and to my dismay, I was seated next to a really strange-looking guy who was covered in tattoos and had a number of body piercings. He was big, had relatively long hair, and looked like a real "biker dude" from a motorcycle gang. We started up a casual conversation. I don't really remember what we talked about, but somewhere in the middle of our conversation, the Lord said to me "hand him three hundred dollars of the money that you won." After wrestling with the idea for a few minutes in my mind, I agreed, and reach into my pocket and took out the money and handed it to him.

"Here," I said, "the Lord just told me to give you this."

His eyes flew open, and he was astonished! He sat there for a second, and then began to cry. He leaned over and gave me a big hug and thanked me. After a few awkward moments, he said to me, "You know, I am on my way back to Las Vegas from Denver to help my mom who is sick, and I didn't know how I was going to pay for some of my expenses when I got there. I had been worried about it, but in desperation I prayed, and then just decided to get on the plane and go. A long time ago, I used to go to church, but recently I have been thinking that I needed to return and to get baptized. Thank you so much for doing this, sir; you don't know how much this means to me."

It was both very humbling and exciting for me to be used by God in this way to help this man. *What a neat, divine assignment!* I thought to myself. I began to perceive that giving this man the money was the reason that God had sent me to Las Vegas in the first place. However, I was about to find out that it wasn't the *only* reason. Surprisingly, even after giving the man three hundred dollars of the money that I had won, I still had plenty of funds in which to enjoy myself. I was able to easily pay for my share of the room, eat very well while I was there, play a lot of poker, and enjoy some real relaxation and recreation time with Bob. The Lord had truly kept His word to me. Not only had He generously provided for all of my needs, but even my own personal recreation and enjoyment! Truly, He is a wonderful Boss to work for. What other employer out there not only takes care of his employee's needs while that employee is out of town on a job assignment, but also even covers all of that employee's personal entertainment expenses as well? What a joy it is working for the Lord! And to my utter surprise and delight, I was about to find out that my "job assignment" from the Lord was not yet done either. Early one morning while we were still in Las Vegas, before Bob and I woke up, I had a dream. In my dream, Bob was asking me a lot of really tough questions about the Lord. They were very hard and deep questions, but as I watched and listened to our on-going dialogue in the dream, I quickly learned the answers to all of his questions. After the dream ended, Bob and I both curiously woke up at about the same time.

Upon waking, Bob immediately said to me, "Can I ask you a couple of questions, Eric?"

"Sure, go ahead." I answered. And then his questions proceeded almost exactly as I had heard them in my dream only moments before—and of course I now knew all the answers! We talked for about two and a half to three hours that morning about God. I could hardly believe it. And I must say that it was very enlightening for both of us. Bob is a professional litigator (which is sort of like an attorney), so he is very intelligent, methodical, and challenging. He liked, and agreed with, all of my responses and answers. Thankfully, God had prepared me for this assignment only moments beforehand by giving me the dream. It was just as He had promised me, saying, "Everything that you will need to do an assignment will be provided for you ahead of time and as you need it, Eric—just go forward in faith and believe!"

ONLY A REMNANT "IN ISRAEL" BELIEVE

Perhaps you, as my reader, are wondering why I referred to Tucker earlier as a type of John the Baptist. This was revealed to me by the Lord in April of 1999. God had already told me in the previous visions that were given to me in the spring of 1995 that a lot of what had happened in the New Testament would be repeated, spiritually speaking. (Although the birth, death, and resurrection of Jesus Christ is *not* going to be repeated—that was only going to happen once and for all.) But many of the other New Testament events, however, are going to be "replayed" in these last days. I realize to some that this statement might seem incredible, impossible, and/or heretical. I can understand your doubts; I had many of my own, too, that is, until the Holy Spirit began showing me both out of the Bible and through divine revelation that it is indeed the truth! Let's take for example the ministry of John the Baptist: Jesus said that John the Baptist was a type of the prophet Elijah. Elijah had lived and ministered some eight hundred and sixty years before John the Baptist was even born, and yet the Bible says that John came "in the spirit and power of Elijah" to prepare a people to meet their Lord—that is, Jesus

Christ (Luke 1:17). Jesus later revealed, after John the Baptist had been killed, that "Elijah will come again and restore all things" before He returns (Matthew 17:11; Mark 9:12). In the visions, the Lord showed me that everything that happened in the New Testament (apart from the birth, death, and resurrection of Jesus Christ) will be done again—only "bigger than it was done the first time." It was also shown to me that instead of there being one John the Baptist (Elijah type) in the future, there would be many; instead of there being one Peter and one Paul in the last days, there would be many Peter types and many Paul types, etc. Each servant of God in these last days will have their own particular part to play—many of them fashioned after the specific individual ministries of New Testament characters. This is what the biblical phrase "coming in the spirit and power of" means.

Duality and/or multiplicity is not too hard of a concept to understand if you realize that the Bible is renown for having types and anti-types, symbols and allegories. It is like an onion that has many different culminating layers within it. Once you begin to understand the characters and what they symbolize and represent, you can begin to see a lot of things that most people are blind to. However, it is impossible to understand the Bible's mysteries, unless the Holy Spirit opens your spiritual eyes and reveals them to you. Otherwise, you will get caught-up in misunderstandings, misinterpretations, and falsehoods. That is why there are so many different churches, denominations, interpretations, misunderstandings, and deceptions all claiming to speak for Christ! Yet, Jesus, Himself, said that it would be so. For He said, "Take heed that no one deceives *you* [My followers]. For many will come in My name [in the name of Christianity], affirming that I am indeed the Christ, but they will deceive many" (Matthew 24:4–5). You need the Holy Spirit to understand the things of God—especially the deep things of God (1 Corinthians 2:7–14). But how does one receive the free gift of the Holy Spirit? It is easy—well, sort of. The Bible gives the following instructions and mandates:

1. *You must first believe.* You must believe that God is who He says He is, and that He is sovereign over your life. And that as your Creator He has full and complete authority to tell you what to do and what not to do, how to live, and how to be. You must believe and acknowledge that you are a sinner (that you have in the past, and still do, regrettably transgress His laws) and that you need to be saved from your sins and from the penalty of eternal death. You must believe and recognize that Jesus Christ was (and is) given to be the propitiation (the atoning sacrifice) for your sins, and that in Him (that is, under His covering of blood) you are forgiven and have been granted a complete and full pardon. And you realize that because He (Jesus) died for you, you must now live for Him—no longer doing your own will, but His.

> He who believes and is baptized will be saved; but he who does not believe will be condemned.
>
> Mark 16:16

> And he brought them out and said, "Sirs, what must I do to be saved?" So they said, "Believe on the Lord Jesus Christ, and you will be saved, you and your household."
>
> Acts 16:30–31

> If you confess with your mouth the Lord Jesus and believe in your heart that God has raised Him from the

dead, you will be saved. For with the heart one believes to righteousness, and with the mouth confession is made to salvation.

Romans 10:9–10

2. *You must repent and be baptized.* Perhaps, you as my reader are wondering what repentance means? "To repent" means to stop going in the direction that you are headed, recognize that you are in error, and turn around and now proceed forward in a new direction. It literally means "to turnaround" and "to chart a new course" recognizing that the old course that you were on was clearly in error and was wrong. Repentance involves an acknowledgement of and a heartfelt remorse for your sins and shortcomings before God; and it also entails a profession of faith that God can and will forgive you for honestly admitting those sins and transgressions against Him. As a result of this acknowledgment, confession, and remorse (collectively called "repentance"), a new believer then proceeds to baptism (total submersion in water) which symbolizes his or her complete and total surrender to God. Baptism is the outward expression and biblical act of "putting yourself to death" or "dying to one's own self" resulting in the total and complete submission of one's own life and will to God in faith. Thus, the new believer is openly declaring that he or she is no longer going to "live for themselves" according to their own carnal will; but is now going to "live for God" according to His divine will and purposes. Repentance and baptism are therefore an official acknowledgment of the supremacy and sovereignty of God over a person's life, existence and will. Repentance and baptism are the free-will expression of a person's total and complete submission and surrender to God.

Now when they heard this, they were cut to the heart, and said to Peter and the rest of the apostles, "Men and brethren, what shall we do?" Then Peter said to them, "Repent, and let every one of you be baptized in the name of Jesus Christ for the remission of sins; and you shall receive the gift of the Holy Spirit."

Acts 2:37–38

Do you not know that as many of us as were baptized into Christ Jesus were baptized into His death? Therefore we were buried with Him through baptism into death, that just as Christ was raised from the dead by the glory of the Father, even so we also should walk in newness of life. For if we have been united together in the likeness of His death, certainly we also shall be in the likeness of His resurrection.

Romans 6:3–5

3. *God gives His Holy Spirit to those who ask Him and to those who obey Him.*

If you then, being evil, know how to give good gifts to your children, how much more will your heavenly Father give the Holy Spirit to those who ask Him!

Luke 11:13

And we are His witnesses to these things, and so also is the Holy Spirit whom God has given to those who obey Him.

Acts 5:32

"Obeying God" literally means doing what He says–both what is commanded of us in the Bible to do as well as what He specifically tells us individually to do. That is why it is so important to read the Bible and to also pray to God and specifically ask Him for His Holy Spirit. We need His Holy Spirit so that we can understand both His Word and His will for our lives. Keep in mind that I had read and studied the Bible all of my life. But I didn't truly get to know God *until He revealed Himself to me through His Holy Spirit.* You can academically study about someone all you want, but you don't truly *know* that person until you *commune* with them—that is, until you experience a two-way relationship with them. This is the "Jew's" problem—spiritually speaking of both the physical Jews of Christ's day and the "fleshly Christians" (religious people) of today. As a whole, they don't know God. They know *about* Him, even memorize a lot of His Words, but they don't *know* Him—that is, by firsthand personal experience. My friends, it *is* indeed possible to *know* Him—to actually hear Him and to see Him! He is just as alive today as He was two thousand years ago. The problem is that a lot of church-going, professing Christians today, especially in our Western churches, believe He is more real as a past figure of history, than as a present-day reality. Therefore, this "unbelief" stunts their spiritual growth and inhibits their actual realization of Him. When you truly get to know Him, He will *"turn your entire world upside down."* Isn't this what the Bible itself declares—that those who knew Jesus and who were proclaiming Him as the *real* and *only* King were turning the "whole world upside down" (Acts 17:6–7)?

Speaking of these things, this is how I found myself at odds with the established institutionalized church. The more I got to know Jesus, the more I found myself being ostracized and persecuted for *knowing Him*! And sadly, most of that persecution came from (and still does come from) professing Christians. I was truly accepted within Christendom when I quietly attended its churches, paid my tithes, went to its colleges, earned its degrees, and paid homage to its clergy; but the minute that I said that Jesus spoke to me—that is, *I had a living encounter with Him*—they kicked me out and completely disfellowshipped me. How remarkable! But the amazing thing is that this is what the "church"—the first-century Jewish congregations—did to Christ also! When He came preaching and testifying that He had had a firsthand encounter with God, they cast Him out and said that He was nuts and demonic (John 8:48, 52; 10:20, 31).

Things aren't any different today, and this is what the Lord has been showing me. That nothing has changed in two thousand years! The church still resists and persecutes those that God sends to them. Ever since God started personally revealing Himself to me, it has gotten me into a lot of trouble. I have been disfellowshipped, abandoned, betrayed, mocked, spit on, kicked, punched, belittled, defrauded, robbed, and bad-mouthed—all for the cause of Christ whom I serve. But this is true biblical Christianity, right? Right! Jesus said that we, His followers, aren't any better than He is; if His own people had done these things unto Him, shouldn't we expect them to do them unto us also? Absolutely. Even the Apostle Paul confirmed this, by saying, "Yes, all who desire to live godly in Christ Jesus will suffer persecution" (2 Timothy 3:12). And the Scriptures attest that the greatest persecution and resistance comes from those who claim that they are His people (1 Thessalonians 2:14–15; Acts 13:27, 44–46; 17:5).

This persecution from those calling themselves "His people" is just another example of the New Testament replaying itself. The

Bible says that "Jesus came unto His own, and His own did not receive Him" (John 1:11). Jesus even told those who were persecuting Him that He had been sent to them by the One that they claimed to "worship" and the One that they called God (John 7:28–29; 8:54) But they didn't *believe* Him (John 6:36; 10:26). That is the point—*His own people don't believe!* That is why the Lord told me to tell His people just one important thing: even after all that He has shown me and revealed to me about the world-shaking events to come, and the incredible good news of what is going to supernaturally happen among His people, He told me to tell them just one thing—*to believe.* He said to me, "Tell My people, who are called by My name [those who call themselves "Christians"] *to believe!* Tell them to believe in Me more than they do, for I am more real than they know. Tell them that I am about to make a move among them that they have never known and that even though a man will tell them these things, yet it is so marvelous that they will not believe it. Tell them that I am even now standing up in My throne." I have preached this message until I am blue in the face and still very few believe me. As a humble lowly servant, there is not much more I can do. Sometimes, I get discouraged; but yet, I know that this is how it is meant to be. As the Bible shows, there is always only a "remnant in Israel" (that is, within Christendom) who truly believe (Romans 9:27; 11:5).

To illustrate this point further of there "only being a remnant" in Christendom who truly believe, I would like to relay a true story that happened a few years ago. Some members of a local Christian church asked me to play with them on their basketball team. Apparently, a group of Christian churches had formed an interdenominational basketball league and a number of different local

Christian churches were participating and sponsoring it. At the time, I didn't know anyone on the team or anyone in the league for that matter, but somehow I got invited to play. During one particular game, about halfway through the season, a man on the opposing team that we were playing got seriously injured. He had fallen on his elbow and hurt it very severely. As all of the players from both teams were anxiously huddled around him, talking about calling an ambulance and a doctor, I went over and said, "We don't need to call a doctor; we have a Doctor who is always with us!"

Surprised, they looked at me, as if to say, "What are you talking about?" Reminding them that we were all Christians and that we professed to worship and follow Christ, I knelt down and prayed for the man. Then I told him to get up and to move his arm. I told him to keep moving it and that within a matter of minutes he would be back in the game shooting three-pointers again.

He looked at me as if to say, "You're crazy! That will never happen. It's too badly injured." Nonetheless, he did as I instructed, and within five minutes he was back in the game shooting three-point shots—and making them, I might add. Everybody in the gymnasium witnessed what happened, including all of the players from four different teams, the officials, the fans, and the ministerial coaches.

A few weeks later, as we were playing in that same Christian basketball league and church gymnasium, another man was gravely injured while playing in a game. He had severely twisted his leg and damaged his knee. As everyone emptied the benches and the stands, quickly rushing to his aid, I stayed back to see if anyone had learned anything from the previous divine healing. To my utter shock and horror and great disappointment, *not one single person* in that entire "Christian" gymnasium exercised any faith whatsoever and called upon our great Physician in heaven to heal him. I was so disappointed and angry. After undeniably witnessing the miraculous healing power of God displayed, only a couple of weeks before, not one professing Christian in that church gymnasium came forward to pray for him and heal him. No one even suggested it! After a few minutes of watching them scramble in panic and desperation, asking each other where the nearest hospital was located, I angrily got up and walked over to those who were huddled around him. I told them all to get back and to get away. I said that I didn't want all of their unbelief negatively affecting this poor man's healing. I also angrily stated that if any of them believed in the true power of God and His sovereignty, then they were welcome to pray with me, but for the other disbelievers to get back. Everyone backed away, except one man. He looked at me and humbly said, "I believe, brother."

With that, the two of us prayed over the injured man, saying, "Lord, Jesus, we know that You always hear us. Please, we pray, heal this man, and forgive us our unbelief that we have just disappointingly displayed before You. In Your name and for Your glory, we ask these things, Lord. Amen."

I then said to the injured man, "Get up."

He looked at me shocked and worried and said, "But I don't have that kind of faith."

As I yanked on his arm, pulling him to his feet, I said, "I do—now get up!"

The other believer and I helped him to his feet, and then we told him to start walking and running in faith. He promptly did, and to his amazement, as well as to everyone else's in the gymnasium, he was instantly healed.

No one said a word to me for the rest of the game, except that one man who believed and who had prayed with me. He was a tall black man, and as I was leaving, he came over to me and said, "I hope to see you again, man of God." Why is it that no one else in that gymnasium believed? Why do people take His name upon them and yet deny His living power? Why do people claim to believe in Jesus and profess to live in Him and celebrate His resurrection from the grave, and yet, by their very works (or lack thereof) they still consider Him to be dead and ancient history? He is alive! He has risen! And upon rising from the dead, He declared to His followers—and to those who believe in Him:

> All authority has been given to Me in heaven and on earth; therefore go into all the world and preach the gospel to every creature. *These signs will follow those who believe*: In My name they will cast out demons; they will speak with new tongues; they will take up serpents; and if they drink anything deadly, it will by no means hurt them; they will lay hands on the sick, and they will recover. As the Father has sent Me, I also send you. Receive the Holy Spirit; if you forgive the sins of any, they are forgiven them; if you retain the sins of any, they are retained. Make disciples of all the nations, baptizing them in the name of the Father and of the Son and of the Holy Spirit, teaching them to observe all things that I have commanded you. And lo, I am with you always, even to the end of the age.
>
> Matthew 28:18–20; Mark 16:15–18;
> John 20:21–23, *emphasis mine*

Why don't we believe Him? We profess to believe in Him. We, as Christians, claim that we know Him. Why, then, don't we do the works that He did? Didn't He say, "Greater works than I have done, *you will do*, because I go to My Father" (John 14:12)? Jesus clearly told us why we don't do the works of God; it is because of our *unbelief* (Matthew 17:19–20; John 6:28–29). I tell you the truth, if we, His people, had faith, even the size of a mustard seed, we would be able to move mountains and heal the masses who desperately need Him and who grievously suffer the world over. Shame on us! We are all dead spiritually. Christ Himself is going to need to first resurrect and revive *us* from the dead before any of us is ever going to do anything profitable to help further His kingdom. Shame on all of us! Of a truth it is spoken of us in the Bible in the parable of the Ten Virgins (representing the church) that while the Bridegroom tarried in coming, we "*all slumbered and slept*" (Matthew 25:5).

I remember a young man a few years ago who came running up to me as I was teaching a Bible study. He was so full of life, vibrant and shining. He suddenly came rushing into the room while I was in the middle of teaching. The Holy Spirit had already told me months earlier that this young man would be coming to me searching for something. When I finished teaching the class and everyone else got up to leave, this young man stayed behind urgently wanting to speak with me. I greeted him, and then he jumped up and stood in the doorway blocking my exit. I asked him, "What do you seek?" He seemed all antsy and nervous, not really knowing what to say but obviously not going to permit me to pass until I had fulfilled his request. Immediately, the Holy Spirit said to me, "He is seeking to be baptized of you."

I then said, "You are here to be baptized, aren't you?"

The young man answered, "I have already been baptized."

"With water?" I asked.

"Yes, sir," he answered.

I then said, "You are here to be baptized with the Holy Spirit, aren't you? For you know that there are two baptisms: one of water and one of the Holy Spirit. Our Father has sent you unto me so that I might lay my hands on you and give you His Holy Spirit, isn't that true?"

"Yes," he humbly replied.

"Okay, then," I said nodding, "as the Lord wills." We both knelt down, and I laid my hands upon his head and asked the Lord to bless Him by giving him His Holy Spirit (Acts 8:17; 9:17). After doing so, we exchanged a few words, and then the young man quickly left. I turned to Dean Sargent, who was standing there next to me observing these things and told him what God had already previously told me: "We will not see this young man again [meaning, at Bible studies or in a Bible class]. For the Lord Himself will teach him all things and will lead him into all truth—even as it is written in the Scriptures" (John 14:26; 16:13; 1 John 2:27).

This young man was worthy of the Lord's Spirit. He had been secretly and privately calling out to God, wanting to know Him and wanting to serve Him with his whole heart. This young man was worthy of Him. He eagerly sought the Lord in faith and found Him. And because of that, God determined to place His Holy Spirit within that young man from henceforth and even forever. I tell you the truth, that young man will live and grow in the Lord and will become a holy vessel and a great warrior for the Lord his God. Oh that there would be this kind of faith and aggressive zeal (and teachable attitude) among the older generations of Israel (Christendom)! What great things would be done in Israel among the people of God today! Didn't Jesus share this same sentiment and lament during His day, saying, "Let the little ones come to Me, and do not forbid them; *for of such* is the kingdom of heaven." (Matthew 19:14). And again, He said, "And from the days of John the Baptist until now the kingdom of heaven has been forcefully advancing, and forceful [aggressive] men lay hold of it" (Matthew 11:12). The Amplified Version of the Bible renders this verse this way:

> And from the days of John the Baptist until the present time the kingdom of heaven has endured violent assault, and violent men seize it by force (as a precious prize)—a share in the heavenly kingdom is sought for with most ardent zeal and intense exertion.
>
> Matthew 11:12, Amplified Version

In the parable of the Unjust Steward, Jesus ended His parable by commending the unjust steward for his shrewd and savvy business dealings. He then commented that "the sons of this world are more shrewd in their generation than the sons of light" (Luke 16:8). In other words, Jesus lamented the fact that even the people of the world (the unbelieving Gentiles) sometimes show more initiative and drive in pursuing the temporal things of this world that they hope to acquire and achieve than do some of the people of His church in their pursuit of the eternal riches and things of God! Why does it seem like the only people who are truly committed and zealous anymore are those who are committed to and zealous for the wrong things? Where are the true Christians who aggressively pursue God and who continually hunger and thirst for His ways and His righteousness? Where are those who long to see the righteous and eternal things of God established on this earth—and who clamor and strive to *know* Him intimately? Don't we realize that our father Jacob was commended and rewarded by God for his aggressive and shrewd behavior in "stealing away" his brother Esau's birthright and paternal blessing? He clearly valued the things of God more than Esau did, and therefore God commended him and rewarded him openly for his *shrewdness* and aggression in pursuing spiritual things (Hebrews 12:16–17; Genesis 25:29–34). Don't we Christians realize that this hungering and thirsting (and striving), in order to *really* know God, pleases Him?! Our father Jacob was blessed because he aggressively wrestled with God and refused to let go until the Lord had blessed him. The young man that I described above who ran up to me to receive from me a "godly reward" ("whosoever receives a prophet because he is a prophet shall receive that prophet's reward") did not care about what the people in my Bible study thought as he bolted into the classroom—totally disregarding all of man's traditional common courtesies and "civil" manners. He didn't care what people thought of him or even what society said in regard to "illegally holding me hostage in that room" until I had blessed him. He didn't think twice about anything in the flesh or how things appeared unto men. He came there for one purpose and for *one sole purpose only*—to receive the kingdom of God and His righteousness which only come through receiving God's Holy Spirit—which this young man clearly longed for and earnestly and aggressively pursued.

Speaking of this, I know a man who just lost out on his opportunity to serve God now and to be accounted "one of our number"—that is to be numbered with the saints and obtain a part in this God-given ministry (Acts 1:17, 25; 10:40–42). Right now, God is looking for people, both men and women, who truly believe and who will serve Him without fear or reservation, people who have been loyal and faithful with "the little" that they have been entrusted with—both with the "little" spiritually that they have been given, as well as faithful with the unrighteous mammon of men that they have been put in charge of (Luke 16:10–12). God is looking for people that He can entrust with *His* resources, *His* power, and *His* judgments in order to righteously govern and administer His authority and government throughout the whole world now and in the kingdom to come. Remember, it is written, that *of the increase of His kingdom and of His government there will be no end,* and that His kingdom and His government will be set up and established upon this earth (Isaiah 9:6–7; Daniel 7:14, 27). Jesus promises that those who persevere and overcome will sit down with Him on His throne and rule the nations with Him with a rod of iron and that He has made us to be kings and priests to reign with Him on this earth (Revelation 1:6; 2:26–27; 3:21; 5:10).

Jesus once said to me regarding this: "Eric, remember, it is written of Me that I am 'the King *of* kings, and the Lord *of* lords' (Revelation 19:16). I have created you to be a king and a lord. In fact, I have made you a king and a lord *now* over a small estate, and I have given you a small area and sphere in which to practice exercising My authority over. I am training you *now* how to rule over much more later. How you lead and rule *now* and how you administer My justice and authority *now* determines what I will entrust you with later. That is why I said and foretold in My parables: 'You good and faithful servant. Because you were faithful with little, you shall be entrusted with much. Here, rule over five cities, or ten cities,' or whatever I shall appoint you over because you were faithful in these little things (Luke 19:12–19). Eric, right now I have committed your body and mind to you, with all of its desires and thoughts, in order for you to bring them into subjection to Me and to rule over them; I have also given you your family and put them in subjection to you; I have given you employees and a company to govern and watch over; as well as some of My people to lead and to help shepherd. I am always watching you to see whether or not you will lead them and rule over them the way that I lead and rule over you—lovingly, mercifully, justly, and fearlessly. You must lead and care for them the same way that I lead and care for you. This is how I am judging you (examining and evaluating you), for all judgment has been committed to Me (John 5:22–23)." This is why we are on this earth in the first place—to believe God and to learn to govern (rule) as He does, to help further expand His kingdom and dominion. We were created to help rule with Him as His sons and daughters!

Getting back to the man that I mentioned above who has seemingly disqualified himself from taking part in serving in this glorious ministry that is now taking place in these last days. The Lord woke me up a week or so ago and talked to me about him. Apparently, he was given a few things by God to "rule" over (govern) and to be accountable for. He was given a number of business accounts, some spiritual and biblical knowledge, and a family (a wife and three children). As a disciple, he was to eagerly pursue God and His ways above all else and teach his family members to do likewise. One day about six months ago though (before the Lord had recently talked to me about him), I was painting in his office, doing some touch-up repairs (he was one of my employees), when the Lord suddenly told me to ask him the following question: "Thus says the Lord God: 'What would you do if you were given more? What would you do with it?'" So I turned around and asked him this according to what the Lord had commanded me.

He seemed utterly shocked by my question. He said, "Why did you ask me that?"

I answered, "I don't know. The Lord just told me to." Later that night, he called me at home deeply concerned about my question. He asked me if we could meet the next day for lunch to discuss it.

The following day we went to a restaurant and talked for a few hours. I told him everything that the Lord had put upon my mouth to tell him about what is soon-coming upon the whole world and what wonderful opportunities and rewards were awaiting those (both in this life and in the age to come) who would pursue His kingdom *first and foremost* in this life above all other things (Matthew 6:33). I also reiterated that the Lord wanted to know what he would do if he were entrusted with more both physically and spiritually. Would he use those things for the glory of the Lord and for the growth of His kingdom? Or would he be lax and irresponsible? Clearly, here was an "open invitation" and opportunity directly from the Lord to join His team. All this man had to do was jump at it! But instead, out of fear and complacency, he did nothing. Just like the fearful and non-committed, lazy, unprofitable servant that Jesus gave the "one talent" to in the parable of the Talents, he went and spiritually buried it (Matthew 25:14–30). Instead of recognizing the incredible opportunity and honor that was being offered him—that is, to serve God and His people and "to be about his Father's business," this man literally did nothing. He completely had a nonchalant attitude about it, and literally didn't do or say anything! In fact, rather than mightily leaping forward in faith and excitement, he turned back in fear and quietly walked away, not saying anything. I was very surprised and disappointed at his laxity, but I didn't think anymore about it until the Lord suddenly woke me up about two weeks ago and began talking to me about him.

Totally unexpectedly, the Lord woke me up at about four o'clock in the morning and said the following to me about this man that I am describing here: "I have given that man some things and put him in charge over a few things in order to see what he would do with them and whether or not he would properly exercise My authority over them. He has not worked hard on his accounts but rather has become complacent; he has not actively and earnestly pursued the knowledge of Me, nor has he made a commitment to follow after Me [symbolized by getting baptized]. The spiritual knowledge I have given him he has become comfortable with and has not hungered for more. His wife and children rule over him, and he has lazily and cowardly let his children do as they please, and not as I have desired or instructed. He is lukewarm about Me and My ways, and therefore I will cause a crisis to develop from within him, which will cause him to have to make a choice. He will either become hot or cold; it is his choice. But he will 'sit on the fence' no longer!" At the time, I didn't fully understand what the Lord was saying to me or planning to do. I kept it to myself and didn't share it with anybody. But I knew in my spirit that God was going to somehow "cause a crisis to arise" in order to cause this man to have to act—either in faith or in fear. Jesus will always let us choose which way we want to go—either forward in faith or draw back in fear (which is unbelief). Remember what was said of that fearful and unprofitable servant that refused to do anything but sit on and bury what he had been given in the parable of the Talents? Jesus, as his Master and Judge, said, "Take that wicked and lazy unprofitable servant and cast him out! For to everyone who has, more will be given, so that he will have abundance; but from him who does not have, even what he has will be taken from him" (Matthew 25:26–29). We are all accountable to God for what we have been given, and everybody has been given something by Him!

One week later, Teresa and I were at our office building, and the man suddenly came up to me distraught and gravely concerned because our company isn't doing well financially (we currently "appear" to be on the verge of bankruptcy), and he informed me that he urgently needed to talk with me and Teresa. All of a sudden, he began panicking, and not intending to, he suddenly informed us that he was leaving our company immediately because he "wasn't sure if he could continue making enough money" in such a dire-looking economy. So without having any other job to go to or any other job prospects on the horizon, he foolishly resigned and walked away from a $90K-a-year job to go look for a new one in a very sluggish faltering economy. I know that God put these foolish thoughts in his head and led him away because the Lord had once told me that in regards to my business, I would neither "have to bring people in nor take them away"; He would do it for me. Apparently, He had already been doing that long before I ever realized it because He told me that He had specifically brought Tony to our company and that Rick had no part in "this inheritance" years before. Although, I don't clearly know yet what "this inheritance" means, I nonetheless know that God is doing something within our company and has been using it as a spiritual "teaching tool" for me and for others. Like I said before, in order to prepare His servants for their future jobs and responsibilities, God often uses our physical circumstances and people we know as spiritual prophetic "types" in order to teach us. This man is a spiritual type; he represents "people who draw back in fear because of how things look"—in other words, people who walk by sight and not by faith. He also typifies "people who are spiritually complacent and negligent"—that is, they are not spiritually hungry and do not value God and what He desires above all else. These people are not fit for and worthy of the kingdom of heaven—that is, "the kingdom which *comes* from heaven."

DEAD OR ALIVE—THE LORD WILL JUDGE US

I know that it sounds incredibly strange, and I am sure that you, as my reader, are probably wondering, *What in the world does my company have to do with things spiritually anyway?* Good question. I have been wondering the same thing for years now as well. As of my writing of this, I am not exactly sure myself yet. But I do know that God is in control, and He is doing something among us that directly corresponds spiritually. Somehow, TW Graphics is going to totally "change inside out" and become a different "ministry" (service) altogether. I don't even know what that means or what that conversion looks like. But a few months ago, Tony and I were in his office, and the Holy Spirit came down upon us and began to show us some marvelous things, about how everything that has been taking place at TW Graphics through the years has merely been a test and a training ground for what God is about to do with us (and through us). I had a vision long ago where I saw huge amounts of different "holy goods and resources" pouring into us to be properly distributed to everyone who was worthy and who had need. In this vision, I saw people donating and offering all kinds of things—such as wheat, corn, barley, jewelry, rice, etc. People were bringing in basket loads, one right after another, to Dwight in the warehouse who was busily trying to receive, inventory, and store all of it and disperse it right back out just as fast as he could. I, in the meantime, was outside the building in the parking lot, preaching and healing the masses of people who were coming to us to be fed and to hear the truth. I don't know what these things mean and how they are going to come about, but I trust God—so much so that my own family (my wife, my in-laws, and even my own parents) are threatening to have me "committed" because I have been watching as TW Graphics, my only financial livelihood, goes "belly-up" right before my eyes and I am not (and haven't been) doing anything about it.

I haven't been trying to save my company or trying to rush back in as a salesperson again (since leaving my job at the Lord's command) because I believe God. I do not live by sight—I live by faith. I know (and believe) what God has told me. Remember that vision about sitting at the poker table while the Lord was dealing and Him instructing me to "go all in" and be willing to lay it all on the line and risk everything since He was the One dealing my cards to me? Well, it is time now—and that is exactly what I am doing! I am either going to "win everything" because I trust God or I am going to lose everything because I trust God—either way let God be praised. Remember the true story in the Bible regarding Shadrach, Meshach, and Abednego, and how the king of Babylon threatened to throw them into the fiery furnace if they didn't fall down and worship the golden image that he had set up? These three men told the king that God was able to deliver them from the fiery furnace, but if He chose *not* to deliver them, either way—live or die—they were not going to disobey

God and worship an idol, come what may (Daniel 3:1–18). The same is true for me—if need be, I will go down believing God.

For those of you who think that I am insane regarding the above statements in allowing TW Graphics (my livelihood and life savings) to just fall apart and disintegrate, let me share with you two dreams that the Lord gave me. About five years ago, right after we had bought our office building (when we were doing well financially) and a few months before God told me to turn everything over to Tony, God gave me two shocking dreams back to back.

In the first dream, I dreamed that I was walking down the streets of a big city (someplace like Los Angeles or New York City), and I looked up into the sky and saw huge tornadoes coming at me and toward the city. Just like everyone else, I too began to panic and freak out at the impending doom. I immediately darted into one of the large "man-made buildings," seeking protection along with everyone else, and I threw myself up against the wall, scared and hovering, trying to cover my head—as did everybody! As I looked around, I suddenly realized that I was taking the exact same posture and reacting the exact same fearful way that everyone else was— even though I was a Christian, and they weren't. Immediately then, that dream ended and a second dream began: I dreamed that I was sitting in my office building, and suddenly once again I looked up and saw a bunch of tornadoes heading toward me. In a panic, I got down on the floor and threw myself up against the wall and covered my head—initially assuming the exact same position that I had taken in the first dream.

Suddenly, however, I heard the Lord's voice tell me to "get up and to courageously stand in the middle of the room—believing." As I did this, it took a great deal of faith for me to stand firm in the middle of my office while violent tornadoes suddenly began to hit all around me. As the harsh winds beat around my head and walls began to disappear and be stripped away, I had to shut my eyes in order to not lose faith and to stand firm through it all. After what seemed like a few intense dangerous moments, the ripping winds and the roaring noise soon stopped, and I suddenly felt a warm summer breeze blow gently through my hair and across my face. Tropical birds began singing, and I could hear calm ocean waves lapping at the beach. I opened my eyes to see that I had been miraculously preserved and protected, and that I was now standing on a beautiful cliff overlooking the ocean with blue skies and a gorgeous peaceful setting all around me. It was like I had been supernaturally transferred by faith to a heavenly place and nothing (or nobody) could touch me. The surroundings were incredibly peaceful and beautiful. It reminded me of being in Hawaii, and it truly felt like paradise all around me. As I peacefully stood on this cliff overhang, looking out at my beautiful surroundings and feeling great, without a single care in this world, I noticed my beloved mother below me on the beach frantically trying to pick up the pieces of my life which were now washing up on the shore as pieces of driftwood. On the pieces of driftwood, it clearly read *TW Graphics*. As I stood on this beautiful cliff, high above it all, the fact that I had lost TW Graphics didn't bother me one bit. As I said before, I believe God and love Him, and I will faithfully see this to the end—no matter what it costs me.

One of the Holy Spirit's primary responsibilities is "to show us things to come" before they actually come to pass (John 16:13); so that when the "things" *do* come to pass, we will be comforted and not caught off guard, all upset and distraught as the Gentiles (unbelievers) are when they are faced with the same opposition, calamity, tragedy, and danger. This is one of the reasons why the Holy Spirit is referred to as our Comforter (John 15:26; 16:7). Jesus said that the Holy Spirit would also "bring into our remembrance everything that He had said unto us" (John 14:26). In this way, the Holy Spirit again comforts us—that is, if we believe what Jesus said to us in the first place!

This was the point of the two dreams above: In the first dream, I was reacting like "the world," like the unbelievers, as the Gentiles do; I was all shaken up and scared. I wasn't putting my faith and trust in God who is able to deliver His own and deliver those who put their faith and trust in Him. Instead, in my first dream, I was reacting in the "natural" (in the flesh)—that is, according to my own judgments and my own carnal human reasoning. But in my second dream, I heard and remembered the words of God, as the Holy Spirit reminded me of them, and I stepped out in faith—and persevered in that belief and I overcame all external forces! My faith in God delivered me and so I was left standing on solid ground in a peaceful state. It is important to remember here, that sometimes, we must *close our eyes* (shut down our natural senses and human reasoning) in order to trust God and believe Him. God does not want us relying on what our eyes and ears tell us, or what our own human reasoning dictates. No, He wants us to solely rely on and believe what *He* tells us—regardless of what the circumstances might "look" like. That is the key! Man needs to learn that he doesn't live by bread alone, but by every word that proceeds out of the mouth of God (Deuteronomy 8:3; Matthew 4:4). "Bread" here represents everything in the natural realm that man looks to and believes sustains him. But Jesus came saying that God gives us the "unnatural" Bread from heaven which is Jesus Himself—and that if any man or woman "eats of Him" and looks to Him, then he or she will never die but will live forever (John 6:32–58).

I always marvel at the fact that most people think that they are alive, when in reality, they are no more alive than a corpse that is being artificially sustained through life-support systems. Let me explain: There are primarily three artificial life-support devices being used in hospitals today to keep a "dead" person alive. All three of these devices deal primarily with keeping a person's blood running through their body. These artificial mechanisms and devices include respirators (for breathing in order to oxygenate the blood), pacemakers/defibrillators (keeping the heart pumping for blood circulation), and dialysis machines (for cleansing the blood). Notice that all three of these devices primarily deal with a body's blood. There is a reason for this—for God reveals in His Word that *for all flesh*—"its life is in the blood" (Genesis 9:4; Leviticus 17:11). In other words, if you take away a body's blood or stop its blood circulation, it has no more life—and is considered officially dead. But, as most people would agree, just because a corpse has blood (life) pumping through it, doesn't make that body profitable or "alive" and functioning. This fact is why many people, year after year, elect to have their loved ones disconnected from "artificial life support" and why many people decide against having the medical field artificially prolong their life should they be permanently injured. To truly live, a person needs to have a functioning purpose whereby they are profitable and their existence means something; otherwise, they are no more alive than a corpse that is being artificially sustained by blood-circulating machines. The point being that just because you have blood or "life" coursing through your veins right now doesn't mean that you are *alive*! Many people just live and breathe, but don't really have any other eternal purpose other than to just perpetuate our species. And even this is in danger of becoming extinct if God doesn't intervene (Matthew 24:22).

Jesus and the Bible both agree with the above statements that refer to us as being "dead" if we aren't in an abiding relationship with God. Notice the following:

Jesus answered one of His followers who had asked to be excused from following Him in order to first go and take care of his father until his father had died. Jesus instructed him, saying: "Follow Me, and let the dead bury their own dead" (Matthew 8:21–22).

In another place, Jesus said to the religious people who refused to come to Him and believe:

> Most assuredly, I say to you, he who hears My word and believes in Him who sent Me has everlasting life, and shall not come into judgment, *but has passed from death into life*... Search the Scriptures, for in them you think you have eternal life; but these are they which testify of Me. But you are not willing to come to Me *that you may have life*... You are from beneath; I am from above. You are of this world; I am not of this world. Therefore I said to you that you will die in your sins; for if you do not believe that I am He, you will die in your sins... Most assuredly, I say to you, if anyone keeps My word he shall never see death.
>
> John 5:24, 39–40, 8:23–24, 51, *emphasis mine*

> He who does not believe the Son shall not see life, but the wrath of God abides on him.
>
> John 3:36

In contrast to our blood being our "life" and sustaining us, Jesus said that whoever drinks *His* blood really has life, and that we, in our current state, are really dead:

> Most assuredly, I say to you, unless you eat the flesh of the Son of Man and drink His blood, *you have no life in you.* Whoever eats My flesh and drinks My blood has eternal life, and I will raise him up at the last day. For My flesh is food indeed, and My blood is drink indeed. He who eats My flesh and drinks My blood abides in Me, and I in him. As the living Father sent Me, and I live because of the Father, so he who feeds on Me will live because of Me.
>
> John 6:53–57, *emphasis mine*

Jesus said that without Him, we don't have life in our present state:

> I have come that they may have life, and that they may have it more abundantly.
>
> John 10:10

Jesus defined "life" as knowing God and His Son, Jesus Christ:

> Father, the hour has come. Glorify Your Son, that Your Son also may glorify You, as You have given Him authority over all flesh, that He should give eternal life to as many as You have given Him. *And this is eternal life, that they may know You, the only true God, and Jesus Christ, whom You have sent.*
>
> John 17:1–3, *emphasis mine*

When you don't know God, both the Bible and God consider you to be "dead" in your sins:

And you [believers] He made alive, *who were dead in trespasses and sins,* in which you once walked according to the course of this world, according to the prince of the power of the air [Satan], the spirit who now works in the sons of disobedience, among whom also we all once conducted ourselves in the lusts of our flesh, fulfilling the desires of the flesh and of the mind, and were by nature children of wrath, just as others. But God, who is rich in mercy, because of His great love with which He loved us, even when *we were dead in trespasses,* made us alive together with Christ, and raised us up together, and made us sit together in the heavenly places in Christ Jesus, that in the ages to come He might show the exceeding riches of His grace in His kindness toward us in Christ Jesus.

Ephesians 2:1–7, *emphasis mine*

And you, *being dead in your trespasses and the uncircumcision of your flesh,* He has made alive together with Him, having forgiven you all trespasses ...

Colossians 2:13, *emphasis mine*

Again, I say, I truly marvel at how many people think that they are alive, but in reality, they are no more alive than a dead corpse that is being artificially kept "alive" by pumping blood through its veins. Perhaps, you, my reader, are wondering then, *What is my purpose? Why did God create us human beings then? What is this "life" about, if God considers us to be "dead" right now anyway?* Great questions! And it is my hope and purpose to answer them by showing that God is calling each and every one of us right now *to believe.* For this is the purpose of our existence in this life: to *believe* God! And it is the purpose of *my* life and my life's testimony and for all of my experiences that I have relayed here in this book. It is the very purpose why I am writing this book and why I am willing to expend my life in service to others—to endure persecution and suffering, so that others might *believe*! As I wrote in the beginning of this book, my whole life is a real testimony to the greatness, mercy, and sovereignty of God. And believe it or not, *yours* is too. For God is working out His divine plan here among us, and it is so marvelous that even though certain people have been sent (and will be sent) to tell us these things ahead of time, yet "we still won't believe" (Habakkuk 1:5; Isaiah 29:14). For it is written: "Eye has not seen, nor ear heard; nor have entered into the heart of man the things which God has prepared for those who love Him" (1 Corinthians 2:9). But God says that He has revealed them to us through His Spirit (1 Corinthians 2:10). That is, He has revealed His mysteries and secrets to His servants—the prophets and apostles (Amos 3:7; Matthew 13:10–17; Ephesians 3:1–5). The Greek word for *apostle* literally means "one who is sent"—that is "one who is sent by God." Yet, most people do not believe those whom God sends. Just as Jesus prophesied, saying, "If they do not hear Moses and the prophets [those things written in the Bible], neither will they be persuaded though one rise from the dead." (Luke 16:31). In other words, if they don't believe those that God had sent to them earlier, then they certainly won't hear and believe Jesus now (who has been resurrected from the dead) speaking either. The point is—people simply don't believe! That is why Jesus said that the work of God right now is for people to *believe* in Him whom God has sent (John 6:29).

The reason that most "Gentile" (nonreligious) people don't believe me is that they don't believe in God anyway—so they won't, for the most part, believe my witness. But the reason that most "Jews" (that is, Christians and/or religious people) don't believe me, is that they are too spiritually proud to consider that maybe they aren't as close to God as they think they are. To listen to me or to believe my testimony (written in this book) in most cases, automatically causes "fleshly Jews" to question why *they* aren't necessarily "hearing from God" in the same way or experiencing the same types of supernatural occurrences. For some reason, my testimony automatically puts them on the defensive and causes them a total "crisis of belief." My testimony usually elicits one of two responses from them: they either humbly admit to themselves that their relationship with God is not all that they purport it to be, and consequently, they begin hungering to know God better, and begin crying out to Him for a closer, deeper, and more meaningful relationship than they've had; or they feel that they need to find some way in their own mind or among themselves to discredit me and consider my testimony to be false and/or demonic. Seldom do I find a person or a church who believes me. But when I do, it is because they already know Him who sent me. Just as Jesus said: "He who receives whomever I send receives Me; and he who receives Me receives Him who sent Me" (John 13:20). This is the purpose of my book, therefore: it is to give a true account of my life story—my witness and testimony of how God uses fallible human beings to serve as messengers and lifelong eye witnesses of His incredible mercy, power, and sovereignty, and that He exercises that power and sovereignty over all of mankind according to His divine will and to fulfill His divine purposes. My true testimony is recorded here for all to see in order to cause people to either believe me (and consequently, be inspired and encouraged to draw closer to God themselves as a result), or to write me off as a kook, mentally unstable, a religious fanatic, and/or a "deceiver of the people." Everything that I have written in this book is the absolute truth, as God is my witness, and I am not a liar. And very soon, the world will see it as such and will know that I have not lied and that God, my God, is faithful and true. Elijah faced the same dilemma in his day: most people in Israel thought that he was a kook, a false prophet, and a "troubler of the people" (1 Kings 18:17). That is, until they saw fire come down from heaven and the Lord openly reveal Himself (1 Kings 18:38–39)!

As you can probably tell by the tone of my writing, I am getting tired. I am getting tired of not being believed. It doesn't matter that I have had a spotless record all of my life of not being a liar or a deceiver. I have never sought a following, never tried to start "my own church," and never charged nor accepted any money (or anything) for my services and for spiritually helping people. I have only tried to faithfully serve God and to be a blessing to His people. And for this reason—and for this reason alone—I suffer. But I suffer gladly, knowing that God will soon vindicate me. And like Elijah, and the prophets before me, I too can say:

> Lord God of Abraham, Isaac, and Israel, let it be known this day that You are God in Israel, and that I am Your servant, and that I have done all these things at Your word. Hear me, O Lord, hear me, that this people may know that You are the Lord God, and that You have turned their hearts back to You again.
>
> 1 Kings 18:36–37

People forget that God is both the judge of the living and the dead, the Jew and the Gentile, those who are "within" Christendom and those who are "without" (Acts 10:42; Romans 3:29; 14:9; 1 Corinthians 5:12–13). These verses mean the "spiritually living" as well as the "spiritually dead," those who are religious and those who aren't. They include *everybody*! It doesn't matter whether you know Him or recognize Him as God right now or not—you still answer to Him, *always*. And everybody is accountable for what they know and when they know it. Everyone is accountable for what they say as well. For Jesus said,

> I say to you that for every idle word men may speak, they will give account of it in the day of judgment. For by your words you will be justified, and by your words you will be condemned.
>
> Matthew 12:36–37

I had to learn the meaning of this verse the hard way one time. Long before I went into the full-time ministry, when God was first training me, I went up to a mountain-town casino to relax and play some poker. It was about a forty-five-minute drive from my house, and I really enjoyed going up there, not only because I enjoyed playing at the small-stakes poker tables, but I really found the ride to be quite enjoyable and relaxing. One particular night (this happened about ten or eleven years ago), I drove up to one of these casinos and quickly lost my money. As I was driving back home, I was so mad because I had lost at poker that I said out loud, "I'm not going back up there anymore!" I didn't mean it of course; it was just one of those things that you blurt out when you are frustrated and mad at yourself. The next night, however, I went right back up there to play some more. Curiously, I lost again, and the same result happened. I quickly drove back down the mountains, cursing myself for losing again, and inadvertently professed that I wouldn't be going up there again.

Early the next morning, the Lord woke me up from my sleep when it was still dark outside and sternly said to me, "Go downstairs. I want to talk to you!" I could tell by the tone of His voice that this was serious and that He was not happy. When I got downstairs to my office, nothing happened right away. I sat at my desk for a few minutes, wondering if I was supposed to be praying or something, because God wasn't saying anything or putting any immediate thoughts into my head. So I got down on the floor to pray, and as I began, He suddenly cut me off and angrily said, "Get up. *I'll* do the talking! Go get your Bible." Scared because of the tone of His voice, I quickly went back to my desk and grabbed my Bible. I didn't know what to do, so I opened it, and immediately it fell open to the verses that said the following: (These verses literally leapt off the page toward my face and I heard the Lord's voice thunder the words as I read them.)

> Do not be rash with your mouth, and let not your heart utter anything hastily before God. For God is in heaven and you on earth; therefore let your words be few. When you make a vow to God, do not delay to pay it; for He has no pleasure in fools. Pay what you have vowed. It is better not to vow than to vow and not pay. Do not let your mouth cause your flesh to sin, nor say before the angel that it was an error [accident or mistake]. Why should God be angry at your voice and destroy the work of your hands?
>
> Ecclesiastes 5:2–6

At that moment, the Holy Spirit then reminded me that I had twice stated that I wouldn't go up to the mountain casinos ever again and that God was holding me to that errant vow that I had so rashly let come forth out of my mouth! As I read those verses again, the Holy Spirit made clear to me that if I did go back up there again, then I was in extreme danger of His judgment. The Holy Spirit repeated His words, by saying, "Why should God have to destroy all the works of your hands, Eric, in order for you to learn this lesson?!" I learned a fearful thing that morning. I have never been back up there since, and I have certainly tried to watch what I say (promise) with my mouth.

I mentioned earlier that I would explain why an angel told me about my nephew's birth while I was attending college. I didn't understand the significance of this, nor even think about it again, until the spring of 1995 when God was giving me those visions and revelations. One day shortly after having seen and heard those "unspeakable things," I asked the Lord if the things were indeed true and if they were going to come to pass. He ignored my question but immediately said the following to me: "Behold, your nephew A.J. shall be great, and he shall stand before Me, even as his name is Aaron. And he shall be great before Me, even greater than you." At that moment, I then suddenly remembered that an angel had announced his birth to me many years before. I also hadn't realized or remembered that his real name was "Aaron"; we had always called him by his initials, "A.J." A few years later, my sister, April, called me one day, and said that she and her husband (A.J.'s dad) were "having trouble with him" (he was being a typical rebellious teenager), and they wanted to know if he could come and live with me for a while so that I could help teach him and instruct him "in the ways of the Lord" as she put it. When I inquired of the Lord regarding this in my mind (as I was still on the phone with my sister), I immediately felt the "heat" of the Presence of God jealously tell me, "No! For I, Myself, will teach him what he must know and how to properly serve Me!" These are the same sentiments that I was also later given from the Holy Spirit regarding the young man who ran up to me years later in order to receive the Holy Spirit by the laying on of my hands. In both cases, God let me know that He would personally teach and instruct His young servants and that I wouldn't have anything to do with these young men's "spiritual training." Clearly, these things are biblical—remember how Jesus came to John the Baptist to have John baptize Him (lay his hands on Him) even though John the Baptist was spiritually "less" than Jesus, but John the Baptist didn't go on to "train" Jesus or to teach Him anything. Likewise, Elisha ended up being "twice the prophet that Elijah was" even though Elijah came before him and served as a type of a "father figure" to him (2 Kings 2:1–15).

I tell you the truth—the generation that comes after me shall be greater than me. For God will raise up many "apostles and prophets" ("two witnesses") that will do many miraculous signs and will astound the whole world, as a final witness, and then the end will come (Revelation 11:1–14; Matthew 24:14). Even now, there are many little "Joshuas and Calebs" and little "Samuels and Davids" and little "Esthers and Deborahs" privately among us, growing up in obscurity and being instructed by the Lord and becoming very strong in Him. Soon, they will be made known and manifested to the world, even though the world will have little regard for them because it is evil and the love of the Father is not in the world. The world does not know Him nor recognize Him or those whom He sends. We, the servants of God, are not of this world, neither do we care for the things of this world. We live to see Him glorified and to see His kingdom take over all of the kingdoms of this earth (Daniel 2:44). To Him be the glory and the power and the dominion, even truly, forever! Amen.

CPSIA information can be obtained
at www.ICGtesting.com
Printed in the USA
FSHW010509200819
61233FS